CYCLICAL CHANGES IN TRADE BALANCES OF COUNTRIES EXPORTING PRIMARY PRODUCTS

CANADIAN STUDIES IN ECONOMICS

A series of studies now edited by Douglas G. Hartle, sponsored by the Social Science Research Council of Canada, and published with financial assistance from the Canada Council

CYCLICAL CHANGES IN TRADE BALANCES OF COUNTRIES EXPORTING PRIMARY PRODUCTS

1927 - 1933

A Comparative Study of Forty-Nine Countries

S. G. TRIANTIS

UNIVERSITY OF TORONTO PRESS

© University of Toronto Press 1967
Printed in the Netherlands
Reprinted in 2018
ISBN 978-1-4875-7334-8 (paper)

PREFACE

THIS STUDY owes a great deal to a number of people. Several of my colleagues in the Department of Political Economy of the University of Toronto kindly spared their time to help me with ideas and comments. In addition, Professor H. G. Johnson, C. P. Kindleberger, and Ilse Mintz were kind enough to read parts or all of the Manuscript. I am most grateful to them for their advice and suggestions.

During two summers I received awards from the Canada Council and I was a member of the Institute for Economic Research at Queen's University. I have greatly appreciated the help received and the research facilities at Queen's. I should further like to acknowledge the painstaking editorial assistance of Miss Diane Dilworth of the University of Toronto Press as well as the Humanities and Social Sciences Research Grant received from the University of Toronto for secretarial assistance.

This work has been published with the help of a grant from the Social Science Research Council of Canada using funds provided by the Canada Council.

I finally wish to thank the Editor of the *American Economic Review* for permission to use material published in the March 1952 issue of the *Review*.

S. G. TRIANTIS

University of Toronto

CONTENTS

TABLES

DIAGRAMS

CYCLICAL CHANGES IN TRADE BALANCES OF
COUNTRIES EXPORTING PRIMARY PRODUCTS

INTRODUCTION

BEFORE THE SECOND WORLD WAR the economic conditions and problems of the large number of countries which exported chiefly primary products and were mostly underdeveloped economies attracted little attention in the Western world. Moreover, this attention was directed mainly to problems of immediate and obvious commercial and financial relations between these economies and the West. For instance, the depression of the early nineteen-thirties aroused some temporary interest in the changes in trade balances of these countries, in so far as these changes affected the ability of these economies to service the foreign capital which they had received and to import Western manufactures. Usually, the less obvious, though very important, problems of potential economic development in these countries were neglected.

Since the war the interest in the development of underdeveloped economies has grown apace, and now academic talent and international organizations are preoccupied with every conceivable facet of the matter. The problem of fluctuations in the foreign trade of these countries is much in the forefront: the position of these economies in the system of international trade and finance has been emphasized, and attention is being directed to the ability of such countries to finance imports, service foreign capital which they might receive, and continue their economic development under varying external circumstances. The main purpose of this study is to analyse and explain past phenomena. While much has been written on the great cyclical episode of the period 1927-33, more than thirty years later the chapter relating to the changes in the trade balances of the countries exporting chiefly primary products is still missing. Our work is directed mainly at filling this gap. However, it is hoped that the perceptive reader will gain considerable insight into various possibilities concerning the current trade problems of such countries.

Our study might have been approached by outlining theories relating to cyclical changes in the balance of merchandise trade and using the available information to test their validity. We have, however, adopted the alternative course, of presenting the statistical and factual information relating to forty-nine countries exporting chiefly primary products and attempting to explain the phenomena observed with the use of traditional, or new, theoretical reasoning. Chapter 1 is a review of the changes in the forty-nine balances in the period 1927-33. In Chapter 2 we consider the approximate determinants of these changes. Chapters 3 and 4 deal with the changes in merchandise exports, and Chapters 5 to 7 with the changes in imports. In Chapter 8 we draw together, and review the relative role of certain factors accounting for the cyclical changes of the forty-nine balances. An Appendix to the study accounts for significant differences between our conclusions and those drawn by Dr. T. C. Chang in his study of *Cyclical Movements in the Balance of Payments.*[1]

As the subtitle of this volume indicates, this is a comparative study. The emphasis is placed on the presentation and explanation of significant differences between the cyclical changes in merchandise balances of countries exporting chiefly primary products, rather than on an exhaustive presentation of familiar factors responsible for the changes in the balances of the great majority of these countries. It is not our purpose, for instance, to discuss in any detail the basic reasons for the decline in imports which followed the decrease in the exports of these countries—these matters have been considered extensively in economic literature. Our concern is to explain why in some countries the relative decline in imports was smaller than the relative decline in exports, while in others it was greater, and why it was much smaller, or much greater, in some countries than in others.

One may expect that few, if any, of the readers of this volume will be unaware of the paucity of statistical and factual information about the great bulk of the countries examined, especially for the period before the Second World War. For example, fairly reliable data relating to national income and its changes, or changes in public and private investment, are available only for a handful of the forty-nine countries; and data relating to such phenomena as the distribution of income and the cyclical changes thereof are even scarcer. In many instances in the preparation of this study the kind of elaborate analysis used in the study of more advanced economies was impossible. Often, it was necessary to rely on indirect evidence, or to devise ways of getting around the obstacles imposed by the lack of certain types of information. However, the study is presented with the belief that the basic conclusions are justified, and that supplemental or more accurate information would not affect them materially.

Some readers of this study might be inclined to compare it to other studies of a similar nature, and might feel disappointed that, unlike those studies, this volume presents few, if any, new estimates of elasticities, marginal propensities, foreign trade multipliers, or other such ratios relating to the economies examined. The author offers no apology. As indicated earlier and again in the last chapter, his purpose was limited: to explain past phenomena, rather than to show a "pattern" of behaviour of the trade balance which may readily serve forecasting purposes. Moreover, estimates of that kind would have been hampered very seriously by the shortage of information. For reasons explained later, the values of some of the foregoing ratios seem to depend also on factors other than those usually noted in the literature, so that the task of estimating these ratios is more involved and requires more information than has usually been assumed.

CHAPTER ONE

CHANGES IN THE TRADE BALANCES OF FORTY-NINE COUNTRIES EXPORTING CHIEFLY PRIMARY PRODUCTS, 1927-33

WE MAY BEGIN OUR INQUIRY with a presentation in this chapter of basic information relating to the cyclical changes, in the period from 1927 to 1933, of the balances of merchandise trade of forty-nine countries exporting chiefly primary products.

I

In the years 1928-9, farming, forestry, fishing, and mining products, in a raw or semi-processed stage, accounted for at least half the total value of merchandise exports of each of the following forty-nine countries:[1]

Argentina	Costa Rica	Guatemala	Netherlands	Poland
Australia	Cuba	Haiti	New Zealand	Portugal
Bolivia	Denmark	Honduras	Nicaragua	Roumania
Brazil	Dominican R.	Hungary	Nigeria	Salvador
Bulgaria	D.E. Indies	India	Norway	Siam
Canada	Ecuador	Irish F.S.	Panama	Spain
Ceylon	Egypt	Latvia	Paraguay	Turkey
Chile	Estonia	Lithuania	Persia	Venezuela
China	Finland	Malaya	Peru	Yugoslavia
Colombia	Greece	Mexico	Philippines	

On the other hand, more than half the exports of each of the following eleven countries consisted of manufactures: Austria, Belgium, Czechoslovakia, France, Germany, Italy, Japan, Sweden, Switzerland, the United Kingdom, and the United States. In the years 1928-9 the merchandise trade (exports plus imports) of the former countries constituted about 36 per cent of world trade, and of the latter countries about 56 per cent. This study is concerned with the trade balances of the former countries, and only a few remarks about the changes in the balances of the latter countries are made in this and the next chapter.

The division of countries into those exporting chiefly primary products and those exporting predominantly industrial goods (referred to henceforth as "primary-exporting" and "industrial-exporting" countries respectively) has been quite common in economic literature. Justification for this division is found in the existence of some common features in the former economies which distinguish them from the latter; notably, features relating to the origin and, hence, certain conditions of supply of their chief exports. However, as we shall see, there were fundamental differences among primary-exporting countries with respect to many other factors bearing on the cyclical changes in merchandise trade; for instance, some other conditions of supply of their exports, or the conditions of demand for these products. As a consequence, there often were more striking differences between the cyclical changes in the trade of various primary-exporting countries than between the changes in trade of primary-exporting and industrial-exporting economies. In the period studied the exports of many primary-exporting countries declined proportionately more than the exports of many industrial-exporting countries, while the exports of others decreased proportionately less.

The foregoing remarks might seem obvious and superfluous. However, the distinction between primary (or, more narrowly, agricultural and mining) and industrial products, and, correspondingly, between countries exporting such goods, has not infrequently been allotted more substance than it may reasonably claim. Numerous differences between countries exporting, for instance, agricultural, or mining, products have been neglected; and "patterns" have been distinguished, which the cyclical changes in the trade balances of these "types" of country reputedly followed in the past and may be expected to follow in the future.[2]

II

Next in order are a few remarks about the foreign trade data presented in this study. Unless otherwise indicated, these data, as well as other data relating to balances of payments, have been obtained from publications of the League of Nations, chiefly the *International Trade Statistics*, the *Balances of Payments*, and the *Statistical Year-Book*, of various years. As far as the content of "merchandise" trade is concerned, gold and silver specie and, as a rule, also bullion have been excluded from both the exports and imports of the countries concerned.[3] To facilitate interperiod and intercountry comparisons of trade all value data have been converted into pre-1933 United States dollars. Accordingly, unless otherwise indicated, throughout this volume percentage changes in values of exports or imports relate to values in gold. Unless otherwise indicated, throughout this study the terms "trade," "exports," "imports," "balance," "deficit," and "surplus" will refer to foreign merchandise trade. Reference to value, or volume, of exports or imports in "1928-9" will denote the arithmetic mean of the values, or volumes, for 1928 and 1929, and similarly for other two-year periods.[4]

III

The basic data relating to the changes in the trade balances of the forty-nine primary-exporting countries between 1928-9 on the one hand, and 1930-1, 1931-2 or 1932-3 on the other, are shown in Table I. Column (5) indicates the countries and periods in which the balances changed favourably (decline in the absolute size of the deficit, or increase in the absolute size of the surplus), or unfavourably. This column is summarized in Table II, which shows the number of countries whose balance changed favourably or unfavourably in each of the three periods considered.[5]

TABLE I

BASIC INFORMATION ON THE CHANGES IN THE PERIOD 1928-33 OF THE MERCHANDISE BALANCES
OF FORTY-NINE PRIMARY-EXPORTING COUNTRIES
(Based on values in pre-1933 US dollars)

Country, and ratio of exports to imports in 1928-9 (1)	Two-year period compared to 1928-9 (2)	Percentage decline in exports (3)	Percentage decline in imports (4)	Favourable (F) or unfavourable (U) change in the trade balance (5)
Argentina	1930-1	51.2	40.9	U
1.18	1931-2	60.5	65.6	U
	1932-3	68.1	72.9	U
Australia	1930/1-1/2	45.9	67.5	F
0.99	1931/2-2/3	53.0	74.0	F
	1932/3-3/4	54.6	72.9	F
Bolivia	1930-1	36.6	37.4	U
1.81	1931-2	65.8	70.2	U
	1932-3	73.5	75.8	U
Brazil	1930-1	40.0	53.5	F
1.08	1931-2	55.2	71.5	F
	1932-3	62.3	71.9	F
Bulgaria	1930-1	4.0	39.8	F
0.82	1931-2	26.2	47.1	F
	1932-3	51.3	63.7	F
Canada	1930/1-1/2	48.3	39.0	U
1.09	1931/2-2/3	63.6	62.6	U
	1932/3-3/4	69.3	73.0	U
Ceylon	1930-1	36.0	37.3	U
1.05	1931-2	57.9	57.0	U
	1932-3	68.7	67.1	U
Chile	1930-1	49.0	25.2	U
1.52	1931-2	73.8	67.3	U
	1932-3	85.7	85.9	U
China	1930-1	46.6	34.1	U
0.82	1931-2	64.7	49.1	U
	1932-3	78.5	62.1	U
Colombia	1930-1	23.5	62.1	F
0.95	1931-3	41.2	74.0	F
	1932-3	54.8	76.4	F
Costa Rica	1930-1	18.9	48.6	F
0.99	1931-2	39.5	62.8	F
	1932-3	54.9	72.2	F
Cuba	1930-1	48.0	43.5	U
1.28	1931-2	63.9	69.5	U
	1932-3	73.2	80.2	U
Denmark	1930-1	14.1	11.1	U
0.94	1931-2	38.3	37.5	F
	1932-3	55.1	56.4	F
Dominican R.	1930-1	39.6	48.7	F
1.06	1931-2	53.7	63.6	F
	1932-3	64.0	69.1	F
D. E. Indies	1930-1	36.9	29.9	U
1.43	1931-2	57.3	53.7	U
	1932-3	66.5	66.2	U
Ecuador	1930-1	23.5	34.3	F
1.09	1931-2	44.1	59.6	F
	1932-3	59.2	73.6	F

Country, and ratio of exports to imports in 1928-9 (1)	Two-year period compared to 1928-9 (2)	Percentage decline in exports (3)	Percentage decline in imports (4)	Favourable (F) or unfavourable (U) change in the trade balance (5)
Egypt	1930-1	47.7	28.3	U
1.02	1931-2	60.0	54.0	U
	1932-3	64.6	64.3	U
Estonia	1930-1	31.5	37.4	F
0.96	1931-2	53.4	61.6	F
	1932-3	67.1	72.9	F
Finland	1930-1	23.7	43.1	F
0.85	1931-2	42.9	63.0	F
	1932-3	51.5	69.4	F
Greece	1930-1	22.2	25.9	F
0.51	1931-2	45.7	46.5	F
	1932-3	60.4	66.2	F
Guatemala	1930-1	26.8	51.7	F
0.86	1931-2	51.6	66.6	F
	1932-3	66.2	77.9	F
Haiti	1929/30-30/1	41.4	40.1	U
1.05	1930/1-1/2	58.9	54.3	U
	1931/2-2/3	60.2	61.2	U
Honduras	1930/1-1/2	25.8	35.6	U
1.64	1931/2-2/3	41.6	52.0	U
	1932/3-3/4	59.8	60.4	U
Hungary	1930-1	20.3	39.9	F
0.82	1931-2	51.4	61.8	F
	1932-3	61.2	71.9	F
India	1930-1	38.1	37.3	U
1.31	1931-2	61.5	55.4	U
	1932-3	69.8	64.9	U
Irish F. S.	1930-1	14.7	14.2	F
0.78	1931-2	42.7	35.8	F
	1932-3	65.2	54.5	F
Latvia	1930-1	23.1	29.5	F
0.80	1931-2	51.4	61.1	F
	1932-3	66.9	73.9	F
Lithuania	1930-1	+3.4 *	1.2	F
0.98	1931-2	21.3	25.5	F
	1932-3	40.5	48.2	F
Malaya	1930-1	41.5	35.1	U
1.01	1931-2	65.5	60.1	U
	1932-3	72.3	70.6	U
Mexico	1930-1	32.1	27.7	U
1.60	1931-2	53.0	57.9	U
	1932-3	68.3	68.2	U
Netherlands	1930-1	23.8	20.7	F
0.73	1931-2	45.7	41.3	F
	1932-3	60.5	53.9	F
New Zealand	1930-1	33.9	29.6	U
1.17	1931-2	52.3	58.1	U
	1932-3	59.3	67.4	U
Nicaragua	1930-1	36.4	43.7	F
0.86	1931-2	53.9	62.7	F
	1932-3	65.0	74.2	F
Nigeria	1930-1	33.3	35.6	U
1.20	1931-2	56.7	61.2	U
	1932-3	63.5	67.3	U

Country, and ratio of exports to imports in 1928-9 (1)	Two-year period compared to 1928-9 (2)	Percentage decline in exports (3)	Percentage decline in imports (4)	Favourable (F) or unfavourable (U) change in the trade balance (5)
Norway 0.68	1930-1 1931-2 1932-3	21.6 42.7 48.9	10.4 39.2 57.8	U F F
Panama 0.25	1930-1 1931-2 1932-3	29.9 46.0 51.7	11.6 37.6 54.5	F F F
Paraguay 1.04	1930-1 1931-2 1932-3	27.0 42.7 54.1	28.5 61.1 70.7	F F F
Persia 1.68	1930/1-1/2 1931/2-2/3 1932/3-3/4	17.1 35.3 46.4	33.4 57.8 65.1	F U U
Peru 1.77	1930-1 1931-2 1932-3	48.8 65.8 70.6	46.1 68.8 76.8	U U U
Philippines 1.15	1930-1 1931-2 1932-3	24.5 35.8 41.5	20.9 36.6 52.5	U U F
Poland 0.82	1930-1 1931-2 1932-3	19.0 44.3 61.6	42.6 64.0 73.9	F F F
Portugal 0.40	1930-1 1931-2 1932-3	19.0 37.2 47.4	23.8 46.7 51.9	F F F
Roumania 0.91	1930-1 1931-2 1932-3	10.8 31.7 45.7	38.3 56.9 62.8	F F F
Salvador 1.19	1930-1 1931-2 1932-3	43.3 61.2 74.0	46.9 65.4 73.0	U U U
Siam 1.40	1930/1-1/2 1931/2-2/3 1932/3-3/4	49.6 62.7 65.1	37.0 60.3 66.3	U U U
Spain 0.74	1930-1 1931-2 1932-3	22.8 59.8 66.7	36.9 62.5 68.5	F F F
Turkey 0.69	1930-1 1931-2 1932-3	19.3 33.7 42.8	45.5 57.6 68.0	F F F
Venezuela 1.67	1930-1 1931-2 1932-3	6.6 23.8 31.6	35.1 63.1 72.5	F F F
Yugoslavia 0.93	1930-1 1931-2 1932-3	18.0 45.9 61.4	22.5 51.2 68.3	F F F

* Lithuania's exports increased between 1928-9 and 1930-1.

TABLE II

Changes in the Merchandise Balances of Sixty Countries in the Period 1928-33

Countries	Number of Countries					
	Between 1928-9 and 1930-1		Between 1928-9 and 1931-2		Between 1928-9 and 1932-3	
	Favour- able change	Unfavour- able change	Favour- able change	Unfavour- able change	Favour- able change	Unfavour- able change
Primary- exporting	27	22	28	21	29	20
Industrial- exporting	5	6	6	5	6	5
Total	32	28	34	26	35	25

The figures in column (1) of Table I show the ratio of exports to imports of each country in 1928-9. A figure greater than 1.00 indicates a surplus, and one smaller than 1.00 a deficit. Combination of these data with those of column (5), discussed in the previous paragraph, shows in each case whether an improvement (deterioration) in the balance involved an increase (decline) in a surplus, or a decline (increase) in a deficit. Of the 27, 28, and 29 primary-exporting countries whose balances improved in each of the three periods considered, 21, 23, and 23, respectively, experienced a decline in their deficit; and of the 22, 21, and 20 primary-exporting countries whose balances deteriorated, 19, 20, and 19 experienced a decline in their surplus. This decline in the surplus or deficit of the great majority of the forty-nine countries is discussed in subsequent chapters.[6]

Perusal of Table I, column (5) shows that, except for four primary-exporting countries, the direction of change in the balance of each country was the same in the three periods considered.[7] Often, even the extent of the change varied little between the second and third period. Accordingly, for the sake of brevity we often concentrate our subsequent discussion on the changes in the second period, 1928-9 to 1931-2. However, interperiod comparisons are made whenever they are required.

CHAPTER TWO

THE RELATION BETWEEN IMPORTS AND EXPORTS IN THE BASE PERIOD

I

IN A PERIOD OF DECLINING EXPORTS AND IMPORTS, such as the period considered, the direction of change in a country's balance can be viewed as depending on (*a*) the ratio between exports and imports in the base period, referred to henceforth as "the original relation," and (*b*) the ratio between the percentage decline in imports and the percentage decline in exports, referred to henceforth as "the import/export decline." The balance will change favourably if ratio (*a*) is smaller than ratio (*b*), and unfavourably if it is greater.[1]

While the *direction* of change in a country's balance depends on the relation between ratios (*a*) and (*b*), the *extent* of change in the deficit or surplus depends on the original values of imports and exports and the sizes of the percentage declines in imports and exports. Hence, if the original imports (exports) are given, the amount of change in the balance depends, in addition to ratios (*a*) and (*b*), on the size of the percentage decline in exports (imports).[2] Alternatively, if again the original imports (exports) are given, the amount of change in the balance depends on the *difference* between the original imports and exports, the *difference* between the percentage decline in imports and the percentage decline in exports, and the size of the percentage decline in exports (imports).[3]

II

We may now examine the relative importance of the original relation and the import/export decline for the change in the balances of the forty-nine primary-exporting countries in the period 1928-9 to 1931-2. In countries in which the one ratio was greater, and the other smaller, than unity, the direction of change in the balance was the joint effect of both relations. In the remaining countries the two ratios were on the same side of unity and, hence, tended to change the balance in opposite directions. The net effect was determined by the ratio which was further from unity.[4]

The values of the two relations for each of the forty-nine countries are shown in Table III, columns (1) and (2), respectively. Column (4) indicates the relation which accounted for the favourable or unfavourable change in the balance, shown in column (3). These two columns are summarized in Table IV, which shows the number of countries in which the original relation (coupled with a general reduction in trade), the import/export decline, or both, were responsible for the direction of change in the trade balance in the period 1928-9 to 1931-2: sixteen, six, and twenty-seven countries respectively. Judging then by the number of countries affected, the original relation was the more important determinant of the direction

TABLE III

THE ORIGINAL RELATION AND THE IMPORT/EXPORT DECLINE AS DETERMINANTS OF CHANGE IN
THE MERCHANDISE BALANCES OF FORTY-NINE PRIMARY-EXPORTING COUNTRIES
IN THE PERIOD 1928-9 TO 1931-2

Country	Original relation *	Import/ export decline †	Favourable (F) or unfavourable (U) change in the balance	Determinants of change in the balance: original relation (E/I), import/export decline (m/x), or both ‡	Sole or main determinant of change in the balance: § original relation (E/I) or import/ export decline (m/x)
	(1)	(2)	(3)	(4)	(5)
Argentina	1.18	1.08	U	E/I	E/I
Australia	0.99	1.40	F	E/I, m/x	m/x
Bolivia	1.81	1.07	U	E/I	E/I
Brazil	1.08	1.30	F	m/x	m/x
Bulgaria	0.82	1.80	F	E/I, m/x	m/x
Canada	1.09	0.98	U	E/I, m/x	E/I
Ceylon	1.05	0.98	U	E/I, m/x	E/I
Chile	1.52	0.91	U	E/I, m/x	E/I
China	0.82	0.76	U	m/x	m/x
Colombia	0.95	1.80	F	E/I, m/x	m/x
Costa Rica	0.99	1.59	F	E/I, m/x	m/x
Cuba	1.28	1.09	U	E/I	E/I
Denmark	0.94	0.98	F	E/I	E/I
Dominican R.	1.06	1.18	F	m/x	m/x
D.E. Indies	1.43	0.94	U	E/I, m/x	E/I
Ecuador	1.09	1.35	F	m/x	m/x
Egypt	1.02	0.90	U	E/I, m/x	m/x
Estonia	0.96	1.15	F	E/I, m/x	m/x
Finland	0.85	1.47	F	E/I, m/x	m/x
Greece	0.51	1.02	F	E/I, m/x	E/I
Guatemala	0.86	1.29	F	E/I, m/x	m/x
Haiti	1.05	0.92	U	E/I, m/x	m/x
Honduras	1.64	1.25	U	E/I	E/I
Hungary	0.82	1.20	F	E/I, m/x	m/x
India	1.31	0.90	U	E/I, m/x	E/I
Irish F.S.	0.78	0.84	F	E/I	E/I
Latvia	0.80	1.19	F	E/I, m/x	E/I
Lithuania	0.98	1.20	F	E/I, m/x	m/x
Malaya	1.01	0.92	U	E/I, m/x	m/x
Mexico	1.60	1.09	U	E/I	E/I
Netherlands	0.73	0.90	F	E/I	E/I
New Zealand	1.17	1.11	U	E/I	E/I
Nicaragua	0.86	1.16	F	E/I, m/x	m/x
Nigeria	1.20	1.08	U	E/I	E/I
Norway	0.68	0.92	F	E/I	E/I
Panama	0.25	0.82	F	E/I	E/I
Paraguay	1.04	1.43	F	m/x	m/x
Persia	1.68	1.64	U	E/I	E/I
Peru	1.77	1.05	U	E/I	E/I
Philippines	1.15	1.02	U	E/I	E/I
Poland	0.82	1.44	F	E/I, m/x	m/x
Portugal	0.40	1.26	F	E/I, m/x	E/I
Roumania	0.91	1.80	F	E/I, m/x	m/x
Salvador	1.19	1.07	U	E/I	E/I
Siam	1.40	0.96	U	E/I, m/x	E/I

Country	Original relation * (1)	Import/ export decline † (2)	Favourable (F) or unfavour- able (U) change in the balance (3)	Determinants of change in the balance: original relation (E/I), import/export decline (m/x), or both ‡ (4)	Sole or main determinant of change in the balance: § original relation (E/I) or import/ export decline (m/x) (5)
Spain	0.74	1.05	F	E/I, m/x	E/I
Turkey	0.69	1.71	F	E/I, m/x	m/x
Venezuela	1.67	2.65	F	m/x	m/x
Yugoslavia	0.93	1.12	F	E/I, m/x	m/x

* Ratio between exports and imports in 1928-9.

† Ratio between the percentage decline in imports and the percentage decline in exports in the period 1928-9 to 1931-2.

‡ E/I indicates that the balance changed in the direction shown in column (3) because of the original relation of exports to imports, and in spite of the relation between the percentage changes in imports and exports. Conversely, m/x indicates that the balance changed as shown in column (3) because of the import/export decline and in spite of the original relation. Finally, E/I, m/x indicates that both factors contributed to the change observed.

§ The basis on which the original relation, or the import/export decline is taken to be the sole or main determinant of the direction of change in the merchandise balance is indicated in the text (pp. 11-14).

TABLE IV

THE ORIGINAL RELATION AND THE IMPORT/EXPORT DECLINE AS DETERMINANTS OF CHANGE IN THE MERCHANDISE BALANCES OF SIXTY COUNTRIES IN THE PERIOD 1928-9 TO 1931-2

	Number of countries		
	Original relation	Import/export decline	Original relation and import/export decline
49 primary-exporting countries Change in the balance:			
Favourable	5	5	18
Unfavourable	11	1	9
TOTAL	16	6	27
11 industrial-exporting countries Change in the balance:			
Favourable	2	0	4
Unfavourable	1	3	1
TOTAL	3	3	5
All 60 countries Change in the balance:			
Favourable	7	5	22
Unfavourable	12	4	10
TOTAL	19	9	32

of change in the balances. It accounts, wholly or partly, for the phenomenon noted in Chapter I: the improvement or deterioration of forty-three of the forty-nine balances involved a decline in the deficit or the surplus respectively.[5] Only the surpluses of Brazil, the Dominican Republic, Ecuador, Paraguay, and Venezuela, and the deficit of China, increased in spite of the influence of the original relation.

We may further divide the twenty-seven countries, in which both relations were responsible for the direction of change observed in the balance, into those in which the greater part of the change in the deficit or surplus was due to the original relation and those in which it was due to the import/export decline. The partitioning of the change in the balance may be based on a variety of alternative premises. In the great majority of primary-exporting countries, changes in exports were the prime moving factor of changes in incomes, prices, and the balance of trade. Accordingly, we shall ascribe to the original relation that part of the actual change in the deficit or surplus of each country which would have occurred had the imports (and that part of the balance of payments which offset the merchandise deficit or surplus) declined by the same percentage by which the exports decreased; the remainder we ascribe to the import/export decline.[6] Table III, column (5) indicates the relation which accounted in each country for either the entire change in the balance (while the influence of the other relation was in the opposite direction) or for the greater part of the change. Columns (3) and (5) of Table III are summarized in Table V, which shows that the original relation was the more important determinant of change in the balance in twenty-six of the forty-nine countries.[7]

TABLE V

THE ORIGINAL RELATION AND THE IMPORT/EXPORT DECLINE AS SOLE OR MAIN DETERMINANTS OF CHANGE IN THE MERCHANDISE BALANCES OF SIXTY COUNTRIES IN THE PERIOD 1928-9 TO 1931-2

	Number of countries	
	Original relation	Import/export decline
49 primary-exporting countries Change in the balance:		
Favourable	9	19
Unfavourable	17	4
TOTAL	26	23
11 industrial-exporting countries Change in the balance:		
Favourable	5	1
Unfavourable	2	3
TOTAL	7	4
All 60 countries Change in the balance:		
Favourable	14	20
Unfavourable	19	7
TOTAL	33	27

The relative importance of the original relation and the import/export decline may be judged also by the part of the arithmetic sum of the changes in the forty-nine balances[8] which is due to each of the two factors. We ascribe to each factor the part indicated in the previous paragraph. For countries in which the two factors operated in opposite directions, the share of the original relation, computed as indicated, is positive or negative depending on whether or not this factor was the decisive one. The share of the import/export decline, which, as indicated, is equal to the actual change in the balance minus the share of the original relation, is correspondingly negative or positive. The negative dollar shares of each factor are deducted from its aggregate positive share. Table VI

TABLE VI

PARTS OF THE CHANGE IN THE MERCHANDISE BALANCES OF SIXTY COUNTRIES IN THE PERIOD 1928-9 TO 1931-2 DUE TO THE ORIGINAL RELATION AND THE IMPORT/EXPORT DECLINE °

	Parts of the change in the balances			
	Part due to the original relation		Part due to the import/export decline	
	in $ million	%	in $ million	%
49 *primary-exporting countries* Change in the balance:				
Favourable (28 countries)	432.6	47.1	486.6	52.9
Unfavourable (21 countries)	639.8	79.0	169.6	21.0
TOTAL	1,072.4	62.0	656.2	38.0
11 *industrial-exporting countries* Change in the balance:				
Favourable (6 countries)	1,373.1	85.5	232.6	14.5
Unfavourable (5 countries)	445.0	45.1	541.2	54.9
TOTAL	1,818.1	70.1	773.8	29.9
All *60 countries* Change in the balance:				
Favourable (34 countries)	1,805.7	71.5	719.2	28.5
Unfavourable (26 countries)	1,084.8	60.4	710.8	39.6
TOTAL	2,890.5	66.9	1,430.0	33.1

° The dollar figures represent (arithmetic) sums of decreases in deficits and increases in surpluses, of increases in deficits and decreases in surpluses, or both.

indicates that the original relation accounted for 62.0 per cent of the arithmetic sum of the changes in the forty-nine balances.[9]

Yet another way of judging the relative importance of the original relation and the import/export decline is to compare the arithmetic sum of changes in the balances which each factor tended to cause, irrespective of whether the actual change in the balance was, in each case, in the same or the opposite direction.[10] Again, the original relation tended to produce a larger total change in the balances of the forty-nine countries than the import/export decline: $1,341.0 and $1,026.7 million, respectively.

III

Tables V and VI indicate that the original relation was more important than the import/export decline in the change in balances, in the period 1928-9 to 1931-2, of the eleven industrial-exporting countries—indeed, more than in the primary-exporting countries.[11] We conclude, that it was the more important factor in the change in balances of all sixty primary- and industrial-exporting countries (see the last section of Tables V and VI).

It is necessary to stress this importance of the original relation because, in some cases, it has been neglected badly. Thus, unfavourable changes in trade balances in the downswing have been ascribed to income elasticities of demand at home and abroad, and other factors, which, taken together, are supposed to account for an alleged import/export decline smaller than unity, when, in fact, the balance turned unfavourably because of the original relation (a surplus in the boom coupled with a general reduction in trade in the downswing), and *in spite of* an import/export decline *exceeding unity*.[12]

One might tend to minimize the importance of the original relation by ascribing the surpluses or deficits of the various countries in the boom to import/export increases in the upswing similar to the subsequent import/export declines, thus suggesting that the import/export change was, in effect, the ultimate determinant of the cyclical change in the balances. For the sake of the argument we may assume that, in each country in the upswing, the import/export change was equal to, and the direction of change in the balance was the reverse of, that observed in the ensuing downswing. Then, the foregoing statement could be made for the seventeen primary-exporting countries in which the import/export decline combined with the original relation to change the balance from a deficit (surplus) in the boom to a surplus (deficit) in the depression, and in which we also found that the import/export decline was the main determinant of the change in the balances.[13] But in all the twenty-six primary-exporting countries in which we found that the original relation was the sole or main determinant of the change in the balance, the surplus or deficit in 1928-9 merely diminished in 1931-2, without changing to a deficit or surplus, respectively.[14] The original relation would therefore be the sole or main determinant of the assumed reverse change in the upswing, of the higher surplus or deficit in the boom.[15]

IV

For the sake of brevity we concentrated our discussion of changes in balances over the cyclical downswing after 1928-9 on the period 1928-9 to 1931-2. We may now compare the three periods 1928-9 to 1930-1, 1928-9 to 1931-2, and 1928-9 to 1932-3. The relative importance of the original relation as a determinant of change in the balance increased over the three periods, particularly between the first and the second. In the first period the original relation was the sole determinant of change in the balance of eight countries and the main determinant in ten (the figures for the import/export decline were nine and twenty-two respectively); the total of eighteen increased to twenty-six in the second period, and to twenty-eight in the third period.[16] Between the first and third period then the original relation displaced the import/export decline as the sole or main determinant in ten countries. The role of the original relation increased also in five countries in which it had been the main determinant in the first period and became the sole in the third, and in another eighteen countries in which the original relation or the import/export decline was the main determinant in both the first and third periods, but the original relation was responsible for a greater part of the change in the balance in the latter than the former period. Only in five of the forty-nine countries was there a decline between the first and third period in the part of the change in the balance for which the original relation was responsible.[17]

This change in the relative importance of the original relation is due, of course, to the change in the value of the import/export decline. In forty-one countries this value was closer to unity in the third period than in the first, and in the other eight countries it was remoter from unity.[18] In thirty-one of the former forty-one countries the value of the import/export decline remained in the third period on the same side of unity on which it had been in the first period (above in twenty-five countries and below in six). In these countries then the relative importance of the original relation as a determinant of the change in the balance either increased (twenty-three countries) or did not change (eight countries). In another eight of the forty-one countries, as well as in four of the eight countries in which the value of the import/export decline was further from unity in the third period than in the first, the import/export decline was smaller than unity in the first period, and greater in the third. In eight of these twelve countries, which had a surplus in 1928-9, and in which the original relation had been the main or the less important determinant of the change in the balance in the first period, it became the sole determinant in the third period; and in two other countries, which had a deficit in 1928-9, and in which the original relation had worked against the actual change in the balance in the first period, it became the main determinant in the third period.

The increase then between the first and third period in the importance of the original relation as a determinant of change in the trade balance is related to the decline towards unity in the import/export decline of twenty-five countries and the increase towards or beyond unity of that of eighteen countries.[19] These changes are in turn due to one or both of the following changes. In all forty-nine countries the percentage decline in exports was greater in the third than in the first period. In the majority of the forty-nine countries the arithmetic difference between the percentage decline in imports and the percentage decline in exports was smaller in the third than in the first period. These two changes are discussed in later chapters.[20]

We have completed our discussion of the role of the original relation in the changes of the balances of the forty-nine countries. In the following chapters we examine the percentage declines in exports and imports. Some remarks on the relative importance of the original relation in particular groups of primary-exporting countries will be made in Chapter 8.

CHAPTER THREE

CHANGES IN EXPORTS OF INDIVIDUAL COMMODITIES

IN THE EXAMINATION of the changes in exports and imports we begin with the former. As explained earlier and, more fully, in Chapter 6, the changes in the trade balances of most of the primary-exporting countries probably started largely from changes in exports, which, through changes in incomes and prices, led to changes in imports.

I

The percentage decline in total exports of each of the forty-nine primary-exporting countries between 1928-9 on the one hand, and 1930-1, 1931-2 or 1932-3 on the other, is shown in Table I, column (3). To facilitate the use of these data, particularly for intercountry comparisons, we have classified the countries in Table VII by the percentage decline in their exports in each of the three periods. Within each class the countries are listed alphabetically. A graphic impression of the percentage decline in exports of the various countries, of their ranking by this criterion, and of the changes in these factors over the three periods may be obtained from Diagrams I, II and III, located in Chapter 6 and designed chiefly to illustrate phenomena discussed in that chapter.

A glance at Table VII shows that in all three periods the percentage declines in exports of the forty-nine countries varied greatly. Thus, the decline between 1928-9 and 1931-2 ranged from 21.3 and 23.8 per cent in the case of Lithuania and Venezuela, respectively, to 65.8 in Bolivia and Peru, and 73.8 in Chile. Generally speaking, the decline in exports of the various countries varied with the type of goods exported and the characteristic conditions of supply of, and demand for, these commodities—although, as we shall see, exports of given goods from various countries were sometimes influenced also by special conditions. We may start our discussion of the first, and more general determinant, namely, of the type of exports, with a detailed examination of the changes in exports of the four Balkan countries, Bulgaria, Greece, Roumania, and Yugoslavia. While these countries had broadly similar economic backgrounds and basic conditions of production, owing to differences in resource endowment they exported a noteworthy variety of goods.

II

On the basis chiefly of significant demand and supply characteristics the Balkan exports may be grouped into four broad classes: Class A, including staple foodstuffs and other commodities facing a low price elasticity of demand; Class B, including non-staple and semi-luxury agricultural products whose price elasticity of demand was higher; Class C, including chiefly raw materials (except fuel)

TABLE VII

FORTY-NINE PRIMARY-EXPORTING COUNTRIES CLASSIFIED BY THE PERCENTAGE
DECLINE IN THEIR EXPORTS IN THE PERIODS
1928-9 TO 1930-1, 1928-9 TO 1931-2, AND 1928-9 TO 1932-3

Percentage decline
in exports

Section A. 1928-9 to 1930-1

i.	0 –15.0	Bulgaria, Denmark, Irish F.S., Lithuania *, Roumania, Venezuela
ii.	15.1–20.0	Costa Rica, Persia, Poland, Portugal, Turkey, Yugoslavia
iii.	20.1–25.0	Colombia, Ecuador, Finland, Greece, Hungary, Latvia, Netherlands, Norway, Philippines, Spain
iv.	25.1–30.0	Guatemala, Honduras, Panama, Paraguay
v.	30.1–35.0	Estonia, Mexico, New Zealand, Nigeria
vi.	35.1–40.0	Bolivia, Brazil, Ceylon, Dominican R., D.E. Indies, India, Nicaragua
vii.	40.1–45.0	Haiti, Malaya, Salvador
viii.	45.1–50.0	Australia, Canada, Chile, China, Cuba, Egypt, Peru, Siam
ix.	Over 50.0	Argentina

Section B. 1928-9 to 1931-2

i.	20.1–35.0	Bulgaria, Lithuania, Roumania, Turkey, Venezuela
ii.	35.1–40.0	Costa Rica, Denmark, Persia, Philippines, Portugal
iii.	40.1–45.0	Colombia, Ecuador, Finland, Honduras, Irish F.S., Norway, Paraguay, Poland
iv.	45.1–50.0	Greece, Netherlands, Panama, Yugoslavia
v.	50.1–55.0	Australia, Dominican R., Estonia, Guatemala, Hungary, Latvia, Mexico, New Zealand, Nicaragua
vi.	55.1–60.0	Brazil, Ceylon, D.E. Indies, Egypt, Haiti, Nigeria, Spain
vii.	60.1–65.0	Argentina, Canada, China, Cuba, India, Salvador, Siam
viii.	65.1–70.0	Bolivia, Malaya, Peru
ix.	Over 70.0	Chile

Section C. 1928-9 to 1932-3

i.	30.1–45.0	Lithuania, Philippines, Turkey, Venezuela
ii.	45.1–50.0	Norway, Persia, Portugal, Roumania
iii.	50.1–55.0	Australia, Bulgaria, Colombia, Costa Rica, Finland, Panama, Paraguay
iv.	55.1–60.0	Denmark, Ecuador, Honduras, New Zealand
v.	60.1–65.0	Brazil, Dominican R., Egypt, Greece, Haiti, Hungary, Netherlands, Nicaragua, Nigeria, Poland, Yugoslavia
vi.	65.1–70.0	Argentina, Canada, Ceylon, D.E. Indies, Estonia, Guatemala, India, Irish F.S., Latvia, Mexico, Siam, Spain
vii.	70.1–75.0	Bolivia, Cuba, Malaya, Peru, Salvador
viii.	75.1–80.0	China
ix.	Over 80.0	Chile

* In the period 1928-9 to 1930-1 Lithuania's exports increased by 3.4 per cent.

whose income elasticity of demand was fairly substantial; and Class D, including
fuels, whose income elasticity of demand was comparatively low.[1] The individual
exports falling in each of these classes, and the rate of decline in these exports
between 1928-9 and 1931-2 are shown in Table VIII. The four classes may be
considered in detail.

III

Class A. This group includes staple foodstuffs and other commodities facing a
low price elasticity of demand: grain, dry beans, tobacco, wine, fodder, and
colza.[2] As indicated in Table VIII, with the exception of wheat, maize, rye, and
Bulgarian fodder, the decline in these exports was relatively heavy; it was greater
than the percentage decline in the total, or the Class B exports of the Balkan
countries.

TABLE VIII

PERCENTAGE CHANGE BETWEEN 1928-9 AND 1931-2 IN THE EXPORT VALUE OF THE MAIN BALKAN EXPORTS

Exports	Percentage change (rise (+), fall (–)) in export value			
	Bulgaria	Greece	Roumania	Yugoslavia
Class A				
Barley	−55.1		−54.9	
Maize	−10.1		+ 2.8	+19.0
Oats			−34.8	
Rye	+11.8		−24.4	
Wheat	+506.8		+831.6	
Other cereals *				−62.1
Fodder (bran, etc.)	+35.7			−49.7
Dry beans			−46.5	−63.4
Tobacco	−58.0 †	−52.4		
Wine		−74.2		
Colza (rape-seed)	−84.8			
Class B				
Cheese	−26.5			
Eggs	+13.2			−37.3
Meat, game, and meat extract			−12.7 ‡	−25.7
Poultry				+118.6
Olives		−30.3		
Olive oil		+ 0.9		
Olive-stone oil		− 7.2		
Haricots	−24.9			
Currants		−23.3		
Raisins		+ 4.1		
Figs		−39.6		
Plums and other fruit				−19.3
Class C				
Building timber			−64.3	−58.3
Hides and Skins	−71.4	−60.0		−64.8
Livestock	−62.2 §		−50.1	−40.1
Essence of rose	−75.8			
Silk cocoons	−88.1			
Hemp				−54.0
Copper and manuf. of (incl. alloys)				−41.3 °
Other metals				−52.3
Class D				
Crude and residual petroleum, and gas oil			+12.9	
Motor spirit			−19.1	
Refined petroleum (kerosene)			−49.3	
Other mineral oils			−49.3	
TOTAL EXPORTS	−26.2	−45.7	−31.7	−45.9

* For Yugoslavia: cereals other than maize.
† Percentage decline between 1928-9 and 1932.
‡ Percentage decline between 1928-9 and the average of the years 1931 and 1933.
§ Includes poultry, which has been listed in Class B. No separate figures are readily available. It may be noted, however, that the exports of a broader group of live animals, including poultry, decreased by 31.5 per cent only, compared to a fall of 77.8 per cent in the exports of oxen, cows and sheep. This difference is discussed later in the text.
° Percentage decline between 1929 and 1931-2.

Owing mainly to the specialized nature of resources, the scarcity of non-farm employment opportunities and the immobility of the Balkan peasant, his lack of capital, and the fairly long gestation period, the short-run elasticity of supply of the goods in this class was small.[3] In the downswing, their supply curve probably shifted somewhat to the right owing to the decrease in the cost of seed, containers, and a few other requisites. In any event, as the typically inelastic demand curve for such goods shifted to the left, their price declined heavily, while the quantity exported declined little or increased. A heavier fall in their export value was avoided because of the low income elasticity of demand for these goods.[4]

These are the basic conditions that determined the decline in the exports of Class A goods from these, and other, countries. However, the output of many Class A goods varies with weather conditions which affected, in different ways, some exports of Balkan grain and the exports of Greek wine.

Between 1928-9 and 1931-2 Balkan exports of wheat, maize, and rye, and Bulgarian exports of fodder either increased, or declined relatively moderately. As Table IX, Part A indicates, in this period the volume of wheat exports of Bulgaria and Roumania increased greatly owing chiefly to bumper crops in the years 1930 and 1931.[5] Since in 1928-9 wheat exports represented a small percentage of domestic production, and since in the downswing stocks could not be greatly increased in view of the fall in prices and the lack of credit and storage facilities, the relative increase in exports was bound to be great. In such circumstances the higher price elasticity of demand for the exports of these countries than for the same types of product in general assumed great practical significance. Probably, Bulgaria and Roumania benefited also from the price-support policies of countries such as the United States, from the relative stickiness of transportation costs, which favoured a shift from overseas to nearby suppliers in times of falling prices, and from the fact that Bulgaria and Roumania were small suppliers of wheat and hence the price elasticity of substitution between their exports and similar exports of their competitors tended to be high.[6]

As Table IX, Part B, indicates, the increase in the volume of maize exports of Bulgaria and Roumania was similarly due mainly to large crops in the years 1929, 1931 and 1932, and the increase in Yugoslavia's exports of maize to exceptionally small crops in the years 1927 and 1928. Owing chiefly to large crops in the years 1930 and 1931 the volume of rye exports of Bulgaria and Roumania increased between 1928-9 and 1931-2 from 14.0 to 42.0 thousand metric tons, and from 24.1 to 56.0 thousand tons, respectively.[7] Finally, the increase in exports of Bulgarian fodder must be ascribed to similar factors, which raised the volume exported from 14.6 thousand metric tons in 1928-9 to 36.7 thousand in 1931-2.

Wine is another product whose output varies considerably with natural factors. In 1930/1-1/2 the wine output of almost every European country close to the Mediterranean Sea (specifically of Bulgaria, Cyprus, France, Greece, Italy, Portugal, and Spain) was lower than in 1927/8-8/9. The total wine output of the seven countries declined by 11.8 per cent.[8] In the period 1926 to 1935 production of wine in Algeria expanded greatly. Between 1927/8-8/9 and 1930/1-1/2 the output of Algerian wine increased by 36.2 per cent.[9] Nevertheless, the total output of the European countries listed above and Algeria decreased in that period by 8.2 per cent. The shift of the typically inelastic supply curve of wine to the

TABLE IX

VOLUME OF BULGARIA'S AND ROUMANIA'S PRODUCTION AND EXPORTS OF
WHEAT AND MAIZE, 1926-34
(Thousand metric tons)

Part A Wheat

| Year | Bulgaria | | Roumania | |
	Production	Exports	Production	Exports
1926	993	36	3,018	272
1927	1,146	39	2,632	210
1928	1,339	21	3,143	28
1929	904	3	2,716	7
1930	1,560	39	3,560	337
1931	1,736	243	3,682	986
1932	1,309	173	1,511	123
1933	1,511	101	3,241	12
1934	1,078	35	2,085	1

Part B. Maize

| | Bulgaria | | Roumania | | Yugoslavia | |
	Production	Exports	Production	Exports	Production	Exports
1926	686	99	5,842	690	3,410	895
1927	533	129	3,531	1,762	2,109	198
1928	508	48	2,769	473	1,819	4
1929	940	79	6,376	375	4,148	167
1930	787	192	4,521	1,181	3,465	503
1931	991	135	6,071	1,027	3,203	225
1932	887	168	5,995	1,739	4,793	185
1933	951	100	4,547	1,072	3,578	601
1934	790	126	4,852	530	5,154	673

SOURCES: Stanford University, Food Research Institute, *Wheat Studies*, IX, Oct. 1932-Sept. 1933, 118, 269 (where also the exceptionally high yields of wheat per acre in the years 1930 and 1931 are shown), and XII, Sept. 1935-June 1936, 165, 400; LN, *Statistical Yearbook 1930/1*, 85, and *1935/6*, 97; *idem, International Trade Statistics*; various years, and IIA, *International Yearbook of Agriculture Statistics, 1929-30*, 295.

left to a large extent offset the effects on price of the decline in demand. Between 1928-9 and 1931-2 the gold price of wine exported from Greece, Portugal, and Algeria declined only by 15-20 per cent.[10] On the other hand, as indicated, the output of wine in Greece and Portugal had decreased (in the former country by as much as 23.3 per cent between 1927/8-8/9 and 1930/1-1/2), while the output in Algeria had increased. Consequently, the quantity of wine exports of Greece and Portugal declined between 1928-9 and 1931-2 by 68.7 and 63.5 per cent, respectively, while that of Algeria increased by 57.1 per cent.

IV

Class B. Non-staple and semi-luxury agricultural products are included in this group: dairy products, meat, poultry, olives, olive oil, vegetables, and fruit. Generally, as indicated in Table VIII, the exports of these commodities either increased, or decreased proportionately less than the total, or the Class A, exports of the Balkan countries.

The short-run elasticity of supply of most commodities in Class B, as in Class A, was small, while generally, the income elasticity of demand for the former goods was greater than the elasticity for the latter.[11] The smaller decline in exports of Class B goods is explained chiefly by the generally greater price elasticities of demand for these, than for Class A, goods. In many cases in which demand was elastic[12] Class B exports were helped also by a larger shift of the export supply curve to the right than in the case of Class A goods.

The price elasticities of demand were generally higher for Class B than Class A goods partly because of the tendency of consumers to shift towards the former goods when prices fall; and partly because the f.o.b. export price constituted a greater part of the price to the foreign consumer in the case of Class B goods than of the bulky commodities of Class A.[13] Since transportation, handling, and warehousing costs were relatively sticky compared to the f.o.b. export prices of agricultural produce (and specific import duties were absolutely sticky), a fall in the f.o.b. price of the goods of Class B tended to affect the quantity demanded more than a proportional fall in the f.o.b. price of Class A goods.[14]

The export supply curve for meat, poultry, and dairy products probably shifted to the right considerably owing to the heavy decline in the price of feed, to the possibility of reducing flocks and herds, and to the tendency of the poor Balkan farmer in the depression to moderate the decline in his cash revenue by reducing his stock of animals and by shifting to the consumption of more staple foodstuffs. Some of these developments were aided by the bumper crops of grains noted earlier.[15] Such factors and the fact that Balkan exports of meat, poultry, and dairy products were, as a rule, a small part of Balkan output in the base period, largely explain the substantial relative increase in the volume of exports of, for instance, cheese and eggs from Bulgaria, and pigs and poultry for Yugoslavia: between 1928-9 and 1931-2 the quantity of these exports rose by 27.8, 76.8, 22.6, and 184.9 per cent, respectively. As with most Class A goods, the supply of Balkan olive and fruit products was affected also by natural conditions. While Spain's output of olive oil declined between 1927/8-8/9 and 1930/1-1/2 by 45.7 per cent, Greek output increased by 16.5 per cent. The quantity of Greek exports of olive oil and olives increased between 1928-9 and 1931-2 by 77.3 and 14.2 per cent, respectively. On the other hand, owing to severe frost in March 1931 the Greek output of currants and figs was exceptionally low in 1931, and the quantity of fig exports declined in that year very heavily.[16]

V

Class C. This class is composed of raw materials (except fuel) and other primary products facing a substantial income elasticity of demand: hides and skins, other agricultural raw materials, building timber, livestock, and metallic minerals. Generally, the decline in these exports, shown in Table VIII, was relatively heavy: it was greater than the percentage decline in the total, or the Class B or D, exports of the Balkan countries.

As indicated, the chief characteristic of the goods included in this class and accounting for the heavy decline in their exports, was a short-run income elasticity of demand which, in all likelihood, was higher than that for any of the other three classes of exports. Another important factor was that these goods (as well as many other Class C, and several Class A goods, exported by the forty-nine primary-exporting countries and listed in Table X) are storable for longer periods than Class B goods and, hence, are more subject to speculation and change in inventories. When industrial output declines heavily, and manufacturers and export and import traders become panicky, as in the downswing after 1929, decreases in prices are accompanied and enhanced by a strong tendency to reduce stocks. As with the exports of Balkan grain and Greek wine, non-cyclical factors also affected the exports of some Class C goods. Thus, Roumanian and Yugoslavian timber exports faced increasing Russian competition, and Bulgarian exports of essence of rose were affected by the long-term decline in demand for this product for church services in Russia and the perfume industry of Western Europe.[17]

While meat and poultry were listed in Class B, livestock is included in Class C. The price elasticity of demand for livestock was probably lower than the elasticity for meat and poultry: its value constituted a smaller part of the cost of the final commodity than in the case of those goods. Since transportation, handling, warehousing and processing costs were relatively sticky compared to the f.o.b. export price of agricultural goods (and specific import duties were absolutely sticky),[18] a decline in the f.o.b. price of livestock tended to affect the quantity demanded less than a proportional fall in the f.o.b. price of meat. The greater decline in exports of livestock than of meat and poultry was probably due chiefly to the greater income elasticity of demand for the former. The Balkan export trade statistics show that, generally speaking, the smaller the size of the animal the less was the decline in exports, since the smaller the animal the closer it came to being a consumer good.[19]

The elasticity of supply and the change in supply in the downswing varied between various types of products included in Class C. As indicated later, such differences on the supply side help to explain differences between the cyclical changes in prices, and quantities exported, of various types of Class C goods.[20]

VI

Class D. Fuels comprise this class. Roumania's total oil exports declined by 21.6 per cent; proportionately less than her total, or Class C, exports.

The short-run elasticity of supply of oil probably exceeded the elasticity of supply of agricultural products included in Classes A, B, and C. Probably, the supply curve shifted to the right owing to the decline in the cost of labour, fuel, repair and maintenance of wells and equipment, and miscellaneous supplies. Furthermore, since fixed costs are a substantial part of total costs, covering only variable costs allows a considerable shift of the supply curve over short periods. On the demand side, it is necessary to distinguish between the various types of oil listed in Table VIII.[21]

The price and income elasticities of demand for the third item (kerosene or lamp oil) should be similar to the elasticities for most goods of Class A, in which kerosene should be included. While the quantity of kerosene exported from Roumania increased by 34.0 per cent between 1928-9 and 1931-2, the low price elasticity of demand led to a heavy decline in the value of kerosene exports.[22]

While the income elasticity of demand for the first two oil items listed in Table

VIII probably exceeded the elasticity for such goods as those included in Class A, it was not high. The volume of industrial fuel used did not decrease nearly proportionately to the volume of other raw materials and industrial output; and the demand for motor spirit was "only moderately sensitive to cyclical changes in income."[23] In any event, the income elasticity of demand for these two oil items was probably smaller than the elasticity for most Class C goods; and it was not large enough to offset the relatively favourable effects of a higher price elasticity of demand for these oil items than for Class A goods. Further, the expansion of aviation in the years considered and the longterm substitution of oil for other fuels in some industries favoured the demand for these two oil items. Other factors which probably favoured Roumania's oil exports were the heavier fall in money costs in less developed economies such as Roumania, production restrictions in the United States, and restrictions of exports from other oil-producing countries.[24]

VII

From the individual exports of the Balkan countries we may extend the discussion to the commodities exported by the other forty-five countries considered in this study. Detailed examination of their trade statistics indicates that the great bulk of their primary exports can be broadly classified in the four classes noted earlier. This classification is shown in Table X. Generally, between 1928-9 and 1931-2 the exports of Class A and C goods declined heavily, while Class B and D exports declined lightly or increased.

The main factors accounting for the differences in the relative decline in value of exports among the goods listed in the four classes were noted in sections III-VI of this chapter. Since changes in the value of exports of given goods consisted of changes in prices and in quantities, we may now inquire into the changes in these two components. In doing so, we shall refer also to some significant differences between the behaviour of values, prices or quantities of exports of goods included in the same class, and between the behaviour of exports of the same type of good from different countries.

VIII

Generally, between 1928-9 and 1931-2 the world output of the staple commodities listed in Class A did not change much. Thus, the output of wheat, rye, rice, cocoa, coffee, tea, sugar, wine, tobacco, groundnuts, and linseed increased or declined by 7 per cent or less. The world output of maize increased by 9.6 per cent, and that of copra declined by 14.0 per cent.[25]

The quantity of world exports of these commodities also tended to change little. Between 1928-9 and 1931-2 the quantity exported of wheat, rice, cocoa, coffee, tea, wine, groundnuts, groundnut oil, linseed, palm kernels, and palm and palm-kernel oil increased or declined by 7 per cent or less. Notable exceptions to the relatively small change in quantity of Class A exports were sugar and copra, which declined by 14.3 and 14.0 per cent, respectively, and maize which increased by 36.4 per cent.[26]

While the quantity of world exports of Class A goods as a rule changed little, the prices of these goods declined heavily. Thus, between 1928-9 and 1931-2 the

TABLE X

CLASSIFICATION OF THE MAIN PRIMARY EXPORTS OF
FORTY-NINE PRIMARY-EXPORTING COUNTRIES

Class A. Staple foodstuffs and other commodities facing a low price elasticity of demand

Maize	Tea	Cottonseed
Wheat	Sugar	Groundnuts
Other cereals	Common wine	Linseed
Flour	Tobacco	Palm oil and kernels
Rice	Bean cake and oil	Kerosene
Dried legumes	Coconut oil	Opium
Cocoa	Copra	
Coffee	Copra-meal and -cake	

Class B. Non-staple and semi-luxury agricultural products

Butter	Tinned fish	Currants	Madeira wine
Cheese	Other fish	Dates	Port
Eggs	Fresh vegetables	Figs	Other fine wines
Bacon	Tomatoes	Oranges	Cigars
Frozen meat	Olives	Raisins	
Other meat	Olive oil	Other fresh or	
Poultry	Bananas	dried fruit	

Class C. Raw materials (except fuel and wood pulp) and other primary products facing a substantial income elasticity of demand

Raw cotton	Hides and skins	Zinc and zinc ores
Wool	Livestock	Silver and silver ores
Silk	Copper and copper ores	Nitrate of soda
Raw jute	Iron, ore and semi-	Wood
Hemp	manufactured	Cork, raw and sheets
Other vegetable fibres	Lead	
Raw rubber	Nickel	
Feathers	Tin and tin ores	

Class D. Fuels, pulp, and paper

Crude and residual petroleum, and fuel oil	Coke and briquettes
Gasoline and motor spirit	Wood pulp
Benzine	Paper
Coal	

gold prices of wheat, maize, rye, barley, rice, cocoa, coffee, tea, sugar, ground-nuts, linseed, palm oil, and palm kernels declined by percentages ranging from 47 to 63 per cent.[27]

The small change in export quantity and large change in price of the goods included in Class A are explained by factors discussed with reference to Balkan exports, chiefly by the low price elasticities of demand and supply for these goods, and for some of them also by the significant effect of changes in traders' inventories. Naturally, differences with respect to these factors, as well as other conditions of supply and demand, resulted in several interesting differences between the changes in prices, quantities, or values of export of various Class A goods. For instance, reference was made earlier to the large increase in the quantity of maize exports; the decline in the price of maize was among the heaviest of Class A goods. Owing to restrictive production policies of the Persian government the quantity of opium exports declined between 1928-9 and 1931-2 by as much as 44.4 per cent. Even between such goods as tea and coffee there were noteworthy differences in demand and especially supply—for instance, with respect to control of production and elasticity of supply, natural variations in yield, and length of the gestation period.[28]

Interesting differences are found also between changes in exports of given goods from different countries. Some of these differences were due chiefly to differences in conditions and policies of supply and export. The output of many Class A goods varied with weather conditions, and the relative change in quantity exported was particularly large in countries in which exports were a small part of domestic output. The quantity and price of exports were sometimes affected also by changes in supply in other important countries. Striking examples of the effects of these factors were found in the discussion of exports of Balkan grain and Greek wine.[29] Again, while the quantity of wheat exported from Argentina and Canada declined between 1928-9 and 1931-2 by 40.5 and 32.4 per cent respectively, the quantity exported from Australia increased by 83.0 per cent, owing chiefly to exceptionally large crops in the years 1930-2 and food shortages in the Far East. In the period considered Brazil's coffee production represented about two-thirds of the world output. While in 1931 and 1932 she destroyed huge quantities of coffee in order to support its price, smaller Latin American coffee exporters, such as Colombia, Costa Rica, or the Dominican Republic, exported as much as possible. Moreover, some of these countries exported coffee of a higher grade than Brazil's, and in times of falling prices the demand for the former tended to decline less: the higher grades of coffee were consumed more by people whose income elasticity of demand was relatively low. Also, a given proportional decline in price tended to favour the more expensive grade of coffee, owing mainly to the relative stickiness of transport, warehousing, and handling costs.[30] Again, while the quantity of tea exported from Ceylon and the Dutch East Indies increased between 1928-9 and 1931-2 by 0.9 and 10.1 per cent, respectively, and that from India declined only by 4.2 per cent, the quantity exported from China decreased by 26.7 per cent. This relatively heavy decline was due chiefly to the expansion of tea production in the U.S.S.R. and the fluctuations in Soviet tea imports.[31]

Other differences between changes in exports of given goods from different countries were due chiefly to differences in demand conditions and policies in traditional export markets. The basic characteristics of demand, indicated earlier for the various classes of exports, were those prevailing in important foreign markets. Sometimes conditions were different in the less important markets. Thus, rice exports tended to decline more or less depending on the country of destination: in some countries (Far East) it was a staple foodstuff (Class A), while in others (many European countries) it shared the characteristics of other Class B goods.[32] Sugar was a necessity for higher income groups, but a semi-luxury for lower income groups in less developed countries. In the depression the latter tended to substitute inferior produce, such as syrups, or to reduce consumption of such foodstuffs more heavily.[33]

Differences between changes in exports of given goods from different countries were sometimes due to the fact that in certain importing countries some Class A goods were subject to specific import duties whose magnitude varied with the country of origin. Thus, British cocoa imports were subject either to a General import duty or to a lower British Preferential duty. When prices declined, cocoa exports subject to the former duty could remain competitive on the British market only if their export price declined relatively more than the price of cocoa exports subject to the lower duty.[34] Finally, changes in policies in traditional markets sometimes affected differently the exports from different countries. Cuba's sugar exports were hit hard by the increase in duties in the Smoot-Hawley tariff. The volume of her raw sugar exports to the United States declined from 4.15 million short tons in 1929 to 1.57 million in 1933. On the other hand, and although total United States sugar consumption decreased, imports from the insular possessions (chiefly, the Philippines, Hawaii, and Puerto Rico) increased.[35]

Exceptionally light decreases in the quantity and value of certain Class A exports, such as those noted, were of decisive importance in some cases: the decline in the total exports of a few countries depending heavily on Class A exports was considerably smaller than the typical decline in the exports of countries exporting such goods.

IX

Between 1928-9 and 1931-2 the world output of dairy, meat, and fish products listed in Class B either increased or declined very little. Thus, the output of butter, cheese, "mutton and lamb," "pork, bacon, etc.," and fish increased by 11.3, 6.0, 5.7, 3.8, and 1.9 per cent, respectively; the output of veal and beef declined by 1.5 and 3.0 per cent, respectively.[36]

The quantity of world exports of these commodities either declined little or increased—in a few cases substantially.[37] Thus, between 1928-9 and 1931-2 world exports of cheese, and fish exports from Norway, Portugal, and Spain declined in quantity by 8.4 and 12.9 per cent, respectively. The quantity of exports of frozen and chilled meat from Argentina, Australia, New Zealand, and Uruguay declined by 0.8 per cent; and the quantity of all meat (excluding livestock, live pigs, and live poultry) exported from Argentina, Australia, Brazil, the Irish Free State, Lithuania, the Netherlands, New Zealand, Paraguay, Poland, Uruguay, and Yugoslavia increased by 1.0 per cent. World exports of butter, and exports of bacon from Denmark and the Irish Free State increased in quantity by 14.3 and 36.8 per cent, respectively.[38]

Adequate estimates of world output for most of the fruits and vegetables listed in Class B are not readily available. Like many commodities of Class A, the output and exports of these goods are subject to the vagaries of nature. Sometimes the effect of poor crops in some countries was balanced by large crops in others. Thus, while the output of bananas in such countries as Colombia, Costa Rica, and Panama declined substantially between 1928-9 and 1931-2, the output in other countries, such as Brazil and Honduras, increased considerably. Consequently, world exports of bananas declined in quantity only by 2.7 per cent.[39] Furthermore, a few of these commodities are storable, and large changes in output due to natural factors were often accompanied by small changes in exports. In 1928-9 production of olive oil in Greece, Italy, and Spain represented more than four-fifths of world output. Owing to great variation in yield, the output of olive oil in the three countries declined between 1927/8-8/9 and 1930/1-1/2 by 27.4 per cent. But their exports of olive oil declined in quantity between 1928-9 and 1931-2 only by 8.4 per cent.[40]

The available data indicate that, unless the output of fruits and vegetables was affected by natural conditions, the quantity of such exports tended to increase. Thus, between 1928-9 and 1931-2 world exports of citrus fruits and grapes increased in quantity by 9.6 and 2.5 per cent, respectively. The quantities of fresh apples, apricots, bananas, grapefruit, grapes, lemons, oranges, peaches, pears, pineapples, and preserved fruit imported by the United Kingdom increased. The quantity of all fresh fruit imported by Denmark, France, Norway, Sweden, and the United Kingdom increased by 7.2, 88.3, 14.3, 20.3, and 20.2 per cent, respectively. Even German imports of fruit increased slightly, by 1.3 per cent. Of the advanced countries only the United States seems to have experienced a fairly significant decline in the quantity of fruit imported.[41]

The decline in price varied more among goods included in Class B than in Class A. Generally, the decline in prices of meat and dairy products was smaller than that of Class A goods. Between 1928-9 and 1931-2, or 1928/9 and 1931/2 the gold prices of bacon, butter, cheese, eggs, beef, chilled beef, ham, mutton, pork, salted cod, and olive oil decreased by percentages ranging from 37 to 50 per cent. The decline in fruit prices was even smaller. Thus, between 1928-9 and 1931-2 the gold prices of apples, bananas, grapefruit, grapes, lemons, oranges, pears, and plums imported by the United Kingdom decreased by percentages ranging from 23 to 38 per cent; and the prices of dried fruit, such as currants, dates, figs and fig cake, plums, prunes, prunelloes, raisins, and sultanas imported by the United Kingdom declined by 20 to 34 per cent.[42]

The conclusion to be drawn from the foregoing, and other, data is that the generally smaller decline in exports of Class B than Class A goods consisted of a smaller decline in price and a somewhat more favourable change in the quantity of the former goods exported. These differences in change of price and quantity exported are explained chiefly by the higher price elasticities of demand for Class B goods and the larger shift of the supply curve of many of these export goods to the right (factors discussed with reference to Balkan exports).[43] It is probable also that the difference in income elasticity of demand between Class A and B goods is smaller in the case of a short-run decline, than of an increase in income. Finally, the output of some products, notably butter, experienced also an upward trend in the period considered.[44]

As one might have expected, differences with respect to the foregoing factors, as well as in other conditions of supply and demand, resulted in interesting differences between the changes in prices, quantities, or values of export of various Class B goods. Thus, in many countries the export supply of meat and dairy products increased considerably owing to such economic factors as were indicated in the discussion of Balkan exports. On the other hand, in the case of fruits and vegetables natural factors were often a more important determinant of supply and, hence, of export quantity and price.[45]

Interesting differences are found also between changes in exports of given goods from different countries. Some of these differences were due chiefly to natural causes operating on the supply side, especially in the case of fruit, vegetables, and fish. Instances relating to the output of olive oil and bananas were noted earlier. While the quantity of Norway's output and exports of fish declined between 1928-9 and 1931-2, Portugal's increased. Differences between changes in supply were caused also by differences in agricultural policies followed in the depression, for instance with respect to export subsidies.[46] Other differences were related to conditions of demand and policies in traditional export markets. Thus, owing to the steeper business downswing in the United States income-sensitive exports directed to that country tended to suffer more than similar exports to such European countries as the United Kingdom. While the quantity of banana imports of the United States diminished, that of Western European countries increased. Between 1928-9 and 1931-2 there was a rise in the quantity of butter exported by practically every important exporting country, notably by Argentina, Australia, Denmark, Estonia, Finland, Latvia, Lithuania, and New Zealand. But owing to German import restrictions, the Netherlands' butter exports declined heavily.[47] From 1932 on several Class B exports of the Irish Free State were affected seriously by the "economic war" with Great Britain.[48] Further, several Class B goods, such as butter, cheese, or olive oil, vary in quality and brand depending on the country of origin. Changes in incomes and relative prices tended to affect differently the quantity demanded of the various qualities.[49] Finally, in some cases long-term developments contributed to the increase in exports of some countries and the decline of similar exports from others. Thus, with minor interruptions, the quantity of frozen meat exported from Australia and New Zealand increased yearly between 1926 and 1935, and that from Argentina and Uruguay decreased.[50]

X

The commodities included in Class C share a common characteristic, namely, a higher income elasticity of demand than for the bulk of the goods included in the other classes. Also, as indicated, many Class C goods are subject to speculation and change in inventories. However, differences between Class C goods with respect to other conditions—of demand and particularly of supply—call for separate consideration first, of agricultural raw materials (including rubber), second, of minerals, and third, of wood.

As in Class A, generally, between 1928-9 and 1931-2 the world output of important raw materials of agricultural origin did not change much. Thus, the world output of cotton, wool, silk, and rubber declined only by 3.0, 2.9, 7.7, and 1.3 per cent, respectively, and the output of flax increased by 12.0 per cent. Of the important agricultural raw materials for which production statistics are available only the output of raw jute and hemp decreased relatively heavily, by 37.2 and 31.6 per cent, respectively.[51]

The change in quantity of exports varied considerably between the various agricultural raw materials. Two broad groups of cases may be distinguished. The quantity of world exports of a few goods whose output decreased slightly, did not change much. Thus, between 1928-9 and 1931-2 the quantity of world exports of wool, cotton, and silk, and of rubber exports from Ceylon, the Dutch East Indies, and Malaya declined by 3.1, 8.9, 12.3, and 3.7 per cent, respectively.[52] On the other hand, the quantity of exports of such goods as hides and skins, hemp, jute, coir, and essence of rose declined heavily. Thus, between 1928-9 and 1931-2 the quantity of hides and skins exported from Brazil, Bulgaria, China, Estonia, Greece, India, Lithuania, Panama, and Spain decreased by percentages ranging from 27 to 74 per cent; the quantity exported from Argentina, Australia, Nigeria, and Paraguay declined by 12 to 21 per cent. In the same period, the quantity of world exports of hemp declined by 37.0 per cent; the quantity of raw jute (and jute gunny cloth) exported from India decreased by 33.7 (and 39.8) per cent; the quantity of coir (and coir yarn) exported from Ceylon declined by 18.9 (and 19.8) per cent; and the quantity of essence of rose exported from Bulgaria decreased by 67.5 per cent.[53]

The decline in price of the agricultural raw materials ranked among the heaviest of the export commodities of the forty-nine countries. Between 1928-9 and 1931-2, or 1928/9 and 1931/2 the gold prices of cotton, agave fibres, flax, hemp, jute, silk, wool, rubber, and hides declined by percentages falling mostly between 60 and 75 per cent.[54]

The heavy decline in the prices of these goods is explained chiefly by the high income elasticity of demand for such goods, discussed with reference to Balkan exports, and the generally low elasticity of their supply.[55] The differences between these goods with respect to change in quantity of export are explained by differences in income elasticity of demand (which tended to be higher, for instance, for hides and skins than for cotton and wool) and by the effect of specific factors, natural or other, on the supply curve, as noted, for example, with respect to jute exports.

As in other exports, some differences are observed between changes in exports of given agricultural raw materials from different countries. They are explained chiefly by differences in the conditions of supply and export. Thus, while the quantity of rubber exported from Malaya was about the same in 1928-9 and 1931-2, and that exported from the Dutch East Indies declined only by 6.8 per cent, the quantity exported from Ceylon declined by 20.0 per cent.[56] In the same period, while the quantity of cotton exported from Egypt declined only by 6.4 per cent, and that exported from the United States, Peru, Persia, Paraguay, or Haiti increased, the quantity exported from India and China declined by as much as 35.6 and 29.0 per cent, respectively. These large decreases in the quantity of cotton exported are related chiefly to the shift in the depression from foreign to domestically produced textiles and, in the case of India, also to large cotton crops in 1927/8 and 1928/9 and an exceptionally small crop in 1931/2.[57]

Unlike the previous groups of commodities, between 1928/9 and 1931/2 the world output of the chief minerals (except fuels, which are included in Class D) exported by the countries considered declined heavily: copper by 36.0 per cent, lead by 28.2 per cent, nickel by 48.0 per cent, silver by 31.2 per cent, tin by 33.3 per cent, zinc by 38.2 per cent, and nitrate of soda by 66.5 per cent. As indicated in Table XI, the quantities of these goods exported from the countries studied declined even more heavily, by percentages ranging mostly between 30 and 65 per cent.[58]

The decline in price of minerals was relatively heavy, though it was smaller

TABLE XI

PERCENTAGE DECLINE IN THE QUANTITY OF MINERAL EXPORTS OF
PRIMARY-EXPORTING COUNTRIES BETWEEN 1928-9 AND 1931-2

Commodity	Country °	Percentage decline (increase: +) in quantity exported
Copper ore	Chile (0.9)	81.9
	Spain (1.0)	51.3
Copper ore and copper	Bolivia (4.2)	78.0
	Mexico (12.5)	66.8
Copper †	Canada (1.6)	62.2
	Chile (35.7)	42.6
	Peru (18.5)	38.0
	Spain (1.6)	29.7
Lead ore	Bolivia (2.5)	63.1
	Peru (0.3)	40.1
Lead	Australia (2.5)	+7.3
	Canada (0.9)	12.6
	India (0.7)	10.4
	Mexico (14.2)	29.3
	Spain (4.4)	15.1
Nickel	Canada (1.6)	53.2
Silver ore and silver	Bolivia (5.5)	16.6
	Canada (1.0)	20.9
	Peru (1.3)	63.6
Silver	Australia (0.7)	20.5
	Mexico (15.3)	52.1
Tin ore	Bolivia (75.3)	52.7
	D.E. Indies (3.2)	43.5
	Nigeria (13.1)	39.8
	Siam (8.2)	+29.3
Tin	D.E. Indies (2.4)	23.8
	Malaya (21.2)	34.7
Zinc ore	Peru (1.4)	over 90.0
Zinc concentrates	Australia (0.9)	74.5
Zinc ore and zinc	Mexico (9.8)	65.0-70.0
Zinc	Australia (0.8)	+ 7.8
	Canada (0.5)	+55.0
	Poland (5.6)	28.9
Nitrate of soda	Chile (44.9)	70.4

° The figures in brackets show the percentage of the value of the country's exports represented by the commodity concerned in the period 1928-9.

† For Canada: "fine copper, contained in ore, matte, regulus, etc." and "blister copper." For the other three countries: "bars and ingots."

SOURCES: LN, *International Trade Statistics,* various years; idem., *Statistical Yearbook, 1936/7,* 152; Australia, Commonwealth Bureau of Census and Statistics, *Oversea Trade,* Bulletin, various numbers; Canada, Dominion Bureau of Statistics, *Trade of Canada,* various years; Mexico, Direccion General de Estadistica, *Anuario Estadistico de los Estados Unidos Mexicanos, 1940* (1942), 670; and Peru, Ministerio de Fomento, *Boletin del Cuerpo de Ingenieros de Minas del Perú,* No. 122 (*La Industria Minera en el Perú 1937,* por Jorge Hohagen) (Lima, 1938), 58-9. See also P. Bower, "The Mining Industry," in M. Perham, ed., *Mining, Commerce and Finance in Nigeria* (London: Faber and Faber, 1948), 18-19.

than that of agricultural raw materials and, generally, slightly smaller than the decrease in price of staple foodstuffs. Between 1928-9 and 1931-2 the gold prices of copper, lead, silver, tin, zinc and Chilean nitrate declined by percentages ranging from 44 to 58 per cent. Because of strict control, the price of nickel remained unchanged throughout the period 1927 to 1932.[59]

The much heavier decline in the quantity exported of metallic minerals than of the agricultural products included in Classes A and B, and most of those included in Class C, is explained by the greater short-run income elasticity of demand for, and the greater elasticity of supply of, the former goods.[60] The greater elasticity of supply explains also the smaller decline in their price than in the price of many agricultural raw materials included in Class C. However, in most of the countries considered, many of which were underdeveloped, the capital-labour ratio was greater in mining than in agriculture; hence in the depression, when only variable costs had to be met, the supply curve in mining shifted to the right more than that in agriculture. Since, in addition, the short-run income elasticity of demand for many metals exceeded the elasticity for several agricultural raw materials (e.g., cotton or wool), the difference in price decline between metallic minerals and agricultural raw materials was not great. (Similar factors account for the difference in price decline between metallic minerals and staple foodstuffs.) The difference in price decline was thus insufficient to offset the effect of the heavier decline in the export quantities of metallic minerals on their export values: these declined more than the export values of any other group of exports considered.[61]

We finally turn to wood. Between 1928-9 and 1931-2 the quantity exported from the countries considered declined heavily: by percentages ranging mostly between 35 and 65 per cent for the various countries and types of wood. The quantity of cork exported from Portugal and Spain decreased by 29.5 and 57.1 per cent, respectively.[62]

The prices of wood declined substantially less than the prices of goods included in Class A and in the previous groups of Class C. Between 1928-9 and 1931-2 the gold prices of the various kinds of unmanufactured or semi-manufactured wood exported from the countries considered declined by percentages ranging from 30 to 45 per cent. The prices of manufactured wood declined by about 22 to 30 per cent.[63]

The relatively heavy decline in the quantities exported of wood and manufactures thereof—comparable only to the decline in the quantities of mineral exports—is explained by the greater short-run income elasticity of demand for wood than for the agricultural products included in Classes A, B, and C, and the greater short-run elasticity of supply, especially in relation to a decline in price. The smaller decline in the prices of wood and manufactures thereof than of agricultural products included in Classes A and C is accounted for by the greater elasticity of supply of the former goods. The smaller decrease in the prices of wood and manufactures thereof than of minerals is explained by the fact that the capital-labour ratio and overhead costs are smaller in the production of the former goods; hence, in the depression, when only variable costs had to be met, the supply curve tended to shift to the right less than it did in mining.[64] However, the relatively moderate decline in wood prices was insufficient to offset the effect of the heavy decline in export quantities on the export values of wood: the decline in these values was among the heaviest of the primary exports considered.

XI

Between 1928-9 and 1931-2 the world output of petroleum decreased slightly, by 5.3 per cent. The decline in quantity of world exports also was relatively small: between 1929 and 1931-2 the quantity of unrefined mineral oil exported from nine important exporting countries decreased by 12.6 per cent, and the quantity of "petrol (motor spirits, etc.)" exported from seven important exporting countries declined by 6.1 per cent. (In 1929 the value of exports of petrol from the seven countries was about one and a half time as large as the value of exports of unrefined mineral oils from the former nine countries.)[65]

Petroleum prices declined less than the prices of most goods in Classes A and C: between 1928-9 and 1931-2 the gold prices of crude oil and petroleum products exported from the countries considered decreased by percentages ranging mostly between 20 and 45 per cent.[66]

The main factors accounting for the relatively small change in the quantity of oil exports, and the smaller decline in the price and value of these exports than in the price and value of exports of Class A and C goods were discussed with reference to Balkan trade: chiefly, the higher price elasticity of demand for oil than for Class A goods, the lower short-run income elasticity of demand for oil than for Class C goods, the greater short-run elasticity of supply of oil than of agricultural products included in Classes A and C, and the long-term growth in the consumption of oil. As indicated in that discussion, in the depression special factors favoured the oil exports of less developed countries. Between 1928-9 and 1931-2 the quantity of petroleum exported from the Dutch East Indies, Venezuela, Ecuador, British Malaya, Persia, and Roumania increased—of the last four countries by more than 20 per cent. The quantity of petroleum exported from Colombia declined by 11.2 per cent; and only the exports of Peru and Mexico declined in quantity by as much as 19.7 and 24.0 per cent, respectively.[67]

Coal was not an important export of the forty-nine countries. It represented more than 3 per cent of the value of exports in 1928-9 only in Poland (14.3 per cent) and the Netherlands (4.3 per cent). Between 1928-9 and 1931-2 the gold price of coal declined much less than the prices of Class A and C goods—only by 15.5 per cent. While the quantity of coal exported from the world's five important exporters (the United Kingdom, Germany, the United States, Poland, and the Netherlands) decreased between 1928-9 and 1931-2 by 22.8 per cent, the quantity exported from Poland declined only by 9.7 per cent, and that from the Netherlands increased slightly.[68]

In addition to fuels, Class D of Table X includes pulp and paper. Like petrol, paper is not usually listed as a primary commodity. However, the importance of paper among the exports of some of the countries considered, the relation between production, or exports, of pulp and paper of these countries, and the similarity of some of the demand and supply conditions for pulp and paper, call for inclusion of paper in our discussion.

Between 1928-9 and 1931-2 the world output of wood pulp decreased by 8.8 per cent, and that of paper by 11.1 per cent. The quantity of world exports of pulp declined very little: the quantity exported from Canada, Estonia, Finland, and Norway decreased by 1.3 per cent, and that exported from these four countries and Czechoslovakia, Germany, and Sweden declined by 3.6 per cent. The decline in the quantity of paper exports was greater, owing partly to the long-term growth of paper production in other countries. Thus, the quantity exported from Canada, Estonia, Finland, and Norway decreased by 17.7 per cent, and that exported from these four countries and Austria, Czechoslovakia, Germany, and Sweden declined by 13.8 per cent.[69]

The prices of pulp and paper declined considerably less than the prices of the great bulk of agricultural products and minerals included in Classes A and C. The gold price of mechanical and chemical wood pulp declined between 1928-9 and 1931-2 by 35.2 and 36.1 per cent, respectively; and the gold price of Canadian newsprint declined between 1929 and 1931-2 by about 22 per cent.[70] The combination of a small decrease in quantity of pulp exports and of a relatively moderate decline in prices of pulp and paper resulted in a considerably smaller decline in the value of exports of pulp and paper than in the value of Class A and C exports of the countries considered.

As with fuels, the main factor explaining the smaller decline in quantity of exports of pulp and paper than of wood and minerals listed in Class C was the lower short-run income elasticity of demand for the former goods.[71] Like petroleum, though probably to a smaller extent, pulp and paper exports were assisted also by long-term growth in consumption. The smaller decrease in price of pulp and paper than of metallic minerals included in Class C is accounted for partly by the foregoing factors, and partly by the fact that the capital-labour ratio was lower in the production of pulp and paper than in mining, so that the shift of the supply curve to the right in the depression, when only variable costs had to be met, was probably smaller. Finally, the smaller decline in the price of pulp and paper than of most agricultural products included in Classes A and C is explained partly by factors similar to some of the foregoing (e.g., the lower income elasticity of demand for pulp and paper than for agricultural raw materials), and partly by the greater elasticity of supply of pulp and paper than of most agricultural products. The last feature constitutes an important distinction between pulp and paper, and Class A goods.[72]

XII

The changes in quantity, price, and value of exports of the various primary products may now be summarized.

The decline in the quantity of exports between 1928-9 and 1931-2 was heaviest for minerals (except fuels) and wood—of the order of 30 to 65 per cent. It was considerable, though somewhat smaller, in the case of a number of agricultural raw materials. The exports of other agricultural raw materials (e.g., wool, cotton, rubber), pulp and paper, and fuels decreased in quantity much less—as a rule by less than 15 per cent. Finally, the quantity exported of foodstuffs, both staple and semi-luxury, either declined little or increased.

The fall in price between 1928-9 and 1931-2 was heaviest in the case of agricultural raw materials—of the order of 60 to 75 per cent. It was progressively smaller for staple foodstuffs, minerals (except fuels), meat and dairy products, and unmanufactured and semi-manufactured wood, in that order. There followed petroleum products, wood pulp and fruits. The decreases in price of paper and coal were among the smallest. With the slight exception of the somewhat heavier decline in price of meat and dairy products than of wood, the prices of goods included in Classes B and D generally declined less heavily than the prices of Class A and C goods. Such a clear distinction is not possible regarding the decrease in export quantities.

On account of factors discussed earlier, the percentage decline in price of primary exports of the countries considered exceeded, as a rule, the percentage decline in quantity of the respective exports, the difference being especially large in the case of agricultural products.[73] One notable exception was wood, explained by the greater elasticity of supply of wood than of agricultural products, and by the fact that the shift of the supply curve of wood to the right in the depression was limited. Other exceptions are found among the minerals included in Class C.[74]

Turning finally to the decline in value of exports we may distinguish two broad groups of exports. Between 1928-9 and 1931-2 Class A and C exports declined heavily. Generally, the decrease was heaviest in the case of minerals (except fuels), and progressively smaller for wood, agricultural raw materials, and staple foodstuffs, in that order. On the other hand, Class B and D exports declined considerably less or increased.[75]

The main factors explaining the relative changes in quantity, price or value of exports of the various types of primary products relate to the demand and supply characteristics of these goods, noted in our detailed analysis. Variations in these conditions, and the contribution of other factors served to explain differences between changes in exports of goods included in a given class, or between changes in exports of given goods from different countries. Differences of this kind were sometimes due to other factors in addition to those discussed: for instance, the varying extent to which different goods were subject to speculation and change in inventories in the various countries, the varying possibilities of commodity substitution, the varying extent and pattern of changes in income in traditional import markets, and various non-cyclical factors. These could not be considered in detail, however, a number of significant instances of their influence were noted.[76]

CHAPTER FOUR

CHANGES IN EXPORTS OF THE VARIOUS COUNTRIES

I

WITH THE HELP of the analysis in Chapter 3 we may survey the main factors accounting for the different rates of decline in total exports of the various countries considered.

For the purpose of the present and subsequent discussion the forty-nine countries may be divided into the following two groups:

Group One		*Group Two*	
Argentina	Haiti	Australia	Lithuania
Bolivia	India	Bulgaria	Netherlands
Brazil	Malaya	Colombia	New Zealand
Canada	Mexico	Costa Rica	Nicaragua
Ceylon	Nigeria	Denmark	Norway
Chile	Peru	Dominican R.	Panama
China	Salvador	Ecuador	Paraguay
Cuba	Siam	Estonia	Persia
D. E. Indies	Spain	Finland	Philippines
Egypt		Greece	Poland
		Guatemala	Portugal
		Honduras	Roumania
		Hungary	Turkey
		Irish F. S.	Venezuela
		Latvia	Yugoslavia

Group One includes nineteen countries, or about two-fifths of the total number of countries. On the other hand, in 1928-9 the countries in this group accounted for three-fifths of the total trade (exports plus imports) of the forty-nine countries: $14.7 of $24.5 billion. As a rule, large exports of primary products consisted mainly of Class A and C, rather than B, goods. As will be indicated subsequently, Class A and C goods predominated heavily among the exports of countries in Group One, while being much less important in Group Two. Accordingly, Group One contains a greater proportion of large traders (countries with a large absolute size of trade) than Group Two. On the basis of the value of trade (exports plus imports) in 1928-9, eight of the countries in Group One ranked among the ten largest of the forty-nine traders; and twelve of the nineteen countries in this group ranked among the nineteen largest. We may now consider the changes in exports of the countries in the two groups.

Among the exports of the countries in Group One, Class A and C goods predominated heavily. In 1928-9 they accounted for a little less than two-thirds of the exports of Canada, China, India, Mexico, or Peru, and for well over two-thirds of the exports of each of thirteen other countries. In Spain, Class A and C goods represented about 53-56 per cent of exports. As a consequence of the marked predominance of Class A and C goods the exports of the countries in Group One decreased heavily.[1] Between 1928-9 and 1931-2 eighteen countries experienced a decline in exports exceeding 54 per cent. The exports of Mexico decreased by 53.0 per cent; if gold exports are excluded, they decreased by 60.8 per cent.[2]

By contrast, the total exports of each of the thirty countries included in Group Two declined in the same period by less than 54 per cent. In 1928-9 Class B and D goods accounted for over half the exports of Denmark, Honduras, the Irish Free State, New Zealand, Norway, Panama, Persia, Portugal, or Venezuela, and about half the exports of Estonia. They were also more important than Class A and C goods among the exports of the Netherlands and Poland. Class A and C goods accounted for less than half the exports also of Latvia and Lithuania. In Ecuador, Finland, Greece, Hungary, Roumania, Yugoslavia, and Turkey, Class A and C exports tended to predominate; but their importance was not nearly as great as in the countries of Group One.[3] Only in the remaining nine countries (Australia, Bulgaria, Colombia, Costa Rica, the Dominican Republic, Guatemala, Nicaragua, Paraguay and the Philippines) did Class A and C goods represent a little less, or more, than two-thirds of exports. The relatively moderate decline in exports of these countries was due chiefly to exceptionally moderate decreases in some Class A or C exports.

Thus, Australia's wheat exports (which in 1927/8-8/9 represented 12.8 per cent of her total exports) declined between 1927/8-8/9 and 1931/2-2/3 relatively moderately, by 36.5 per cent. Large Australian wheat crops in the years 1930/1 to 1932/3 and abnormal circumstances in the Far East, notably the great flood of the Yangtze River in 1931, contributed to a huge increase in Australia's wheat exports to China and Japan.[4] The volume of her wheat exports to China, Manchukuo, Hong Kong, and Kwantung rose from an insignificant amount in the crop year (August-July) 1927/8 and 74 thousand metric tons in 1928/9, to 664, 844, and 918 thousand tons in 1930/1, 1931/2, and 1932/3, respectively. In the same crop years, her wheat exports to Japan increased from 87 and 153 thousand tons to 481, 584, and 487 thousand, respectively. Her total exports of wheat rose from 1,924 and 2,956 thousand tons to 4,145, 4,254, and 4,088 thousand respectively.[5] Probably, Australia's wheat exports benefited also from the price-support policies of countries such as the United States, and the considerably heavier decline in the gold value of Australia's currency compared to the currencies of other important wheat-exporting countries. The decline in Australia's total exports was also moderated by the increase in her gold exports.[6]

For reasons indicated earlier, Bulgaria's exports of grain (which in 1928-9 represented 10.0 per cent of her total exports) *increased* between 1928-9 and 1931-2 as by much as 52.8 per cent. Her exports of eggs (a Class B good which in 1928-9 represented 10.3 per cent of her total exports) increased by 13.2 per cent.

Some small Latin American coffee-exporting countries gained in the depression at the expense of Brazil.[7] Between 1928-9 and 1931-2 Brazil's coffee exports declined by 63.0 per cent. On the other hand, the coffee exports of Colombia, Costa Rica, and Guatemala (which in 1928-9 represented 63.3, 65.2, and 77.0 per cent of their total exports, respectively) decreased only by 41.4, 36,2, and 56.4 per cent, respectively. Nicaragua's coffee exports declined by almost as much as Brazil's (by 62.4 per cent); but the represented only 58.5 per cent of her total exports in 1928-9 compared to 71.2 per cent in Brazil.[8] Another 17.4 per cent of Nicaragua's exports and 12.0 per cent of Guatemala's consisted of bananas, a Class B good: between 1928-9 and 1931-2 Nicaragua's banana exports increased by 6.9 per cent, and Guatemala's decreased only by 12.4 per cent.[9]

The exports of sugar and sugar cane of the Dominican Republic (which in 1928-9 represented 60.0 per cent of her total exports) declined between 1928-9 and 1931-2 only by 52.4 per cent, mainly because they had decreased very considerably already in 1929 owing to non-cyclical factors.[10] For reasons indicated earlier, the Republic's exports of coffee (which in 1928-9 represented 8.9 per cent of its total exports) also declined relatively moderately, by 46.8 per cent between 1928-9 and 1931-2.

From 1926 on production of tobacco in Paraguay increased steadily and substantially. Between 1927/8-8/9 and 1930/1-1/2 output increased by 29.5 per cent. Consequently, Paraguay's tobacco exports (which in 1928-9 represented 7.0 per cent of her total exports) increased in quantity considerably, and declined in value between 1928-9 and 1931-2 only by 30.4 per cent. In the same period Paraguay's exports of quebracho extract declined in quantity by 14.2 per cent, while Argentina's increased by 2.8 per cent. However, owing to the much smaller fall in price of the former, the value of Paraguay's exports of quebracho extract declined only by 40.3 per cent.[11]

Finally, in the downswing after 1928-9 the Philippines gained well-known advantages in the United States market at the expense of her competitors. In 1928-9 sugar represented 31.7 per cent of the Philippines' exports; and between 1928-9 and 1931-2 the value of her sugar exports increased by 8.9 per cent.[12]

This concludes the discussion of the main factors accounting for the differences in relative change in value of exports among the various primary-exporting countries.

II

The foregoing analysis related chiefly to intercountry comparisons of the decline in exports between 1928-9 and 1931-2. We may now briefly survey the changes in the decline in exports over the three periods, 1928-9 to 1930-1, 1928-9 to 1931-2, and 1928-9 to 1932-3.

First we may note the general change in the decline in exports of the forty-nine countries. Comparison of the percentage declines in exports in the three periods, shown in Table I, or in Diagrams I, II, and III in Chapter 6, indicates that in all countries the percentage decline in exports was greater in the second period than in the first, and in the third period than in the second; and that in all countries, except Bulgaria and Honduras, the former difference was greater than the latter. The median value of the percentage declines in exports of the forty-nine countries was 27.0, 56.6 and 61.6 per cent, in the three periods respectively; and the range changed from +3.4 to −51.2 per cent in the first period, to −21.3 to

—73.8 per cent in the second period, and —31.6 to —85.7 per cent in the third.

Another comparison may be made, of the average (arithmetic mean) yearly percentage decline in exports of the countries in the three periods. Between the first and third period the average decline in exports of twenty-seven countries increased, and of twenty-two countries diminished. But while between the first and second period as many as thirty-five countries experienced an increase, between the second and third period only ten countries did so.[13]

As one might have expected, over the three periods there were changes in the ranking of the various countries by percentage decline in exports. However, there was a noteworthy stability in the broad relationship of declines in exports of the countries listed in the two groups. With very few exceptions, the percentage declines in exports of the countries in Group One exceeded the declines in exports of the countries in Group Two in all three periods.[14]

The range of the percentage changes in exports of the forty-nine countries remained approximately the same over the three periods: 54.6, 52.5 and 54.1 percentage points in the three periods respectively. However, this reflects the inclusion of the extreme values of percentage changes in exports. The following differences between various decile values of percentage decline in exports of the countries considered indicate that the differences between the percentage changes in exports of the countries diminished progressively over the three periods:

	1st to 9th Decile	2nd to 8th Decile	3rd to 7th Decile	4th to 6th Decile
1928-9 to 1930-1	34.2	24.3	15.9	10.2
1928-9 to 1931-2	31.0	21.7	15.2	8.0
1928-9 to 1932-3	27.5	17.2	11.8	4.8

As indicated earlier, in all countries the percentage decline in exports was greater in the second period than in the first, and in the third period than in the second. But these differences were generally greater in countries whose exports had declined moderately in the first period than in countries whose exports had declined heavily,[15] and this is reflected in the foregoing changes in the differences between decile values of percentage decline in exports. It is reflected also in the fact that of twenty-eight countries whose exports declined in the first period by less than 33 per cent, all except Panama and the Philippines experienced between the first and third period an increase in the average yearly percentage decline in exports, while of twenty-one countries whose exports declined in the first period by more than 33 per cent, all except Bolivia experienced, between the first and third period, a decrease in the average decline in exports.[16]

These observations about the noteworthy stability, over the three periods, in the broad relationship of declines in exports of the countries listed in the two groups, and about the decrease, over the three periods, of the differences between the declines in exports of the forty-nine countries, reflect chiefly the following two relations between the relative declines of the various types of commodity exports distinguished earlier.

First, generally speaking, the decline in Class A and C exports from their 1928-9 level tended to exceed the decline in Class B and D exports in all three two-year periods of the business downswing. So did, therefore, the decline in the total exports of countries that exported, respectively, such goods.

Second, the excess of the decline in Class A and C exports over the decline in Class B and D exports diminished between the earlier and later stages of the business downswing. In the earlier stages the prices or quantities of Class A and C exports declined precipitately. These goods were more storable, and they were subject to speculation and inventory depletion to a considerably greater degree than Class B and D goods. But in later stages the excessive reduction of inventories ceased, and even some restoration took place.[17] Also, compared to the final demand for non-durables, such as foodstuffs or fuels, the final demand for the more durable goods of Class C, such as metals, wood, hides, and textile materials, was bound to decline heavily in the short run and to recover in the longer period. Thus, while the quantity of world exports (or of total exports from the important exporting countries) of such goods as cheese, frozen meat, bacon, fish, bananas, olive oil, or coal was smaller in 1933 than in 1931 or 1932, the quantity of exports of cotton, wool, rubber, jute, nickel, or wood was greater. The quantity of exports of copper and tin also increased between 1932 and 1933. Also, while between January 1933 and January 1934 the gold price of several foodstuffs (e.g., beef, butter, wheat, rice, and cocoa) and fuels (petroleum, petrol, and coal) declined, the prices of cotton, wool, rubber, jute, copper, tin, and timber increased.[18]

It was indicated earlier that between the first and third period twenty-two of the forty-nine countries experienced a decrease in the average yearly percentage decline in exports.[19] Sixteen of these countries belong to Group One and Class A and C goods predominated heavily among their exports. (The three countries of Group One whose average decline in exports did not decrease were Bolivia, whose average decline in exports remained almost the same, Mexico, whose percentage decline in exports in the first period was the lowest of the nineteen countries, and Spain, in whose exports the predominance of Class A and C goods was not marked.) Class A and C goods represented a little less, or more, than two-thirds of the exports of four of the remaining six countries whose average yearly percentage decline in exports decreased between the first and third period, namely, Australia, the Dominican Republic, Nicaragua, and the Philippines.

III

The discussion of changes in exports in this and the previous chapter may be concluded with one or two warnings.

The decline in exports in the years after 1928-9 varied considerably among the various primary-exporting countries, or, more narrowly, among countries that exported chiefly agricultural goods, or mining products. Hence, it is impossible to distinguish any single pattern applicable to the cyclical change in exports of all, or even the great bulk of countries in each of these categories. It is perhaps somewhat more legitimate to generalize about the cyclical changes in exports of countries which exported broadly similar types of primary products. However, even in this, more limited, undertaking, the discussion and examples presented (e.g., relating to the differences in the decline in exports of the "coffee economies") suggest caution and a readiness to allow for qualifications or exceptions.

Sometimes hasty conclusions have been drawn about the nature and causes of balance of payments difficulties of primary-exporting countries. Thus, it has been noted that "both Australia and New Zealand are agricultural countries, but New Zealand is to a much greater extent pastoral. In 1930-1 butter, cheese, eggs, and meat accounted for 66 per cent of the exports from New Zealand and only 14 per cent of those from Australia, 37 per cent of the latter's exports being wool and 21 per cent wheat and flour. Thus *non-food products are of greater importance* to Australia, *which was materially to her advantage during the depression.*"[20] But, as indicated earlier, it was precisely the food exports of Australia that decreased moderately in the downswing, compared with the decrease in wool, hides and skins, and total exports. In New Zealand too, between 1928-9 and 1931-2 the exports of meat, butter, and cheese declined only by 37.1, 34.1, and 48.2 per cent, respectively, compared with the decrease of 52.3 per cent in total exports, and 73.4 and 73.7 per cent in the exports of wool and hides and skins.

Attention may be drawn also to the tendency to relate the balance of trade and payments difficulties of certain primary-exporting countries in the downswing examined to the concentration of the exports of these countries on a small number of goods. Thus, it has been suggested that in the depression holders of British Empire securities fared better than creditors of Latin American countries, partly because "the exports of the larger Dominions and colonies are comparatively well diversified."[21]

Certainly, concentration of a country's exports on a small number of commodities exposes the country inordinately to the risk of a long-term or short-term decline in the foreign demand for one or two particular goods. But whether this country will fare better or worse than others in the event of a cyclical decline of business in general is an entirely different question: our analysis indicates that the answer depends on the kinds of goods exported and the cyclical changes in demand and supply to which they are subject (as well as on any demand or supply conditions peculiar to the countries concerned), rather than on the concentration or diversification of exports.[22] In the period considered such countries as Colombia, Costa Rica, Honduras, or Venezuela (all Latin American) had an extremely concentrated export trade: in 1928-9 one or two commodities accounted for four-fifths or more of the exports of each of these countries. Yet, the percentage decline in the total exports of each of these countries in the downswing was smaller than that of the great bulk of primary-exporting countries; and it was smaller than the percentage decline in the imports of the respective countries. On the other hand, countries such as Canada or India in the British Commonwealth, or China, had a much more diversified export pattern: in 1928-9 a dozen or more commodities were required to make up three-quarters of their exports. The percentage decline in their exports was much greater than the decline in the exports of the countries noted previously; and it exceeded the percentage decline in the imports of the respective countries.

CHAPTER FIVE

CHANGES IN IMPORTS OF INDIVIDUAL COMMODITIES

THE PERCENTAGE DECLINE in total imports of each of the forty-nine primary-exporting countries between 1928-9 on the one hand, and 1930-1, 1931-2 and 1932-3 on the other, is shown in Table I, column (4). As with the exports, the decline in total imports of each country varied with (*a*) the percentage decline in the various types of individual imports, and (*b*) the share of these goods in the country's total imports. This chapter is devoted to a general discussion of these two factors.

I

It might seem desirable to discuss separately the decline in the value of every item imported by the forty-nine countries: there are differences in the demand and supply conditions and in the effects of changes in incomes and prices between almost any two import commodities. However, such an undertaking is impossible owing to the nature of the League of Nations statistics, as well as to limitations of time and resources. For instance, in the statistics many items are reported in classes rather than individually, and these classes range in size from such small ones as "flour" or "fruit" to such all-inclusive ones as "other foodstuffs" or "other articles." Moreover, the grouping of individual imports, or the content of a given class, varies considerably from one country to another, and even from period to period. Quite often even single commodity items in the statistics seem to represent different goods in different countries or periods.

For these and other reasons, some grouping of the various imports into classes of goods having broadly similar demand and supply characteristics is clearly necessary. Unfortunately, the League of Nations statistics do not allow complete freedom in the classification of imports. Thus, foodstuffs cannot be grouped separately, for instance, into the two classes we distinguished with respect to exports, because a large part (sometimes as much as one-half or three-quarters) of the imports of food into the various countries is included in "other foodstuffs."

On the basis of the available data the bulk of the imports of each of the countries considered has been distributed into the following eight classes.[1]

I. Food—in addition to foodstuffs this class includes tobacco, raw or manufactured.

II. Capital goods—cement, iron, other metals, and wood, in a raw, semi-manufactured, or manufactured state.

III. Textiles—includes wool, cotton, and silk, in a raw, semi-manufactured, or manufactured state, but excludes the items which are included in Class VII below.

IV. Fuel—petroleum, coal, lignite, and products thereof.

V. Paper—paper, cardboard, and stationery.

VI. Hides—hides, skins, and furs, in a raw, semi-manufactured, or manufactured state.

VII. Containers—bags and sacks, and hemp and jute, and manufactures thereof.

VIII. Chemicals—chemicals, colours and dyes, paints, drugs, soap, perfumes, and manures.

At some points in the following discussion we are able to subdivide some of these classes into smaller groups of imports. For example, for a number of countries the changes in imports of "raw and semi-manufactured textiles" (including usually cotton—and sometimes also wool and silk—raw, yarn, and thread) are compared with the changes in imports of manufactured textiles; or, various subclasses of chemicals are distinguished.

II

We may start with a survey of the extent of decline in the various classes of imports in the periods 1928-9 to 1930-1, 1928-9 to 1931-2, and 1928-9 to 1932-3. Table XII shows the range of percentage decline of each class of imports in forty-seven primary-exporting countries, in each of the three periods.[2]

We have eliminated extreme values by showing as limits in each period the fourth smallest, and the fourth largest percentage decline in each class of imports. In each period the first five classes of imports (capital goods, food, textiles, containers, and hides) declined relatively more than the last three classes (fuel, paper, and chemicals). Thus, in the three periods the smallest decline of each of the first five classes of imports exceeded 7, 37, and 47 per cent, respectively, except for the smallest decline in the imports of capital goods in the period 1928-9 to 1930-1[3]; and the largest decline of each of these five classes of imports exceeded 51, 69, and 77 per cent, in the three periods respectively. On the other hand, the smallest and largest percentage declines of the last three classes were smaller than these values, respectively.

Tables XII and I show also that the percentage decline in the various classes of imports, and in the total imports of the various countries, increased over the three periods, the increase being greater between the first and second, than between the second and third, periods. This increase was not necessarily proportional for the various classes of imports. For instance, as indicated in Table XII and discussed later, compared to the decline in the other imports of many countries the decline in their imports of capital goods was relatively slow in earlier, and fast in later, stages.

Range data provide no information about the distribution of the values in the ranges, and end values may mislead. Particularly when the ranges of decline are as similar as those of the first five, or the last three classes of imports, no impression can be gained about the relative decline of the various classes of imports in individual countries and the change in this relation over the three periods: for example, about the number of countries and the periods in which food imports declined relatively more than textile imports. In order to examine further the behaviour of the various classes of imports in the downswing we ranked them by their percentage decline in each country, in each of the three periods. Considerable differences were observed in the relative decline of the various classes of imports in the various countries. While, in a given period in some countries,

TABLE XII

RANGES OF DECLINE OF EIGHT CLASSES OF IMPORTS OF FORTY-SEVEN PRIMARY-EXPORTING COUNTRIES BETWEEN 1928-9 AND 1930-1, 1931-2, AND 1932-3 °

Import class	1928-9 to 1930-1		1928-9 to 1931-2		1928-9 to 1932-3	
	Smallest decline %	Largest decline %	Smallest decline %	Largest decline %	Smallest decline %	Largest decline %
Food	20.9 (Irish)	56.0 (Latvia)	44.1 (Hung.)	76.5 (Austr.)	58.2 (Norw.)	81.0 (Cuba)
Capital goods	3.0 (Latvia)	61.9 (Domin.)	38.2 (Irish)	81.4 (Salv.)	55.1 (Irish)	85.8 (Bol.)
Textiles	11.2 (Norw.)	51.6 (Hond.)	37.2 (Norw.)	69.1 (Austr.)	51.0 (Roum.)	77.8 (China)
Hides	17.9 (Yug.)	63.1 (China)	43.8 (Phil.)	81.0 (Chile)	55.4 (Phil.)	89.6 (Col.)
Containers	24.4 (Salv.)	57.6 (Siam)	44.9 (Nig.)	70.7 (Bol.)	47.3 (Mal.)	82.6 (Ecu.)
Fuel	+0.7 (Irish) †	40.8 (Greece)	22.3 (Phil.)	60.1 (Cuba)	42.3 (Port.)	73.6 (Arg.)
Paper	0.4 (Irish)	40.5 (Brazil)	19.5 (Lith.)	61.2 (Col.)	42.3 (Neth.)	69.8 (Latvia)
Chemicals	6.4 (Port.)	42.1 (Pol.)	21.2 (Den.)	56.5 (Siam)	30.2 (Bulg.)	69.7 (Pol.)

° Of the forty-nine primary-exporting countries no estimates are possible for Costa Rica and Turkey in all three periods, Mexico and Panama in the last two periods, and Honduras and Nicaragua in the last period. Data for the individual imports of Honduras in the year 1927/8 are not readily available; the comparison in the first two periods is with the year 1928/9 alone.

The countries which experienced the indicated declines in imports are shown in brackets. In order to eliminate extreme values we show the countries with the fourth smallest, and the fourth largest percentage decline in each class of imports. We have no data for estimating the decline in imports of hides in twelve, ten, and eleven countries, in the three periods respectively, and the decline in imports of containers in twenty-four, twenty-two, and twenty-one countries. Therefore, for hides we show the countries with the third smallest and largest percentage decline in imports, and for containers the countries with the second smallest and largest percentage decline. For a very small number of countries we lack data for estimating the decline in some of the other classes of imports.

† In the period 1928-9 to 1930-1 the fuel imports of the Irish Free State, Latvia, Lithuania, and Malaya increased. The rise was smallest in the first country.

food imports declined relatively more than imports of capital goods, in others they declined less. It was therefore advisable to estimate the frequency in ranking; that is, the number of countries in which, in a given period, the percentage decline in a given class of imports was the greatest among the declines of all classes of imports of the respective countries, second greatest, and so on, and similarly with each of the other classes of imports.

For practical purposes the eight classes of imports of each country were ranked into five ranks: greatest decline in import value, second greatest, third greatest, fourth greatest, and fifth greatest or lower decline in import value. For several countries data for one or two (for Persia three) classes of imports are not available, either because these countries imported insignificant amounts of these goods, or because in at least one of the two-year periods which are being compared these items have been included in "other articles" or other generic classes. It was necessary to make allowance for this fact.[4] If, for example, the data show that imports of capital goods ranked first in terms of percentage decline in thirty countries and hide imports in fifteen, but data for imports of capital goods are available for forty-five countries, while for hide imports only for twenty-eight, one cannot conclude that imports of capital goods declined the most: in seventeen countries hides have not been given "a fighting chance." The following method of "correction" and construction of Table XIII was adopted.

Proceeding vertically in the first of five columns we noted the number of countries in which the imports of capital goods, food, textiles, and so on, declined relatively more than every other class of imports of the respective countries. In the second column we noted the number of countries in which the various classes of imports held second place in terms of relative decline; and so on for the other three columns. Then we assumed that, had there been data for hides, for instance, for the countries for which there are none, the number of these cases would have been distributed among the five ranks in the same way as the cases for which data are available. However, if hide imports occupy first place in terms of decline in more cases than those shown originally, the score in the first column of other classes of imports cannot be as great as originally shown. Therefore, the "firsts" of these other classes were reduced proportionately to their original scores by the number by which the "firsts" of hides or other classes of imports were raised. These reductions were added to the score of the respective goods in the second column: to the extent that they could not have scored "firsts," they would have competed for "seconds." Further, to the hides and other classes of imports in the second column we added the proportion of "not available" cases which according to our earlier assumption would have been "seconds." Since with these two additions the second column showed a total number of countries exceeding the actual, all scores in that column were reduced proportionately. These reductions from the "seconds" of the various classes of imports were added to their "thirds," and the process was continued. Finally, the results were converted into the percentages shown in Table XIII.

This Table shows that in the period 1928-9 to 1931-2, for instance, the imports of food declined relatively more than every other class of imports in 13.0 per cent of the countries considered, and the imports of capital goods did so in 32.4 per cent of the countries. Or, moving horizontally, we find that the imports of food

TABLE XIII

FREQUENCY OF RANKING OF EIGHT CLASSES OF IMPORTS BY THEIR RELATIVE DECLINE IN EACH
OF FORTY-SEVEN PRIMARY-EXPORTING COUNTRIES BETWEEN
1928-9 AND 1930-1, 1931-2, AND 1932-3 °

Import class	Greatest relative decline	Second greatest relative decline	Third greatest relative decline	Fourth greatest relative decline	Fifth greatest or lower relative decline	Total
	(1)	(2)	(3)	(4)	(5)	(6)
		(percentages of the total number of countries)				
Section A: 1928-9 to 1930-1						
Food	11.0	24.1	20.6	17.8	26.5	100.0
Capital foods	12.2	26.5	13.9	12.8	34.6	100.0
Textiles	7.3	17.2	23.1	15.9	36.5	100.0
Hides	35.3	19.1	24.0	9.7	11.9	100.0
Containers	31.8	9.8	11.4	9.4	37.6	100.0
Fuel	2.4	3.3	3.9	9.9	80.5	100.0
Paper	—	—	1.7	11.6	86.7	100.0
Chemicals	—	—	1.4	12.9	85.7	100.0
TOTAL	100.0	100.0	100.0	100.0	400.0	800.0
Section B: 1928-9 to 1931-2						
Food	13.0	22.6	27.4	14.1	22.9	100.0
Capital goods	32.4	19.1	14.7	14.8	19.0	100.0
Textiles	1.6	19.9	20.9	20.5	37.1	100.0
Hides	37.8	18.6	15.5	12.8	15.3	100.0
Containers	13.0	16.6	12.9	17.3	40.2	100.0
Fuel	2.2	1.6	5.0	11.0	80.2	100.0
Paper	—	—	1.7	3.6	94.7	100.0
Chemicals	—	1.6	1.9	5.9	90.6	100.0
TOTAL	100.0	100.0	100.0	100.0	400.0	800.0
Section C: 1928-9 to 1932-3						
Food	24.8	23.2	17.3	13.4	21.3	100.0
Capital goods	32.5	24.6	19.2	10.8	12.9	100.0
Textiles	2.4	13.5	24.5	21.6	38.0	100.0
Hides	31.2	25.3	13.3	15.5	14.7	100.0
Containers	9.1	3.7	16.9	16.0	54.3	100.0
Fuel	—	5.9	6.3	9.4	78.4	100.0
Paper	—	—	1.9	5.6	92.5	100.0
Chemicals	—	3.8	0.6	7.7	87.9	100.0
TOTAL	100.0	100.0	100.0	100.0	400.0	800.0

° The figures in the table are percentages of the total number of countries (considered in each period) in which the decline of a given class of imports ranked as indicated in the column headings.

Of the forty-nine primary-exporting countries the following have been omitted in the periods indicated, because the data for their individual imports either are entirely lacking or permit estimates of declines in only less than five classes of imports: Costa Rica and Turkey in all three periods, Guatemala in the period 1928-9 to 1930-1, Nicaragua in the periods 1928-9 to 1930-1, and 1928-9 to 1932-3, and Honduras, Mexico, and Panama in the period 1928-9 to 1932-3. As a consequence of these exclusions the number of countries considered are forty-five, forty-seven and forty-three, in the three periods, respectively. For the periods 1928-9 to 1930-1, and 1928-9 to 1931-2 the base period used for Honduras is the year 1928-9 alone; and in the second of these periods we compare for Mexico and Panama 1928-9 with 1931 alone.

ranked first in terms of relative decline among the imports of 13.0 per cent of the countries examined, second in 22.6 per cent of the countries, and so on.

With the help of Tables XII and XIII, as well as supplementary data, we may discuss the decline in each of the eight classes of imports.

III

I. *Food.* The decline in food imports between 1928-9 and 1931-2 was relatively heavy. It ranked first in over one-eighth of the countries considered, exceeding or equalling the scores of five other classes of imports. This score of food imports was greatly exceeded by the respective scores of imports of capital goods and hides. However, when the countries in which the decline in each class of imports ranked first, second, or third are taken together, the difference between the scores of imports of food on the one hand, and capital goods, or even hides, on the other, is small compared to the difference between the scores of food and any of the other five classes of imports.

The factors accounting for the changes in international trade in foodstuffs were outlined in Chapter 3. While it has not been possible to divide the food imports of the countries considered into the two classes of foodstuffs, the available statistics indicate clearly that imports of Class A goods declined more heavily than imports of Class B commodities; also, that the former goods usually represented a considerably larger share of the food imports of the various countries than the latter. These factors largely account for the relatively heavy decline in food imports.

In many of the countries considered the imports of several foodstuffs declined relatively more than similar imports of more advanced industrial countries. Thus, in the latter countries, rice shared the characteristics of Class B goods, while in several of the former countries it was a staple foodstuff. Some other Class A goods—for instance sugar, coffee, or wheat—probably had a greater income elasticity of demand in the less developed countries. The peasant or the worker in small towns either tended to substitute inferior local produce for these "semi-luxuries"—he used, for example syrups, other beans, or maize—or he tended to reduce his consumption of such goods more heavily than the consumer in the more advanced countries. There are few data relating to import quantities and changes thereof. Some estimates of sugar, coffee, tea, and cocoa imports suggest that the decline in the quantities of these imports was relatively greater in less developed than in more advanced countries.[5] Probably, the income elasticity of demand for many Class B goods also was higher in the former countries.[6]

Comparison of the three periods shown in Table XIII indicates that, as the downswing progressed, the decline in food imports increased faster than the decline in most other classes of imports: the percentage of countries in which the decline in food imports ranked either first, or first, second, or third increased. The main reasons for this change were the following. In many of the countries examined, a shift in consumption from imports to domestic substitutes and an increase in local production were more feasible in the case of food than of many other goods. However, these changes required some time. In the meanwhile these countries could not substantially reduce food imports by drawing on inventories: unlike stocks of many industrial raw materials in advanced countries, stocks of imported foodstuffs in most of the countries considered were, as a rule, very modest. For these reasons restrictions of imports were frequently directed first against other goods, notably textiles, and only later were extended to food. Changes in relative prices also contributed to the faster increase in the decline in value of food than of other imports as the downswing progressed: prices of important foodstuffs (e.g., wheat and rice) declined substantially even in 1933, while prices of other classes of imports (e.g. textile materials, finished textiles, fuel, and even capital goods), either declined less or increased during this later stage of the depression.[7]

II. *Capital Goods.* Between 1928-9 and 1931-2 the imports of capital goods declined more heavily than every other class of imports, except hides. Their relative decline ranked first in almost one-third of the countries considered, and held fifth place or lower in only less than one-fifth.

There are significant differences between various types of capital goods. For instance, the period which usually elapses between the order and delivery of various capital goods and, hence also, between the downturn in business and the decline in their imports may differ substantially.[8] Or, they may be the object of private or governmental expenditures, and in the downswing the change in these two types of expenditure may differ considerably. It is therefore unfortunate that it has not been possible to divide this class of imports into smaller groups reflecting such characteristics.

Nevertheless, some basic factors relating to the bulk of imports of capital goods may be noted. Purchases of such goods were more sensitive to changes in income than purchases of most of the other classes of goods. Investment (including purchases of some consumer durables) depended on rising incomes, expenditures, and governmental revenue, optimism and readiness to innovate, favourable terms of trade for the farmer, and, in many of the countries considered, also on capital imports. The last depended on good business conditions in the capital-exporting countries (as well as the speculative spirit of the late nineteen-twenties), and on expanding exports, incomes, and governmental revenues in the capital-receiving countries. Even slight reversals of these factors were bound to affect seriously the imports of capital goods.[9] Further, the elasticity of supply of many capital goods, particularly of those in a semi-manufactured or manufactured state, was greater than that of agricultural products. These factors go a long way to explain the heavy decline in the volume and value of imports of capital goods.

Comparison of the three periods shown in Table XIII indicates that, as the downswing progressed, the decline in imports of capital goods increased faster than the decline in every other class of imports; in the period 1928-9 to 1930-1 it ranked first in only about one-eighth of the countries considered, and in about one-third it ranked fifth or lower, in the period 1928-9 to 1932-3 the position was the reverse. The greater part of this change occurred between the first and second periods considered. It reflects mainly the time lag between the initiation of capital projects in the boom and the delivery of the capital goods required from abroad.[10] In consideration of changes in trade balances this lag may be quite important: the period during which the decline in imports of capital goods is moderate compared to the decrease in other imports and in the exports of the respective countries may extend over a large part of the downswing.

III. *Textiles.* In all three periods considered, textile imports declined less than the previous two important classes of imports. For instance, in the period 1928-9 to 1931-2 their relative decline ranked first in only 1.6 per cent of the countries considered, and first, second, or third in 42.4 per cent. The respective scores for food were 13.0 and 63.0 per cent, and for capital goods 32.4 and 66.2 per cent.

The income elasticity of demand for textiles exceeded the elasticity for many staple foodstuffs. On the other hand, it was smaller than the elasticity for many capital goods and materials used in their production. In addition to the fact that consumption fluctuates less than investment, there were limits, social as well as physical, to the temporary substitution of repair labour for purchases of new clothing. For instance, in many Mediterranean and Latin American countries the life of machinery was extended as much as possible,[11] but people would "starve" in order to buy new clothes. Also, while labour could be substituted temporarily for certain types of machinery when these were entirely worn out, this was not possible for clothing. Turning to the price elasticity of demand one would have to distinguish between the various types of textiles, which varied from necessity to luxury. If one may generalize, one may say that the elasticity of demand for textiles was greater than the elasticity for staple foodstuffs and, probably, for many capital goods and materials used in their production. The elasticity of supply and the change in the conditions of supply of textiles in the downswing also tended to vary, depending partly on whether the article was in a raw, semi-manufactured, or finished state.

One may summarize the argument by saying that the value of textiles bought tended to decline less than that of staple foodstuffs chiefly because of the higher price elasticities of demand and supply for textiles; because of the greater income elasticity of demand for textiles the quantity bought tended to decline more than that of staple foodstuffs.[12] The value of textiles bought also tended to decline less than that of many capital goods and materials used in their production, chiefly because of the lower income elasticity of demand for textiles. For the same reason, the quantity bought of the former goods also tended to decline less than that of the latter.

It is interesting to divide the class of textile imports on the basis of the degree of manufacture of the various articles: purchases of imported cloth or clothing, for instance, may change differently than imports of materials for domestic production of textiles. The available data make it possible to distinguish two textile subclasses: first, raw and semi-manufactured textiles (including cotton, wool and silk, raw, yarns, and threads) and second, finished textiles (including cotton, woollen and silk tissues, piece goods, and apparel). It is perhaps needless to say that the data are not fully adequate for this subdivision and that there is some overlapping between the two subclasses.[13] Of thirty-four countries for which this division has been possible in the period 1928-9 to 1931-2, twenty-seven experienced a relatively greater decline in the value of imports of finished, than of raw and semi-manufactured, textiles.[14] In thirteen of these countries the difference between the two changes was as high as 25 to 60 percentage points (in

TABLE XIV

PERCENTAGE CHANGE BETWEEN 1928-9 AND 1931-2 IN THE QUANTITY OF TEXTILE IMPORTS OF TWENTY-FOUR PRIMARY-EXPORTING COUNTRIES

Country	Percentage change in the quantity of cotton imports		Country	Percentage change in the quantity of wool imports	
	Raw cotton, yarn, and thread	Finished textiles °		Raw wool and yarn	Finished textiles °
Bolivia	−66.7	−74.4	Brazil	−60.0	−81.0
Brazil	−47.3	−92.3	Bulgaria	+59.5	−95.0
Bulgaria	+29.2	−66.7	Estonia	−12.5	−66.7
Ceylon	−9.5	+4.0	Finland	−24.6	−65.1
Chile	−34.6	−71.1	Greece	−8.3	−48.3
China	+72.2	−63.0	Hungary	−41.0	−71.1
Colombia	+76.9	−29.7	Latvia	+5.0	−75.0
Cuba	+72.7	−36.4	Norway	−1.1 †	−17.1
Estonia	−42.2	−62.5	Portugal	+50.0 °	−58.3 ✦
Finland	−11.5	−61.1	Roumania	−24.0	−13.0
Greece	+140.5	−32.8			
Guatemala	−21.9	−30.0			
Hungary	+12.8	−83.1			
Latvia	−16.7	−58.5			
Lithuania	+94.1	−20.0			
Mexico	−45.5	−60.0			
Nicaragua	−22.2	−28.8			
Norway	−1.1 †	−11.6			
Persia	+79.2	−31.1			
Poland	−26.1	−52.6			
Portugal	+12.1 ‡	−42.9 §			
Roumania	+8.9	−56.0			
Salvador	−12.4	−15.6			
Spain	+31.4	−81.2			

° Tissues, piece goods and apparel.
† All textile fibres.
‡ Only raw cotton.
§ Includes cotton yarns.
° Only raw wool.
✦ Includes woollen yarns.
SOURCE: LN, *International Trade Statistics*, various years.

Cuba and Lithuania, while imports of finished textiles declined—by 64.2 and 28.3 per cent, respectively—imports of raw and semi-manufactured textiles increased).

For twenty-four of the thirty-four countries, the League of Nations statistics make it possible to compare also the changes in the quantity imported of raw and semi-manufactured cotton textiles (including raw cotton, yarns, and threads) on the one hand, and of finished cotton textiles (including tissues, piece goods, and apparel) on the other hand. A similar comparison for woollen textiles is possible for ten of these twenty-four countries. Table XIV indicates that, with the exception of the cotton imports of Ceylon and the wool imports of Roumania, the quantity of imports of finished textiles declined relatively more than the quantity of imports of raw and semi-manufactured textiles. Indeed, in eleven of the twenty-four countries the quantity of imports of raw and semi-manufactured cotton textiles increased—in most cases very considerably. For ten of the twenty-four countries, and India, it has been possible also to subdivide the group of imports of raw and semi-manufactured cotton textiles into raw cotton, and cotton yarns, and threads. In eight of these eleven countries the quantity of imports of cotton yarns and threads declined relatively more (increased relatively less) than the quantity of imports of raw cotton.[15] We conclude that the smaller the degree of manufacture of the various textile goods, the smaller (greater) was the decline (rise) in the quantity of imports.

The phenomenon described in the previous two paragraphs should be ascribed largely to the higher income elasticity of demand for imports of finished, than of raw and semi-manufactured textiles. When incomes declined, the broad masses in many of the countries considered tended to substitute coarser domestic manu-factures (in effect, the services of lower priced and less efficient domestic labour, technology, and equipment) for imported ones, and, hence, to depend relatively more on imports of raw and semi-manufactured textiles. In many countries in which domestic production of finished textiles supplied a large share of the market, even a small shift to domestic manufactures could entail a large propor-tional decline in imports of finished goods. In some countries tariff changes also contributed to the substitution of domestic for foreign textile manufactures.[16]

As indicated earlier, in seven of the thirty-four countries, namely, Estonia, the Netherlands, Norway, Canada, Ceylon, Egypt, and Poland, the relative decline in the value of imports of raw and semi-manufactured textiles exceeded that of finished textiles—though in only the first three of these countries was the differ-ence greater than 10 percentage points. These exceptions to the generally greater decline in the value of imports of finished textiles are accounted for partly by the relative contribution of price changes to the change in the import values of the two textile subclasses. Four of the seven countries (Estonia, Norway, Poland, and Ceylon) are included in Table XIV. The table shows that in the first three of them the quantity of imports of raw cotton, or wool, and yarn declined relatively less than that of finished cotton or woollen textiles.[17] In addition, in Poland, the only one of the four countries for which the League of Nations presents more detailed data, the quantity of imports of raw cotton declined relatively less than that of cotton yarns and threads, and the quantity of imports of raw wool in-creased while that of woollen yarn declined. But the heavier decline in the prices of raw cotton and wool than of finished textiles more than offset the effect on the change in the value of imports of the lighter decline in the quantity of the former goods. Furthermore, Canada, the Netherlands, and Norway had a much higher standard of living than most of the countries considered, and they likely held relatively larger stocks of raw and semi-manufactured textiles than the poorer countries. In these more advanced economies the incentive to shift to domestical-ly manufactured substitutes when incomes declined was probably smaller, and the possibility of drawing down stocks of raw and semi-manufactured material was greater.[18]

In concluding the discussion of the changes in imports of the two subclasses of textiles we may note that in 1928-9 finished textiles accounted for the greater part of the value of all textile imports in thirty-one of the thirty-four countries[19]—in most of them they represented over three-quarters, and in many as much as 85-95 per cent of the total.[20] Accordingly, the percentage decline in value of all textile imports of the various countries was closer to the heavier decline in the value of imports of finished textiles than to the lighter decline in the value of imports of raw and semi-manufactured textiles.

Comparison of the three periods shown in Table XIII indicates that, as the downswing progressed, the decline in imports of textiles increased more slowly than the decline in other classes of imports: the percentage of countries in which the decline in textile imports ranked either first, or first, second, or third diminished. This change is the reverse of, though weaker than, the change in the relative decline in imports of food and capital goods, noted earlier, and is explained by reference to analogous factors. Thus, the reduction in inventories in the early stages of the downswing was probably more important in the case of textiles than of food, or capital goods taken as a whole. The time lag between order and delivery of imports was smaller for textiles than for many capital goods. Compared to the prices of important foodstuffs (e.g., wheat and rice) which declined substantially in 1933, prices of cotton, wool, and finished textiles either recovered, or decreased only slightly at that stage.[21] Finally, restrictions of imports frequently affected textiles earlier than other goods. In sum, as the downswing progressed, the decline in imports of food and capital goods increased relatively to the decline in imports of textiles: of food largely because of the greater decline in price, and of capital goods largely because of the greater decline in quantity of imports.[22]

IV. *Hides.* In both periods 1928-9 to 1930-1, and 1928-9 to 1931-2, the decline in imports of hides was the heaviest: it ranked either first, or first, second, or third in more countries than the decline in every other class of imports, and fifth or lower in fewer countries. In the third period, 1928-9 to 1932-3, it was preceded only by the decline in imports of capital goods.

The income elasticity of demand for this class of imports tended to be fairly high. In addition to shoes, this class includes many semi-luxuries or luxuries, and the leather, skins, and furs used for their manufacture. (For some classes in the poorer countries even shoes were not a necessity.) Also, it was quite possible to extend considerably the life of many of these articles. Furthermore, inventories of hides and skins could be run down; and, unlike textile raw materials, most countries produced hides and skins of some type, which, in times of falling incomes, could be substituted for superior imports. The elasticity of foreign supply of hides was probably low (raw hides are by-products), and the supply curve may have shifted to the right considerably, owing to decreases in various costs of processing and to the tendency in the exporting countries to reduce stocks in anticipation of further price declines. Owing to these factors the decline in price of these imports was particularly heavy. Volume data available for some of the countries considered indicate also a fairly heavy decrease in the quantities imported.

Table XIII indicates that, over the three periods considered, the decline in hide imports lost somewhat in ranking.[23] On the one hand, as the downswing progressed the need for replacements, postponed in earlier periods, increased; the possibilities of scaling down inventories diminished; and the competition of food (through greater decline in price) and, particularly, of capital goods (through greater decline in quantity of imports) for the higher places in ranking of import declines became stronger.[24] On the other hand, the shift to domestic substitutes tends to be more effective the longer the period given for adjustment. It seems that the influence of factors such as the latter did not quite offset the effects of the former on the ranking of the decline in hide imports.

V. *Containers.* As indicated in Table XIII, in the period 1928-9 to 1931-2, the decline in imports of containers ranked well behind the decline in imports of capital goods, or hides. It ranked also behind the decline in food imports.[25] In the next period, 1928-9 to 1932-3, these differences in ranking increased.

It is not always clear from the available statistics and the nature of the imports and exports of each country whether the containers (which include chiefly bags, sacks, and material for their manufacture) carried the imports of staple foodstuffs, but were listed separately in the trade statistics, or whether they were imported empty to be used in export or domestic trade. In the former case, the price elasticity of demand was probably low since the cost of the containers was a small part of the total cost of the imported merchandise. The income elasticity of demand should be similar to that for the produce they carry, which in the case of staple foodstuffs was quite low. The elasticity of supply of the materials used for the construction of these containers was also quite low. However, the elasticity of supply of manufactured containers was probably much higher. Finally, the supply curve may have shifted to the right owing to the reduction in some manufacturing costs. Imports of empty containers into most of the countries considered tended to share the foregoing features. Probably then, imports of containers generally declined less than imports of capital goods, or hides, chiefly because of the smaller income elasticity of demand for containers; and less than imports of food mainly because of the greater elasticity of supply of manufactured containers.

Over the three periods shown in Table XIII the decline in container imports receded greatly in ranking. In the first period, 1928-9 to 1930-1 it was among the heaviest, ranking first in 31.8 per cent of the countries considered, and first, second, or third in 53.0 per cent. The elasticity of supply of manufactured containers was probably smaller in the shorter period; and, most likely, inventories were reduced in both exporting and importing countries. In later stages, when it became clear that the volume of staple food exports was being maintained fairly well, and the price of containers had decreased considerably, inventories may have been replenished. Also, the competition of food and, particularly, capital goods for the higher places in ranking of import declines became stronger.

VI. *Fuel.* As indicated in Table XIII, the decline in fuel imports between 1928-9 and 1931-2 was relatively moderate: in four-fifths of the countries considered it ranked fifth or lower.

The main factors accounting for the moderate decrease in the international trade in liquid fuel were discussed in Chapter 3. Analogous factors, relating particularly to the elasticities of demand, explain also the moderate decline in coal imports (although, probably, the greater use of coal in capital goods industries, whose output tended to decline more heavily, and the long-term substitution of other forms of power for coal in some industries, contributed to the greater decline in coal than oil imports observed in a large number of countries).[26] It would seem also that in many of the countries considered substitution by "coarser" domestic products in times of falling incomes was much less possible in the case of fuel than of some foodstuffs or manufactured goods.

The ranking of the decline in fuel imports was practically the same in the three periods considered. Compared to annual consumption, in most of the countries considered inventories of fuel were quite small, owing partly to the shortage of capital and storage facilities. Hence, the influence on imports of reductions in inventories in the early stages of the downswing tended to be limited. Further, since in the period 1928-9 to 1930-1 the decline in fuel imports ranked first, second, or third in only very few countries, the tendency of the decline in imports of food and, particularly, capital goods to increase greatly as the downswing progressed, could not materially affect the ranking of the decline in fuel imports.

VII. *Paper.* The decline in paper imports was the lightest of all classes of imports. In the periods 1928-9 to 1931-2, and 1928-9 to 1932-3, it ranked fifth or lower in well over nine-tenths of the countries considered.

This phenomenon should be ascribed chiefly to the relatively low income elasticity of demand for paper. While it has not been possible to divide this class of imports into smaller groups, the statistics indicate that newsprint was dominant. It has been observed that, quite often, when business sales decline, advertising tends, in fact, to increase. However, this factor was less significant in many of the less developed countries, in which newspaper advertising was practised on a very small scale compared with North America. In these countries the income elasticity of demand for paper was low because newsprint had become a necessity for the consumer: partly owing to the small expense involved, partly because newspapers were the chief medium of political and other communication in the years considered,[27] and partly because newspapers were used widely for wrapping and other elementary household purposes. Furthermore, unlike some other imports, for instance certain foodstuffs or hides, the possibility of substituting domestic produce when incomes declined was usually negligible. The price elasticity of demand for paper also was low; and, since only variable costs had to be met in the depression, the supply curve shifted to the right. These factors go a long way to explain the relatively greater decline in the price than in the quantity of paper purchased.[28]

Over the three periods considered the decline in paper imports lost slightly in ranking. The change occurred mainly between the first and second period. In the earlier stages the value of imports was probably affected also by a tendency to scale down stocks of paper, while in later stages other classes of imports, noted earlier, competed more strongly for high ranking.

VIII. *Chemicals.* The decline in the imports of chemicals between 1928-9 and 1931-2 was among the smallest of the eight classes of imports: in about nine-tenths of the countries considered it ranked fifth or lower. This ranking did not change materially over the three periods considered.

For the most part, imported chemicals were manufactured goods, based on minerals and a few animal or farm materials. Accordingly, the elasticity of supply of these goods was generally greater than that of foodstuffs, textile fibres, or hides; and in the downswing the supply curve probably shifted to the right. The income, and price, elasticities of demand for the various goods of this class vary considerably. On the basis of the available data it has been possible to distinguish two or more subclasses of chemicals in the imports of thirty-three countries.[29] The general ranking of the decline in these subclasses of chemical imports is the following, proceeding from the largest decline to the smallest: (a) soap, perfumery, cosmetics; (b) fertilizers; (c) paints, colours, dyestuffs, varnishes; (d) drugs or pharmaceutical products; and (e) other chemical products.

The crucial factor accounting for the order of ranking of the declines in imports of subclasses (a) (c) and (d) seems to have been the income elasticity of demand. For subclass (a) this elasticity was high: perfumery and cosmetics were luxuries, and most of the countries considered produced soap and imported only the better qualities, which in times of falling incomes tended to give way to the cheaper domestic substitudes. The income elasticity of demand for dyes and colours should be similar to that for domestically produced textiles and other goods in whose production they were used. Since in most of the countries considered such textiles were partly substituted for imports, and since in many countries fairly adequate substitutes of imported dyestuffs were not readily available, the decline in the volume of subclass (c) imports was frequently very moderate. Finally, because of the nature of subclass (d) imports the income elasticity of demand for these goods was probably quite low. The decline in subclass (b) imports, was due chiefly to the increase in scarcity of credit to, and working capital of the farmer, and to the short-term decline in emphasis on soil conservation.[30]

This completes the examination in this chapter of the relative changes in the various imports of the forty-nine countries in the downswing after 1929. Of course, there were variations among the countries regarding the rate of change of given types of imports. Some variations resulting from differences in the economic and social structure of these countries were noted in the discussion of individual import classes. Others relate, for instance, to differences between the countries in the rate of economic expansion in the boom or contraction in the downswing, in the possibilities over the short run of substituting domestic products for imports, or in the type and rate of response of consumers and producers to various kinds of economic change (which, in turn, vary with institutional, social, political, and other conditions). Some of these factors are considered in following chapters.

IV

We now proceed to the second part of our analysis, namely, the examination of the share of the various goods in the total imports of the various primary-exporting countries.

The range of the share of each of the eight classes of imports in the total imports of the various countries in 1928-9 is shown in Table XV.[31] As a rule, the first three classes of imports (capital goods, food, and textiles) were far more important than the other classes. Each of the former classes of goods represented

TABLE XV

RANGES OF THE SHARES OF EIGHT CLASSES OF GOODS IN THE IMPORTS OF FORTY-EIGHT
PRIMARY-EXPORTING COUNTRIES IN 1928-9 °

Import class	Share in total imports of individual countries		
	Lowest percentages	Highest percentages	
Capital goods	10.7 (China),	11.5 (Ceylon)	37.2 (Roum.), 40.0 (Mex.) †
Food	8.2 (Roum.),	8.5 (Hung.)	42.1 (Mal.), 44.4 (Ceylon)
Textiles	9.7 (Mal.),	10.2 (Braz., Ven.)	35.7 (Bulg.), 36.3 (Persia)
Fuel	0.8 (Roum.),	1.3 (D.E.I.)	14.3 (Mal.), 17.0 (Arg.)
Chemicals	1.6 (Norw.),	1.8 (Mal.)	7.5 (Lith.), 7.6 (Mex.)
Hides	0.3 (Bol.),	0.6 (China)	4.4 (Latv., Ven.), 4.5 (Bulg.)
Paper	0.9 (Norw.),	1.0 (Bol.)	4.5 (N. Zeal.), 5.4 (Austr.)
Containers	0.4 (Neth.),	0.7 (Mal.)	4.4 (Chile, Dom.), 5.1 (Siam)

° Two outside limits—the first and second highest, or lowest—are shown, and the countries in which the percentages noted were observed are shown in brackets. Of the forty-nine primary-exporting countries, no estimates have been possible for Turkey. For Honduras the estimates are for the year 1928-9 only. For the following classes of imports estimates could not be made for the number of countries shown in brackets: fuel (2), hides (11), paper (6), and containers (24).

† In Venezuela the share of capital goods in imports was exceptionally high: about 46 per cent.

anywhere from 8 to 46 per cent of a country's imports, compared with 0 to 8 per cent accounted for by chemicals, hides, paper, or containers. Fuel was somewhat more important than the last four classes, representing from about 1 to 17 per cent of imports. The combined share in imports of capital goods, food, and textiles ranged from about 55-60 per cent (in Argentina, Denmark, Hungary, and the Netherlands) to about 77-81 per cent (in Bulgaria, Colombia, and Nigeria).

Range data provide no information about the distribution of the values in the ranges. Therefore, we ranked the eight classes of goods by their relative importance, that is, by their share in the imports of each country in 1928-9. Since there were differences in the rank of each class of imports in the various countries, we estimated the frequency in ranking. The results are shown in Table XVI.

The primary data and Tables XV and XVI suggest the following remarks about the import structure of the countries considered in 1928-9. The imports of most of these countries were generally much more diversified than their exports, and this was true both of large countries, such as Australia or Brazil, and of smaller ones, such as Bolivia, Colombia, or Egypt.[32] Capital goods were the most important class of imports, ranking first in almost two-fifths of the countries considered. They were followed by food and textiles, which were of roughly equal importance. It is to be noted that food bulks larger among the imports of many of these countries than of some advanced industrial economies. Fuel occupies fourth place in the majority of the countries considered, although in several countries it ranked fifth or sixth, and in a few second or third. Chemicals ranked fourth in a number of countries, but in the majority they were in fifth, and in some in a lower, position. Containers, paper and hides usually ranked fifth or lower in importance.

It is not possible to consider in detail the great number of factors which

TABLE XVI

FREQUENCY OF RANKING OF EIGHT CLASSES OF GOODS BY THE SIZE OF THEIR SHARE IN THE IMPORTS OF EACH OF FORTY-EIGHT PRIMARY-EXPORTING COUNTRIES IN 1928-9 *

Percentages of the total number of countries

Import class	Largest share (1)	Second largest share (2)	Third largest share (3)	Fourth largest share (4)	Fifth largest or lower share (5)	Not shown in League of Nations statistics (6)	Total (7)
Capital goods	39.6	37.5	22.9	—	—	—	100.0
Food	33.3	25.0	37.5	4.2	—	—	100.0
Textiles	27.1	31.2	37.5	4.2	—	—	100.0
Fuel	—	6.3	2.1	56.2	31.2	4.2	100.0
Chemicals	—	—	—	33.3	66.7	—	100.0
Hides	—	—	—	2.1	75.0	22.9	100.0
Paper	—	—	—	—	87.5	12.5	100.0
Containers	—	—	—	—	50.0	50.0	100.0
TOTAL	100.0	100.0	100.0	100.0	310.4	89.6	800.0

* The figures in the Table are percentages of the total number of countries in which the share of a given class of imports in the country's total imports ranked as indicated in the column headings. Of the forty-nine primary-exporting countries, no estimates were possible for Turkey. For Honduras the estimates are for the year 1928-9 only.

account for the differences in the share and rank of each class of goods among the imports of the various countries. However, some general remarks will be useful in our subsequent analysis.

Generally, the share of capital goods in imports (shown in Table XVII) was highest (almost one-third or more) in countries exporting minerals, for instance in Bolivia, Chile, Mexico, Peru, and Venezuela. It was high (about one-quarter to one-third) also in certain countries (some of them large or fairly advanced) which exported wood products or cereals, for example, in Finland, Norway, Yugoslavia, Canada, and Argentina; also, in several countries among whose exports coffee predominated heavily, for instance, in Brazil, Costa Rica, Guatemala, and El Salvador. Roumania exported petroleum, wood and cereals, and Colombia coffee and petroleum; capital goods constituted well over one-third of their imports. On the other hand, the share of capital goods in imports was relatively low (about one-fifth or less) in countries exporting Class B goods (non-staple and semi-luxury foodstuffs), for example, in Denmark, Honduras, the Irish Free State, and Lithuania. It was low (in a few cases barely exceeding one-tenth) also in a number of countries (some of them very poor) which exported such Class A goods as tea, rice, beans, and sugar, or such Class C goods as cotton, jute, silk, and rubber, for instance in Ceylon, China, Cuba, Egypt, and Siam.

In many cases, differences in the share of capital goods in imports reflect differences in the intensity of the boom and in the rate of investment in the various countries. For instance, in countries like Venezuela, Colombia, and Brazil the boom was intense, based mainly on rapid expansion of oil production and foreign investment in the first two countries, and on expansion of coffee production, bumper crops, foreign investment, and credit and price inflation in Brazil. On the other hand, the profitability of producing non-staple and semi-luxury foodstuffs did not rise greatly in the boom of the late nineteen-twenties and the markets for such exports as sugar or rubber were not particularly strong. Accordingly, the boom was generally much milder in countries exporting such goods. (The developments in the various countries referred to here are described more fully in Chapter 7.)

In addition to the rate of economic expansion a number of other factors account for differences in the pattern of demand and domestic supply in the various countries, and hence for differences in the share and rank of capital goods among their imports. Thus, generally, countries which exported minerals depended heavily on imported equipment and other capital goods. So did some large countries whose development depended on large-scale investment in social overhead capital (transportation, public utilities, and the like). On the supply side, the production of manufactured and semi-manufactured capital goods was more advanced in certain more developed economies. In Denmark the boom was not intense. However, the relatively low share of capital goods in her imports (less than one-fifth) was probably due also to factors such as those just noted: investment in farming to a large extent involved the use of local resources; the country was small and had been provided in earlier periods with much of the necessary social overhead capital; and its capital goods industries were better developed than those of many other countries studied. Finally, the share and rank of capital goods in imports varied also with the dependence of each country on such imports as food, textiles, or fuel. For instance, the high share of capital goods in the imports of Argentina or Australia (over one-third) is explained partly by the high degree of self-sufficiency of these economies in food—the latter represented only about one-tenth of their imports.

The share and rank of food among the imports of the various countries depended largely on the volume, nature, and development of their food resources; also, on other factors which determined the general pattern of demand and domestic supply and, hence, the other import requirements. Argentina's resources of grains and semi-luxury foodstuffs were ample and well developed, her fuel resources were scarce, and the boom, accompanied by inflow of foreign capital, called for a substantial volume of imports of capital goods. Consequently, in 1928-9 food represented only about one-tenth of her imports, and it ranked fourth among the eight classes of imports. The importance of food was about the same among Hungary's imports. On the other hand, in tea-producing Ceylon, sugar-producing Cuba, and coffee-producing Haiti food represented between one-third and one-half of imports.[33] As Table XV shows, the share of food in imports varied among the countries studied more than the share of any other class of imports.

The importance of fuel among imports also depended on the volume, nature, and development of the country's fuel resources, as well as on the development of industry, transportation, and other fuel-using activities, and the competition of other goods for share and rank in total imports. The great variety of possible combinations of these factors is reflected in the considerable variation in the share and rank of fuel among imports: from less than 1 per cent and last place in Roumania , which was well endowed with oil and coal resources, to about 17 per cent and second place in Argentina.[34]

Unlike food and fuel, the relative importance of textile imports depended less on the natural resources of the various countries, since few of them produced a significant part of the raw materials they required. It depended more on the state of development of the country's textile industry, the pattern of demand for textiles, and the competition of food, capital goods, and other commodities for share and rank in imports. While in countries like China, Egypt, Nicaragua, Nigeria, or Persia textiles ranked first among imports and represented from well over one-quarter to over one-third of imports, in countries with well-developed textile industries, such as Canada, Denmark, the Netherlands, or Norway, textiles ranked after capital goods and food and accounted for only 10-15 per cent of imports. However, they ranked third and represented less than one-fifth of imports also in several less developed countries which imported substantial amounts of food and capital goods, for example, in Peru and Costa Rica.

V

The discussion in this chapter has provided many useful insights into the rates of decline of the various types of imports, and the relative importance of these goods among the total imports of the countries considered. But in contrast with the analysis of exports, this discussion cannot supply any ready indicator of the relative rate of decline in total imports of the various countries. In the earlier analysis some conclusions were possible as to the type of country (depending on the composition of exports) that experienced a heavier or lighter decline in exports. This was so because differences between patterns of exports were great, while differences between declines of the same type of exports from different countries were, as a rule, much less significant. But in the case of imports, differences in composition are much smaller, and hence differences between the countries respecting the decline of the same types of imports become significant.

Our main problem is the cyclical changes in trade balances, hence we are interested less in comparisons between the declines in total imports of the various countries, and more in the relation of the decline in each country's imports to the decrease in its exports. A given commodity may be more important among the imports of one country than another. In addition, in the downswing it may decline more heavily in the former country. Yet, both this particular import and the total imports of the former country may decline less than its exports, while in the latter country the converse occurs. For instance, in 1928-9 capital goods were much more important among the imports of Chile than of Persia (32.4 and 14.5 per cent of the total, respectively). They also declined between 1928-9 and 1931-2 much more heavily in the former country (69.0 compared with 50.2 per cent). Yet Chile's imports of capital goods declined proportionately less than her total exports, and so did her total imports, while Persia's imports of capital goods, and her total imports, decreased proportionately more than her total exports. Putting the matter differently, imports of capital goods may be less "helpful" to the balance of trade of one country than, for instance, fuel imports are to another country—even though these fuel imports tend to decline proportionately less than the capital goods imports of either country—if the imports of capital goods of the former country decline less than its exports, while the fuel imports of the latter decrease more than its exports.

An attempt is made in the following chapters to bring forward the factors accounting for the variation, among the countries studied, of the relation between the decline in imports and the decrease in exports. The discussion will make use of the analysis in this chapter. On the other hand, it will provide further insight into factors responsible for differences between the countries in the pattern of imports and, mainly, in the rate of decline of similar imports.

CHAPTER SIX

RELATION BETWEEN THE DECLINE IN IMPORTS AND THE DECLINE IN EXPORTS OF THE VARIOUS COUNTRIES

IN THIS AND THE NEXT CHAPTER we examine the main factors accounting for differences between the countries considered in the relation of the percentage decline in imports and the percentage decline in exports. Changes in the value of imports consisted, as a rule, of changes in both the prices and quantities of imports. Changes in import quantities were related to changes in incomes or in relative prices of imported goods and domestic substitutes. The first section of this chapter is occupied by a preliminary discussion of the changes in incomes and prices in the countries studied.

I

Generally speaking, income changes may originate in changes in domestic factors relating to employment and productivity, or changes in the volume of exports or the terms of trade. In the great majority of the countries examined changes in foreign trade factors were by far the more important. Compared to these, "autonomous" changes in domestic factors were fairly limited. Moreover, given such changes, their effects on the whole economy also tended to be comparatively limited. These matters may be considered in more detail.

Except for a very few of the countries studied, satisfactory data for estimating the ratio of foreign trade (exports or imports) to national income in the period considered are not readily available. The factors which influence this ratio have not been thrashed out fully in economic literature. Historical evidence and comparison of a large number of countries point to a negative correlation between the ratio of foreign trade to national income and the size of a country's population, the diversity of its natural resources, or the size of its area; and to a positive correlation between the trade/income ratio and the degree of compartmentalization of the country's economy, the facilities for international trade, the rate of the country's economic expansion (particularly if expansion is induced largely by growing foreign markets), or the similarity of the country's social fabric and patterns of life to those of countries with which transportation and communication are relatively easy.

In the great majority of the countries considered the small size of the population was an important factor limiting the possibilities of domestic specialization, of use of indivisible equipment and methods of large-scale production, and of establishment of industries producing substitutes for imported goods. Other factors contributing to the dependence of many of these countries on imports and exports were the limited diversity of their natural resources and their small area: transportation costs isolate the interior of a small country from foreign products and markets less than the interior of a large country. These matters may be illustrated by reference to data for the year 1953 relating to forty-one of the forty-nine countries.[1]

In thirty-two countries, or about four-fifths of the forty-one countries, the ratio of foreign trade (arithmetic mean of exports and imports) to national income exceeded 15 per cent (in twenty-four countries it exceeded 20 per cent).[2] The population of each of these countries was smaller than 20 million. Nigeria was the only major exception, while in Egypt and the Philippines the population was 22 and 21 million, respectively. In the remaining nine countries the trade/income ratio was smaller than 13 per cent.[3] Their population exceeded 20 million, except for Yugoslavia (17 million) and Portugal (whose trade/income ratio was 12.8 per cent).

Generally, a large area contains a greater diversity of resources than a small area. Accordingly, a country's area may serve as a crude measure of the diversity of its resources as well as of the indicated impediments to foreign trade due to transportation costs. Of the thirty-two countries whose trade/income ratio exceeded 15 per cent, twenty-three had an area smaller than 500 thousand square kilometres (the group includes Thailand whose area is 514 thousand square kilometres).[4] Fifteen of these had an area smaller than 150 thousand square kilometres. Of the nine countries whose trade/income ratio was smaller than 13 per cent, seven had an area exceeding 500 thousand square kilometres. As with population, Yugoslavia and Portugal were the two exceptions.[5]

Given the diversity of resources, the trade/income ratio tends to vary with the type of resources possessed by the various countries. Underdeveloped countries with large resources of industrial raw materials might be expected to trade heavily. This factor undoubtedly contributed to a high trade/income ratio in the late nineteen-twenties in several of the countries examined, for instance Bolivia, Chile, and Malaya.

Like the small size of the population, various internal obstacles to the movement of goods and productive factors in a considerable number of the countries studied limited the possibilities of domestic specialization and large-scale production for domestic markets. Unfavourable topography (e.g., in Bolivia), underdeveloped transportation and credit facilities, a relatively limited degree of monetization of the economy, or "inter-provincial" taxes are some of the natural, institutional, and economic factors which tended to compartmentalize these economies. These conditions, and the absence of similar obstacles to the international trade of these countries (indeed, the supply of adequate credit, transport, and other facilities by other countries), tended to "turn their economies outwards"—to raise the ratio of foreign trade to national income.

The ratio of foreign trade to national income tends to vary also with the rate of economic expansion at home and abroad. In a large number of the countries considered, which were less developed and frequently stagnant, the short-term variation in the trade/income ratio tended to be more pronounced than in more developed and normally advancing economies. In the former countries cyclical unemployment of resources was usually not significant: the consumption/income ratio was fairly high; small-scale farming and enterprise were important and, hence, a large part of the domestic saving was matched directly by real investment (repair, improvement, and building of homes and business or farm structures); prices and wages (to the extent that wage-labour was significant) were flexible;[6] and considerable compartmentalization of the economy insulated some sectors from developments in others. The conditions of supply of resources (including elasticity and mobility) were such as to make increases in output difficult, particularly over short periods. In most of these countries economic expansion in the late nineteen-twenties originated chiefly in changes, often large ones, in external factors. Early increases in demand and prices in the export industries, whose expansion was often assisted by foreign capital, tended to absorb such resources as had been cyclically underemployed (e.g., in mining) and to lead to increases in domestic prices. The increase in production of types of goods that could be imported became less profitable, and the demand for imported capital and consumer goods for which no close substitutes were being produced, increased. Hence, exports and imports tended to rise greatly as a proportion of the national income.

Undoubtedly, the last factor examined, namely, the rate of economic expansion at home and abroad, raised the trade/income ratio of a large number of the countries considered in the late nineteen-twenties well above that indicated for 1953. For instance, the ratio of such countries as Brazil or Mexico exceeded the 15 per cent mark. We may conclude that in the boom of the late nineteen-twenties the trade/income ratio was 20-25 per cent or more in the great majority of the forty-nine countries.[7] Notable exceptions were China and India, in which the ratio was lower than 10 per cent.

While exports, and hence also their large changes in the downswing, were so important, autonomous changes in domestic factors relating to employment and income were much less significant.

Adequate data for estimating the relative importance of domestic investment in the countries examined in the late nineteen-twenties are not readily available. Investment and its ratio to national income varied chiefly with the rate of economic expansion, and this rate varied considerably among the countries studied. In some countries, for example China, the Irish Free State, or Greece, the boom was very mild, while in others, for instance Venezuela or Colombia, it was intense. But even in the latter countries, the rapid expansion of exports early in the boom tended to absorb such resources as had been cyclically underemployed. Also, much of the investment in certain export industries (e.g., mines) or in public utilities and transportation systems required a considerable amount of equipment and materials of foreign origin. The consequence was that a large part of the investment expenditure was directed to imports rather than to the services of domestic productive resources.

Furthermore, much of the investment in these countries was "export-induced" and "export-financed." To a large extent, the profitability and prospects of public utilities, transportation and even manufacturing, the supply of capital for investment in these and other sectors of the economy, and the revenues of government depended, directly or indirectly, on the fortunes of the country's exports. Moreover, as indicated, much of the investment expenditure on services of domestic productive resources was possible only if accompanied by sizable imports of equipment and materials, and therefore it depended on foreign exchange resources, obtainable chiefly through increases in exports. Even capital imports, which in the nineteen-twenties helped in financing private investment and public works in several of the countries studied, depended considerably on business conditions and prospects in the capital-exporting and capital-receiving countries, and hence tended to vary with the level and profitability of international trade.

We may conclude then that, in the great bulk of the countries considered, in the downswing after 1928-9 the primary changes in income resulting from the large declines in exports were very much greater than the autonomous changes in domestic factors.[8] The repercussions of the former changes also were relatively greater than the repercussions of the latter: partly because of circumstances discussed earlier (e.g., the dependence, direct or indirect, of a large part of domestic investment on exports), and partly because of the following features characteristic of the great majority of the countries studied.

Less developed economies are considerably compartmentalized and exhibit less domestic specialization and domestic trade than more advanced countries: a smaller percentage of the goods produced is exchanged and, on the average, these goods are carried through shorter time and smaller space. In view of this compartmentalization of the economy, the effects of a given disturbance (for instance, a decline in exports or domestic investment) tend to be the more widespread the more numerous the points of impact.[9] The over-all change in each sector of the economy will consist of the initial disturbance and its repercussions. The magnitude of the repercussions in each sector will tend to vary less than proportionately with the variation in the magnitude of the disturbance in that sector for the following reason.

Economic behaviour is conditioned by the value and changes of various economic variables, for instance, income. The conditioning factors include the rate of change of these variables, namely, their percentage change per unit of time. The larger the absolute change in the independent variable per unit of time, the larger is usually the absolute change in the dependent variable; the proportional change in the latter variable may be smaller or greater than the proportional change in the former variable (the "elasticity" may be numerically smaller or greater than unity). What is significant for our present discussion is that as the percentage change in the independent variable per unit of time varies, the relation between the changes in the two variables tends to vary: the absolute magnitude of change in the dependent variable may vary more than proportionately with the absolute magnitude of change in the independent variable, or less than proportionately. (Given the original values of the dependent and independent variables, the "elasticity" too varies with the size of the percentage change in the independent variable per unit of time.)[10] There are reasons for expecting that when income declines as a consequence of a decline, for instance, in exports or domestic investment, the marginal saving/income ratio in a given period (particularly in the periods shortly after the decline in income) will tend to be greater the greater the percentage decline in income per unit of time, and the marginal consumption/income ratio will tend to be smaller.[11] Hence, the magnitude of the repercussions of a decline in exports or domestic investment in an isolated sector of an economy will tend to vary less than proportionately with the variation in the magnitude of the initial disturbance in that sector.

It follows from the foregoing two paragraphs that, in the type of country considered, a decline of a given magnitude in exports or domestic investment tends to have greater (smaller) over-all effects the more wide-spread (concentrated) is its immediate impact.[12] We may now consider the typical distribution of the impact of changes in exports and investment in the countries studied.

In most of the countries studied, such as several of the European agricultural countries or, even more, countries like Brazil or Cuba, the whole economy was export-oriented.[13] Changes in the fortunes of important export crops affected directly the incomes of thousands of farmers, distributors, transportation systems, banking and financial institutions, and export merchants, as well as the government revenue. In addition, in many countries in which the balance of payments tended to deteriorate in the downswing, the primary restriction of the volume of money associated with the decline in exports was followed by a secondary restriction because of the reduction of the usually small reserves of these countries. Briefly, the impact of a change in exports was felt directly in every nook and cranny of the economy.[14] On the other hand, the impact on services of domestic productive resources of a change in important types of investment expenditure, for instance in governmental construction (which, in any event, was to a large extent, in effect, export-induced and export-financed), tended to be concentrated in particular sectors or areas of the economy. For the reasons advanced earlier, the over-all effects of such a change on the economy tended to be smaller than the effects of a change in exports of equal magnitude.

Reference was made twice to the variation of government revenue with exports. In many of the countries studied the tax system relied heavily on indirect taxes and on various forms of taxation of earnings from production, distribution, or export of major crops or minerals. Thus, to a large extent tax revenue depended, directly or indirectly, on foreign trade.[15] However, in the downswing government finance on current account frequently tended to have counter-cyclical effects on total expenditure and prices. In many countries typically inflexible items, such as the service on domestic government debt, military expenditure, and salaries and pensions of the civil service claimed a large part of government expenditure. This fact combined with other factors, political, social and institutional, to render government expenditure on current account highly inflexible in the downswing. Governments were forced to run deficits financed by bank credit.

We may summarize the foregoing argument. In the great majority of the countries studied the changes in incomes in the downswing after 1928-9 originated largely in changes in foreign trade factors: the quantity of exports or the terms of trade.[16]

The changes in the downswing in the quantity of imports of the countries studied must be related largely to changes in their incomes, discussed above, or to changes in the relative prices of imported goods and domestic substitutes. In these countries changes in the prices of such substitutes over short periods were the product, direct or indirect, chiefly of changes in exports: changes in income and expenditure originated mainly in, or were closely related to, changes in exports, and over short periods the elasticity of supply of substitutes for many imported goods tended to be limited.

Having settled these matters, we may revert to our main task: the examination of the relation between the percentage decline in imports and the percentage decline in exports of the various countries in the period studied. This relation exhibited a certain pattern which we shall outline and endeavour to explain. Later we shall consider the influence on this relation of such factors as changes in tariffs, subsidies, exchange rates, exchange controls, or other policies, which, though important in some countries, does not seem to have contributed to the general pattern which we are about to discuss.

II

Generally, in the period 1928-9 to 1931-2 the percentage decline in total imports varied among the countries considered directly with the percentage decline in their exports. However, the variation of the former percentage was substantially smaller than the variation of the latter;[17] and while in countries whose exports declined relatively moderately the percentage decline in imports tended substantially to exceed the percentage decline in exports, in countries whose exports declined relatively heavily the former percentage tended to be equal, or smaller than the latter. Accordingly, the import/export decline, defined in Chapter 2 as the *ratio* between the percentage decline in imports and the percentage decline in exports, tended to exceed unity in countries whose exports declined relatively moderately, and to be close to, or smaller than unity in countries whose exports declined relatively heavily.[18] And the *difference* between the percentage decline in imports and the percentage decline in exports tended to be substantially positive in the former countries and close to zero or negative in the latter.

In our further consideration of the variation between the countries in the relation between the percentage decline in imports and the percentage decline in exports, we may for brevity refer either to the ratio of the two percentages (the import/export decline) or to the algebraic excess of the percentage decline in imports over the percentage decline in exports, which we may call the "responsiveness of imports." (It should be noted that this term is used only for brevity and is not intended necessarily to imply causal relation between the decline in exports and the decline in imports.)[19] We shall refer mostly to the responsiveness of imports: in both verbal analysis and diagrammatic presentation variations in the difference between the two percentage declines are easier to follow than variations in their ratio. Consequently, the discussion will include certain factors which contributed to variations between the countries in responsiveness of imports, though not in import/export decline.

A ready impression of the variation in responsiveness of imports between the countries studied is obtained from Diagrams I, II and III: the diagram for each of the three periods, 1928-9 to 1930-1, 1928-9 to 1931-2, and 1928-9 to 1932-3, relates the import responsiveness of each of the forty-nine countries to the percentage decline in the country's exports.[20]

As in earlier discussion, we may concentrate at first on the second of the three periods. The scatter plot in Diagram II slopes downwards from left to right and crosses the horizontal line of zero responsiveness of imports.[21] The responsiveness of imports (and the import/export decline) varies inversely with the percentage decline in imports of the countries.

Before analysing further the inverse variation of the responsiveness of imports

DIAGRAM I. PERCENTAGE DECLINE IN EXPORTS° AND RESPONSIVENESS OF IMPORTS BETWEEN 1928-9 AND 1930-1 OF FORTY-NINE PRIMARY-EXPORTING COUNTRIES

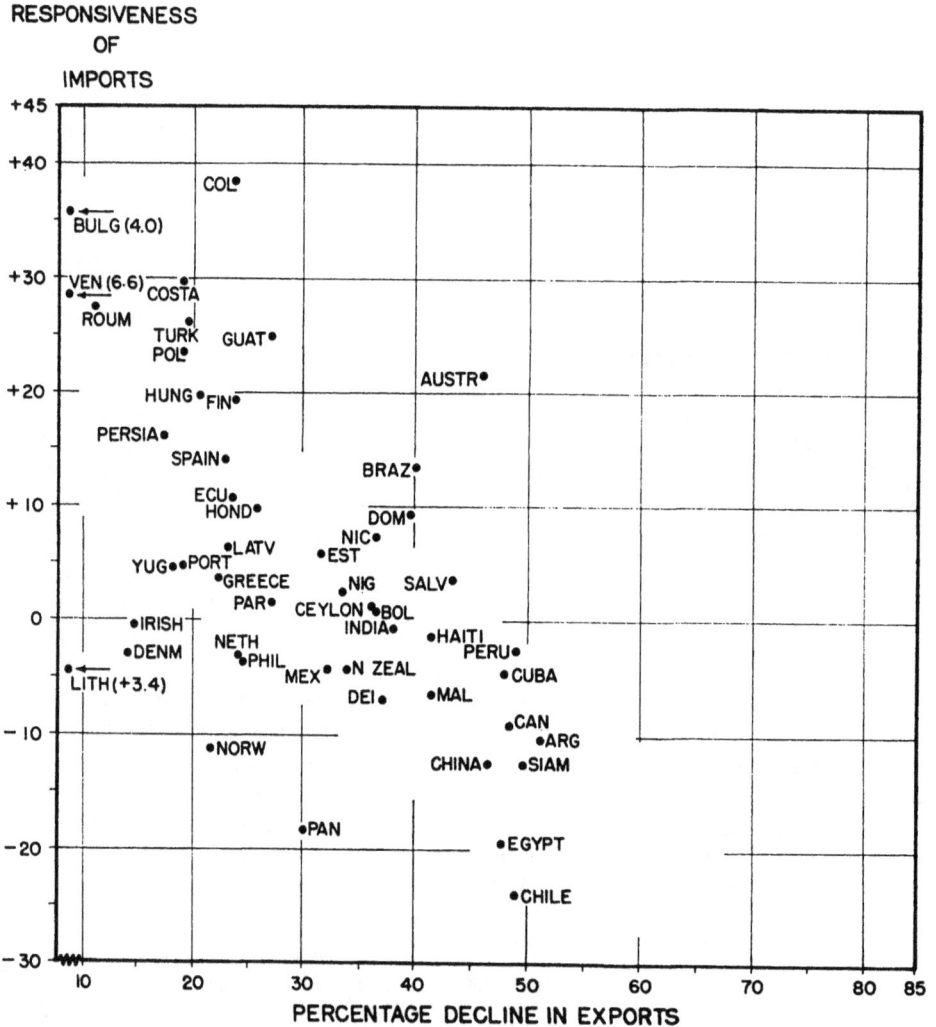

RESPONSIVENESS
OF
IMPORTS

+45

+40

COL●

BULG (4.0)

+30 VEN (6·6) COSTA
      ROUM
        TURK GUAT●
        POL●

                              AUSTR●
+20   HUNG ●FIN●

     PERSIA●
        SPAIN●
                        BRAZ●
        ECU●
+10   HOND●
                        DOM●
                      NIC●
            ●LATV   ●EST
  YUG●●PORT
        ●GREECE   ●NIG   SALV●
        PAR● CEYLON ●BOL
              INDIA●
0   ●IRISH   ●HAITI
    ●DENM   NETH   PERU●
            ●PHIL
  LITH (+3.4)   MEX● ●N ZEAL   ●CUBA
              DEI●   ●MAL
                              ●CAN
-10   ●ARG
        ●NORW   CHINA● ●SIAM

                ●PAN
-20   ●EGYPT

                        ●CHILE

-30 ⋀⋀⋀
    10   20   30   40   50   60   70   80 85
              PERCENTAGE DECLINE IN EXPORTS

° Lithuania's exports increased by 3.4 per cent.

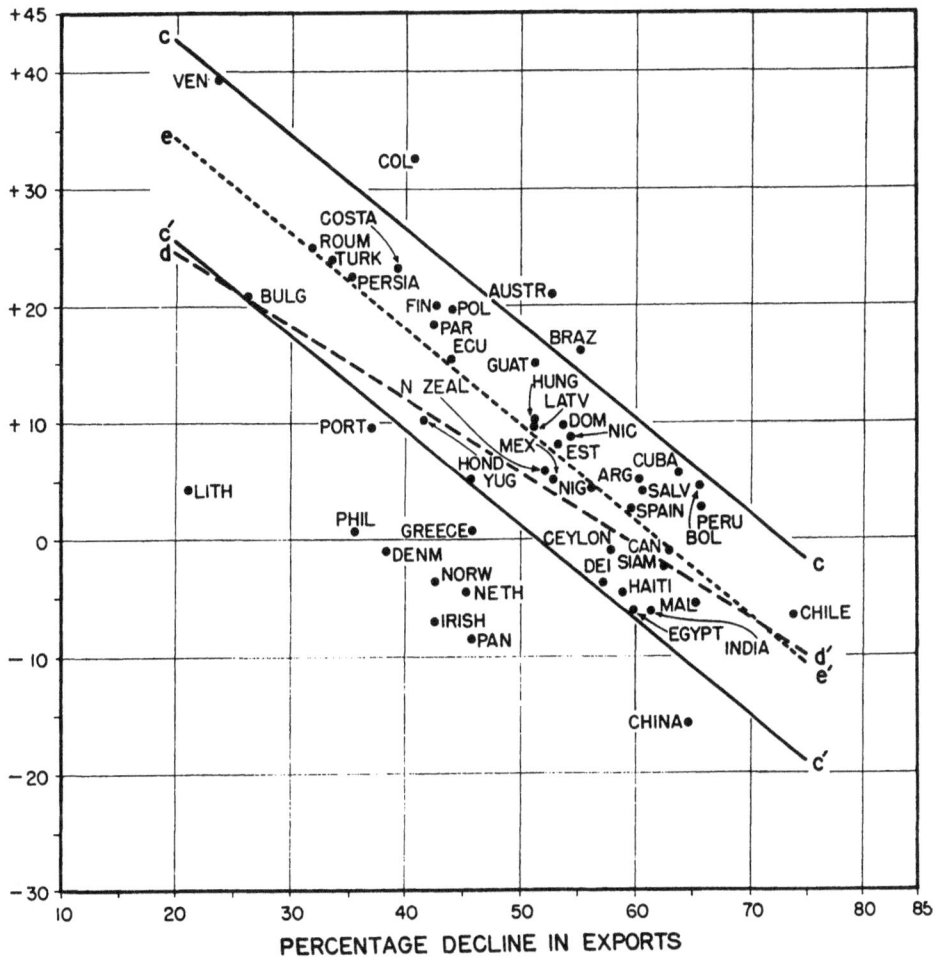

DIAGRAM II. PERCENTAGE DECLINE IN EXPORTS AND RESPONSIVENESS OF IMPORTS BETWEEN 1928-9 AND 1931-2 OF FORTY-NINE PRIMARY-EXPORTING COUNTRIES

RESPONSIVENESS
OF
IMPORTS

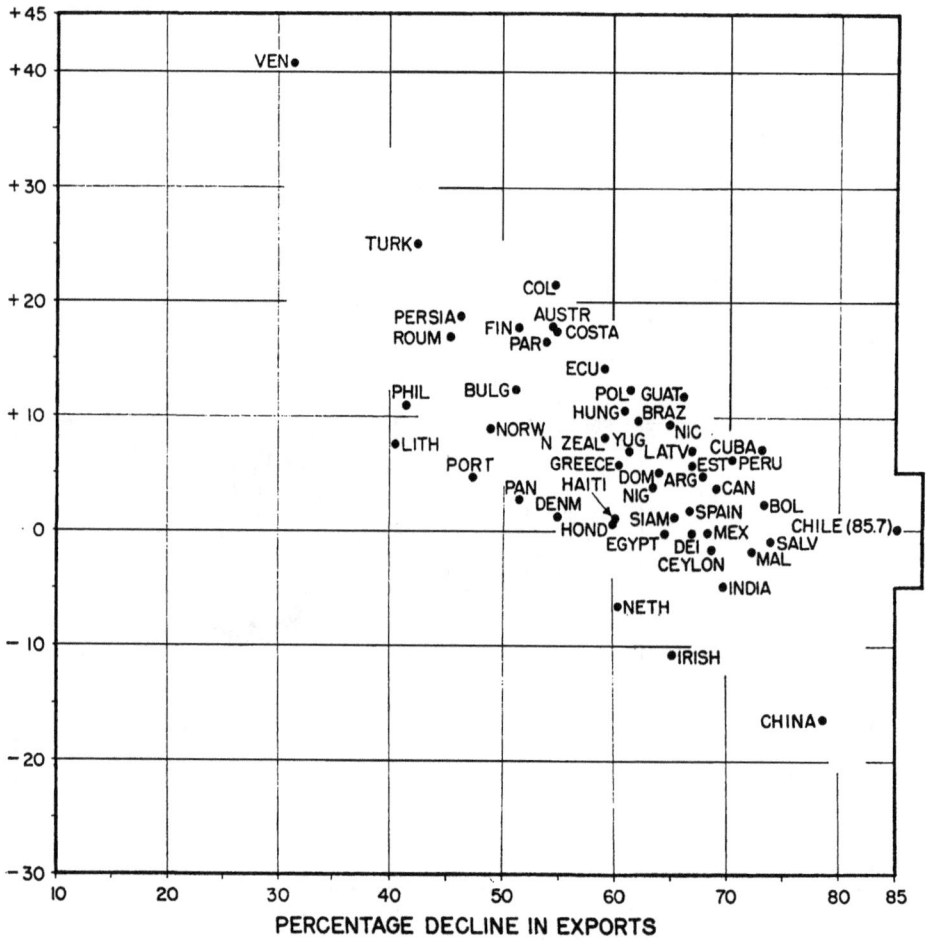

(or of the import/export decline) with the percentage decline in exports, we may pause to emphasize the significance of this relation for explaining the variation of cyclical change in trade balance among the various countries. The original relation between exports and imports (discussed in Chapter 2), the nature of a country's exports which accounted largely for the relative decline in exports (discussed in Chapters 3 and 4), and the relation just observed would have enabled one in 1928-9 to predict successfully the deterioration or improvement in the trade balances of the great bulk of primary-exporting countries. For instance, a country starting with a surplus in 1928-9 and exporting mainly Class A or C goods might have been expected to experience a large deterioration in its balance, because of (a) the effect of the original relation between exports and imports, (b) the probability of a large decline in exports, and (c) the likelihood of a low responsiveness of imports (or import/export decline) following the heavy decline in exports.[22] A full comparison of the countries listed in the two groups of Chapter 4 with respect to these three factors will be found in the concluding chapter. In the remainder of this chapter we consider the main factors accounting for the observed inverse variation of import responsiveness and percentage decline in exports. (Throughout the reader will bear in mind that the discussion will concern the variation among countries only of the responsiveness of imports, not of the extent of change in the trade balance. As indicated, the latter depends also on the difference between the original imports and exports, and the size of the percentage decline in exports.) Other factors explaining differences in import responsiveness between various countries are examined in the following chapter.

III

From the foregoing survey of the responsiveness of total imports we may turn to the responsiveness of the eight classes of imports. Following the same presentation we have drawn diagrams for the period 1928-9 to 1931-2, which relate the responsiveness of each of these classes of imports (the algebraic excess of the percentage decline in a given class of imports over the percentage decline in total exports) to the percentage decline in total exports. For the sake of economy we present here only Diagrams IV-VI, relating the responsiveness of imports of capital goods, food, and textiles (the three important classes of imports) to the decline in exports of forty-five countries.[23]

With the exception of chemicals, in whose diagram no clear pattern is discernible, the diagrams for the various classes of imports show the same general pattern as Diagram II (which relates the responsiveness of total imports to the decline in exports): the seven scatter plots slope downwards from left to right at slopes which are similar to the slope of the plot in Diagram II; and they all cross the horizontal line of zero responsiveness of the respective imports. (Lines dd' in Diagrams II, IV-VI are not related to the slope of the plots; they may be ignored at this stage.) The vertical position of the scatter plots varies, reflecting the extent of decline of the various imports. If the position of the seven plots is measured roughly by the percentage of the countries shown in each diagram which lies above, or below, the horizontal line of zero responsiveness, their order from top to bottom (from greater to smaller responsiveness) is the following: hides; capital

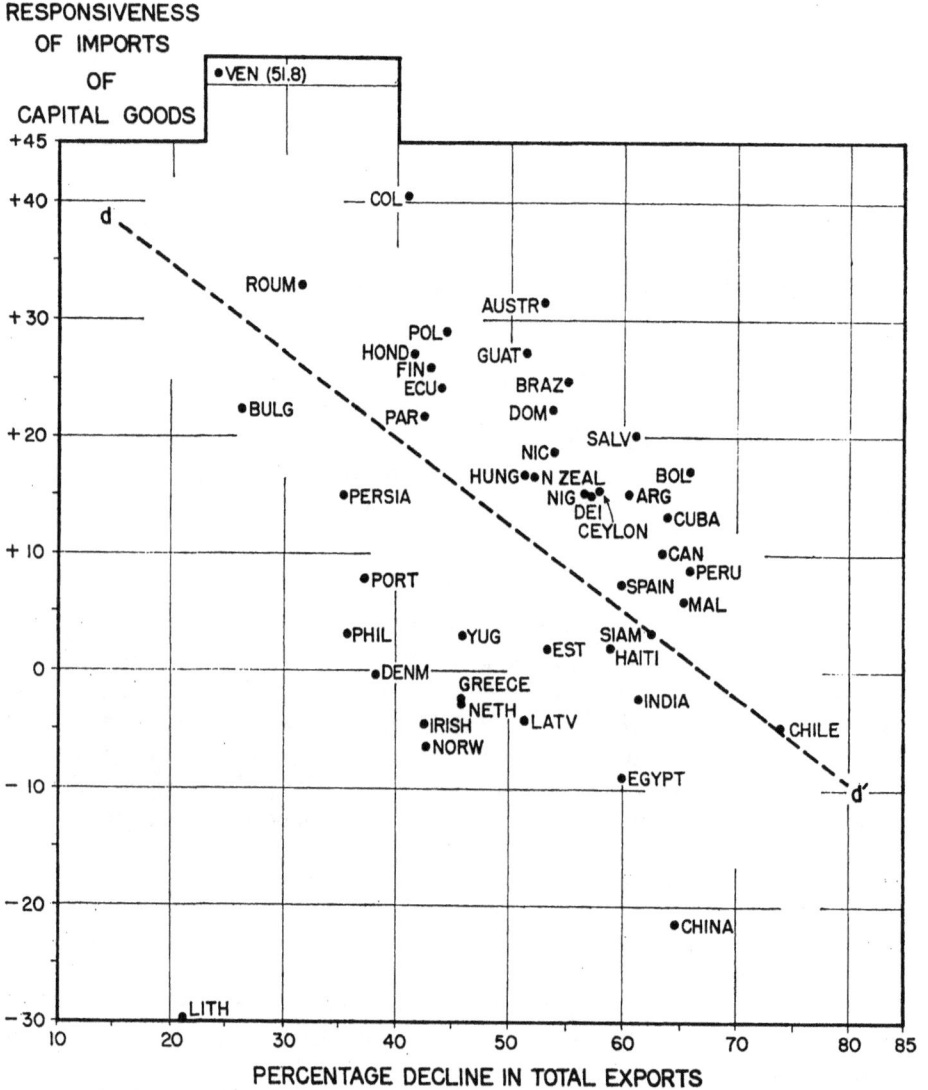

RESPONSIVENESS
OF IMPORTS
OF
CAPITAL GOODS

PERCENTAGE DECLINE IN TOTAL EXPORTS

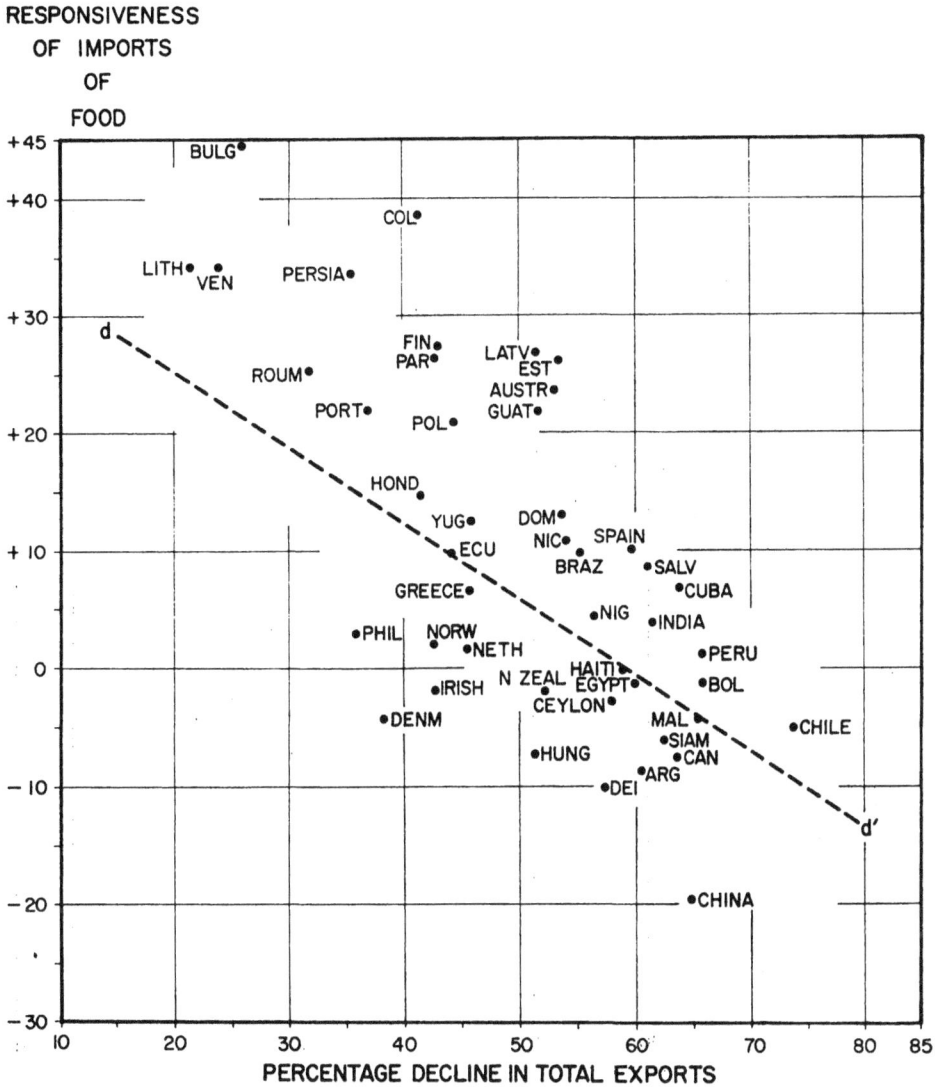

DIAGRAM V. PERCENTAGE DECLINE IN TOTAL EXPORTS AND RESPONSIVENESS OF IMPORTS OF FOOD BETWEEN 1928-9 AND 1931-2 OF FORTY-FIVE PRIMARY-EXPORTING COUNTRIES

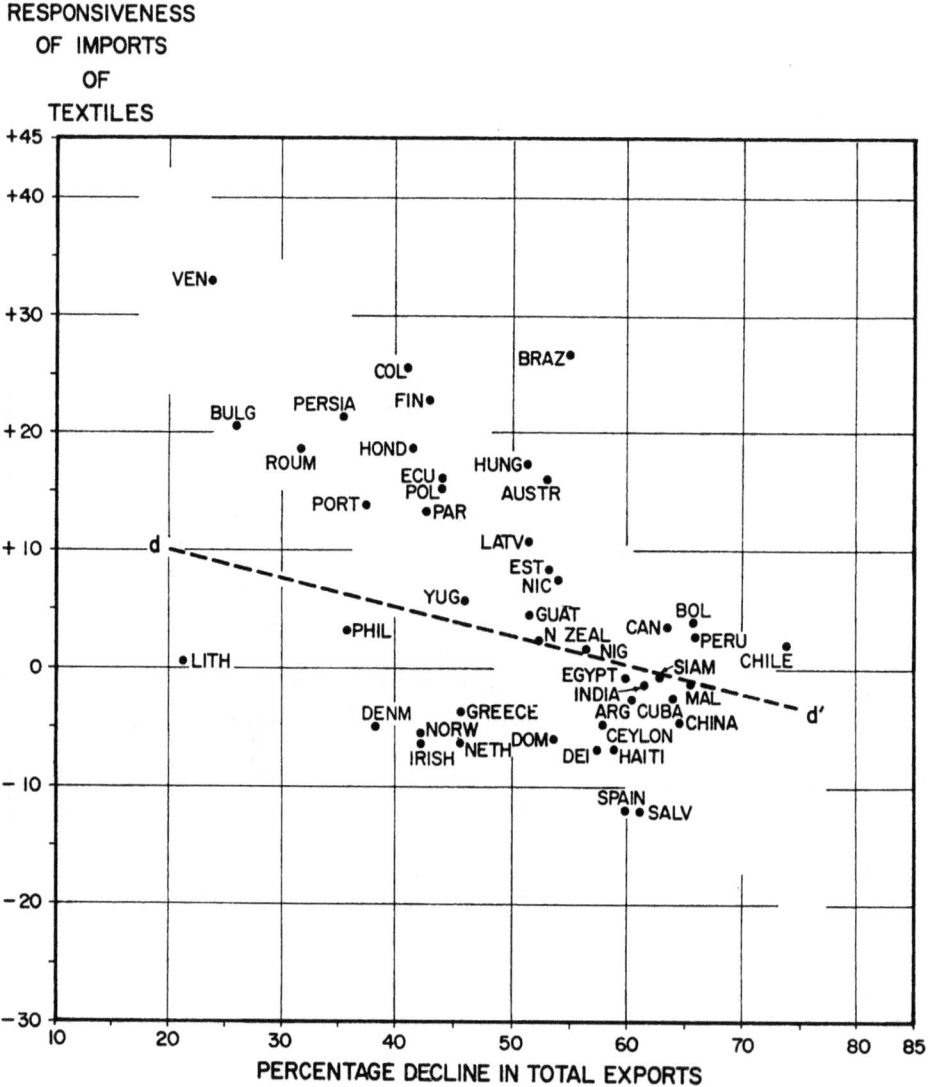

DIAGRAM VI. PERCENTAGE DECLINE IN TOTAL EXPORTS AND RESPONSIVENESS OF IMPORTS OF TEXTILES BETWEEN 1928-9 AND 1931-2 OF FORTY-FIVE PRIMARY-EXPORTING COUNTRIES

goods; food; containers and textiles, with a small difference between them; and fuel and paper in roughly the same position.

It appears then, that the pattern of the responsiveness of total imports of the various countries was a composite of broadly similar patterns of the responsiveness of the individual classes of imports, rather than, as might have been the case, a composite of different patterns of responsiveness of the various imports.

IV

We may now look into the main factors responsible for this tendency of the responsiveness of imports to vary inversely with the percentage decline in exports of the countries studied—in other words, for the tendency in the period examined of the percentage declines in the various types of imports and in total imports to vary among the countries considered less than the percentage declines in their exports.[24]

Changes in the value of imports consisted, as a rule, of changes in both the prices and quantities of imports. We may first concentrate on the price component.

While the change in quantity of given types of imports varied substantially between the countries, the decline in price of given imports of the bulk of these countries was broadly uniform. This uniformity of price decline tended to equalize the percentage decrease in the value of given imports of the various countries: the effect on import value of a given decline in price tends to be relatively greater the smaller the decrease in quantity imported. Hence, the uniform decline in price tended to reduce the differences between the countries in the decline in value of imports which would have resulted from the decline in quantity alone. This equalizing effect is greater the greater the decline in import price.[25] The equalizing effect of uniform price declines extended further to the total imports of the various countries: in contrast with the exports of the countries considered, there was a considerable similarity between their import patterns.[26] We conclude that the broadly uniform and substantial decline in price of given goods imported by the bulk of the countries was an important factor limiting the variation between the countries in the percentage decline of the various types of imports, and of total imports. No comparable equalizing force operated on the percentage decline in exports of these countries. As a consequence, the responsiveness of imports tended to vary inversely with the percentage decline in exports of the countries studied.

V

We may now turn to the quantity component of the change in import values.

The data required for comparing changes in the quantity of similar goods imported by the various countries are very scanty. Thus, changes in the quantities imported by at least twenty countries could be estimated only for the following commodities: coffee, tobacco (raw, semi-manufactured, and manufactured), cotton (raw, semi-manufactured, and manufactured), "paper and manufactures," and "coal, coke, and conglomerates."[27]

Unlike the responsiveness of import values, in which case a pattern of inverse variation with the percentage decline in exports of the various countries could be clearly distinguished, no clear pattern can be seen in the variation between the countries of the responsiveness of imports quantities (the algebraic excess of the percentage decline in the *quantity* of a given import over the percentage decline in the *value* of total exports). If any tendency at all can be detected in the data, it is for the responsiveness of import quantities to vary in the same general way as the responsiveness of import values, namely, inversely with the percentage decline in exports of the various countries. Although such a relation is only slightly noticeable and may be entirely spurious, some factors contributing towards that kind of a relation, as well as factors working in the opposite direction, may be noted. (Owing to the shortage of information it is impossible to test some of the arguments advanced; and, since the discussion concerns an uncertain phenomenon, the hasty reader may prefer to skip the remainder of Section V.)

The quantity of a country's imports tends to change with a change in its income or in the relative prices of imported goods and domestic substitutes. We may first consider the relation of the change in quantity of imports to the change in value of exports through the change in income. In the countries and period considered changes in national income originated largely in changes in exports. For the present time we may neglect the influence on income of other factors.

An explanation of a possible tendency of the responsiveness of import quantity to vary inversely with the percentage decline in exports might be sought in traditional trade and income theory. If we assume stable prices, and imports decline as a consequence of a decline in export income, the relation between these two changes will be equal to the product of the marginal propensity to import and the export multiplier, or to $g/(g + a)$, where g is the marginal propensity to import, and a is the "marginal propensity not to spend."[28] We may assume for the moment that $g/(g + a)$ was the same for the various countries; also, that in the base period the ratio of imports to exports (the inverse of the "original relation") was the same in the various countries and greater than $g/(g + a)$ (i.e., that all the countries had the same small relative surplus, a balanced trade, or the same relative deficit). It would follow that the percentage decline in imports of each country would be smaller than the percentage decline in exports, and that it would vary between the countries directly and proportionately with the percentage decline in exports. Hence, the responsiveness of import quantity would vary inversely with the percentage decline in exports.[29] On the other hand, if we assumed that in the base period the ratio of imports to exports was again the same in the various countries, but now smaller than $g/(g + a)$, the responsiveness of import quantity would vary directly with the percentage decline in exports.[30]

We may now allow for differences between the countries in the original relation. If $g/(g + a)$ and the percentage decline in exports are the same in all countries, the responsiveness of imports will vary directly with the original relation.[31] And if, while $g/(g + a)$ is again the same, the percentage decline in exports varies, a country with a substantially larger original relation than another country, may have a higher responsiveness of imports even though the percentage decline in its exports exceeds that of the other country.[32] The direct variation between countries of the responsiveness of import quantity with the original relation, combined with a possible direct variation between countries of the original relation with the percentage decline in exports (to be considered presently), could result in a direct variation of the responsiveness of import quantity with the percentage decline in exports.

The foregoing argument proceeded on the assumption that "imports declined as a consequence of a decline in export income." However, in the countries and period considered imports changed also as a consequence of changes in other credit items of the balance of payments; and the decline in merchandise exports was accompanied by changes in other debit items besides imports. If in the downswing these other items of the balance of payments declined proportionately more than the merchandise exports, the responsiveness of import quantity would tend to vary between the countries inversely with the original relation. In this case then, the inverse variation of the responsiveness of import quantity with the original relation, combined with a possible direct variation between countries of the original relation with the percentage decline in exports (to be considered presently), would result in an inverse variation of the responsiveness of import quantity with the percentage decline in exports. We may now consider the actual relationships in the countries studied.

Most of the countries which in the downswing experienced a moderate decline in exports had a deficit in 1928-9, and most of the countries whose exports declined heavily had a surplus.[33] In the boom a number of deficit countries were recipients of foreign capital, and some of the surplus countries used part of the surplus to service foreign capital invested in their territories and to accumulate precious metals or foreign exchange reserves. One might expect that in the ensuing downswing the abrupt cessation of the capital flow to deficit countries contributed towards a greater percentage decline in imports than in exports; and, on the other hand, that in surplus countries, the heavy decline in the service of foreign capital (cyclically or by default), and the use of accumulated holdings of precious metals and foreign exchange to finance expenditures and imports, contributed towards a smaller percentage decline in imports than in exports. It might appear then that among the countries a possible inverse variation of the responsiveness of import quantity with the percentage decline in exports was due to a direct variation of the original relation with the percentage decline in exports, and an inverse variation of the responsiveness of import quantity with the original relation.

In fact, it is not possible to place any emphasis on such an explanation of the general variation among the countries in the responsiveness of import quantity. It has been impossible to obtain, for any sizeable group of the forty-nine countries, either a significant correlation between the percentage decline in exports and the value of the original relation, or a significant partial correlation (after eliminating the influence on the responsiveness of imports of the percentage decline in exports) between the responsiveness of imports and the value of the original relation. Failure to obtain a significant correlation of the latter kind might have been expected. The deficits and surpluses of the various countries in the boom were balanced, in effect, by a great variety of combinations of non-merchandise items rather than in the simple fashion noted, and the changes in these items were similarly varied: some of these items declined proportionately less than the merchandise exports of the respective countries, and some more.[34]

Similarly varied was the need for public policies to restrict imports, as well as the combination of policies adopted and their effectiveness.

Another explanation of a possible tendency of the responsiveness of import quantity to vary inversely with the percentage decline in exports may be sought in the tendency of $g/(g + a)$ to vary among the countries. In order to simplify the argument in the previous paragraphs we assumed that $g/(g + a)$ was the same for all countries. Obviously, this was not the case. Some factors accounting for differences in $g/(g + a)$ in the countries studied are discussed in the next chapter. They explain why at given percentage declines in exports some countries had a smaller $g/(g + a)$ and a smaller import responsiveness than others. As far as our present discussion is concerned, it may be argued that, *ceteris paribus*, $g/(g + a)$ tended to vary inversely with the percentage decline in the value of exports in a given period: as indicated earlier, the marginal consumption/income ratio in a given period tends to be smaller the greater the percentage decline in export income per unit of time, and the marginal saving/income ratio tends to be greater. On this count the responsiveness of import quantity will tend to vary inversely with the percentage decline in exports.[35]

The decline in exports of the countries studied was accompanied also by substitution of domestic for foreign goods; partly because of a tendency to substitute inferior domestic goods (e.g., coarser types or qualities of textiles) for foreign goods when incomes decline, and partly because of changes in relative prices of foreign goods and domestic substitutes. As indicated, the decline in prices of imports of the bulk of the countries studied was broadly uniform. On the other hand, in view of the all-pervasive influence of changes in exports in most of the countries studied, incomes and domestic prices generally tended to vary directly with the relative decline in the value of exports of the various countries.[36] The tendency then to substitute domestic for foreign goods on account of changes in incomes and relative prices was probably greater in the countries whose exports declined more heavily. However, according to our earlier argument, the relative decline in income and expenditures probably varied between the countries less than proportionately with the variation in the percentage decline in exports;[37] hence, so did probably also the relative decline in prices of domestic substitutes. Also, the difficulties of substitution in consumption and investment (psychological, social, physical, institutional, and technical obstacles on the demand side, and difficulties in expanding the domestic production of substitute goods) tend to increase more than proportionately with the extent of substitution called for in a given period. Consequently, *ceteris paribus*, the amount of substitution effected in a given period probably tended to vary less than proportionately with the variation in the percentage decline in exports, and this contributed towards an inverse variation of responsiveness of import quantity and percentage decline in exports.[38]

In conclusion, the reader might be reminded that the discussion has been concerned with the responsiveness of import quantities. As explained earlier, the broadly uniform decline in imports prices tended to make the responsiveness of import values vary among the countries studied inversely with the percentage decline in exports.

VI

   The analysis in sections II-V related chiefly to intercountry comparisons of the responsiveness of imports in the period 1928-9 to 1931-2. We may now briefly survey the changes in this responsiveness over the three periods 1928-9 to 1930-1, 1928-9 to 1931 2, and 1928-9 to 1932-3. The factual background is found in columns (3) and (4) of Table I and Diagrams I, II, and III.

   Generally , the responsiveness of imports of the countries studied tended to increase substantially between the first and second period, and to change little between the second and third period. Thus, the median responsiveness increased from +2.3 to +5.1 and to +5.8 in the three periods respectively; and the range of responsiveness changed from −23.8 to +38.6, to −15.6 to +39.3, and to −16.4 to +40.9. Between the first and third period the responsiveness of twenty-seven countries increased, and of the remaining twenty-two diminished.[39] But while between the first and second period as many as thirty-two countries, or about two-thirds of all countries, experienced an increase in responsiveness, between the second and third period only twenty-two countries, or a little less than half of all countries, had a similar experience.[40]

   As one might have expected, over the three periods there were changes in the ranking of the various countries by responsiveness of imports: in one period the responsiveness of a given country was greater than that of other countries, and in another period it was smaller. However, there was a noteworthy stability in the broad relationship of responsiveness of imports of the countries: with very few exceptions, the same countries had a relatively high or low responsiveness in all three periods.[41]

   The range of responsiveness of the forty-nine countries decreased between the first and second period, from 62.4 to 54.9 percentage points, and increased between the second and third period, from 54.9 to 57.3 percentage points. However, the latter change reflects the inclusion of the extreme values of responsiveness. Comparison of Diagrams I, II, and III, or of the following differences between various decile values of responsiveness of the countries considered, indicates that the differences in responsiveness between the countries diminished substantially between the first and second, and the second and third, period:

	1st to 9th Decile	2nd to 8th Decile	3rd to 7th Decile	4th to 6th Decile
1928-9 to 1930-1	40.0	26.0	14.4	6.7
1928-9 to 1931-2	29.4	23.3	11.2	4.6
1928-9 to 1932-3	20.0	14.5	9.4	3.9

   This decline of the differences in responsiveness was the result of a decrease in the responsiveness of most countries which in the first period had a high responsiveness and, to a larger extent, an increase in the responsiveness of countries which had a low responsiveness. Of twenty-one countries whose responsiveness in the first period exceeded +4.5, sixteen experienced a decrease in responsiveness between the first and third period; and of twenty-eight countries whose responsiveness in the first period was +4.5 or less, twenty-two experienced an increase—or, if we neglect the countries with a responsiveness of −1.0 to +4.5, of nineteen countries whose responsiveness was smaller than −1.0, seventeen experienced an increase.

The foregoing observations about the increase over the three periods compared in the responsiveness of low-responsiveness countries, and the decline in responsiveness of high-responsiveness countries reflect the changes in a number of factors.

The prices of important exports (predominantly Class A and C goods) of the low-responsiveness countries declined precipitately in the earlier stages of the downswing; in later stages the difference between the decline in price of such exports and of many manufactured goods imported by these countries either increased little or decreased.[42] Then, as far as the price component of the values of exports and imports is concerned, there was a tendency for the responsiveness of imports of low-responsiveness countries to decline little, or to increase, in the later stages of the downswing. Further, the longer the period considered the greater was the possibility of curtailing investment, of effectively applying policies to restrict expenditure and imports, of substituting domestic for imported goods, and, generally, of responding and adjusting to changes in exports, incomes, and relative prices. Also, certain factors which were partly responsible for the early low responsiveness of these countries weakened or disappeared over the longer period: for instance, foreign exchange reserves which had been accumulated in the boom were run down and this necessitated further curtailment of expenditures and imports. Some other factors which tended to increase in the later periods the responsiveness of certain low-responsiveness countries are noted in the next chapter.

The responsiveness of high-responsiveness countries tended to decline over the three periods. It was indicated that of the countries whose responsiveness in the first period exceeded +4.5 sixteen experienced a decrease in responsiveness between the first and third period. The average yearly percentage decline in exports of thirteen of these countries increased. It appears that the decline in responsiveness which tended to accompany this increase in the rate of decline in exports more than offset the increase in responsiveness of the respective countries made possible by the longer period available for response and adjustment. Of the remaining three high-responsiveness countries, whose responsiveness decreased between the first and third period, Australia, and to a smaller extent Brazil, had an exceptionally high responsiveness in the first period. Moreover, Australia's economy experienced an early revival from the depression and from 1932 on her tariffs were adjusted downwards. Such factors, which contributed to the decrease in responsiveness of some high-responsiveness countries, are noted in the next chapter.

As Diagrams I, II, and III indicate, the inverse relation between responsiveness of imports and percentage decline in exports of the countries examined is a fundamental characteristic of all three periods considered. As one might have expected, the decline over the three periods in the variation among countries of the percentage decline in exports[43] was accompanied by a decline in the variation of responsiveness. The relationship between import responsiveness and percentage decline in exports is reflected also in the fact that of twenty-four countries whose ranking by percentage decline in exports increased (i.e., which developed a higher percentage decline in exports relative to the other countries) between 1928-9 to 1930-1, and 1928-9 to 1932-3, twenty-one receded in ranking by responsiveness (i.e., developed a lower responsiveness relative to the other countries), and of twenty-four countries whose ranking by percentage decline in exports decreased, seventeen advanced in ranking by responsiveness.[44]

FURTHER EXAMINATION OF THE RELATION BETWEEN THE DECLINE IN IMPORTS AND THE DECLINE IN EXPORTS

IN THIS CHAPTER WE EXAMINE other factors accounting for differences between the countries studied in the relation between the percentage decline in imports and the percentage decline in exports.

In Diagram II thirty-eight of the countries studied form a narrow scatter plot sloping downwards from left to right, reflecting the inverse variation of the responsiveness of imports with the percentage decline in exports. Thirty-six of these countries lie between the parallel lines cc and $c'c'$, and the other two (Brazil and Portugal) lie close to these lines. The remaining eleven countries (Australia, Colombia, China, Denmark, Greece, the Irish Free State, the Netherlands, Norway, Panama, the Philippines, and Lithuania) lie at a considerable distance above or below the main body of countries: they had a responsiveness of imports considerably greater or smaller than that of countries which had similar percentage declines in exports and are included in the narrow scatter plot.

While it is necessary in this chapter to account for the exceptional position of these eleven countries, we shall also present factors explaining smaller differences between the responsiveness of imports of various countries: the position of the two countries lying outside but close to line cc and $c'c'$, and differences in the responsiveness of groups of countries lying between these lines. Starting then with the countries in the upper left corner of Diagram II and proceeding clockwise along the periphery of the scatter plot we shall discuss, in effect, significant determinants of the responsiveness of imports and, hence, of the changes in the period studied in the trade balances of various primary-exporting countries.

I

Diagram II indicates that in the period 1928-9 to 1931-2 the responsiveness of imports of Colombia and Australia was higher than that of countries with similar percentage declines in exports. Though to a considerably smaller extent, the import responsiveness of Venezuela and Brazil was also relatively high.

An important factor accounting for the exceptional responsiveness of imports of Colombia is the high rate of economic expansion which she experienced in the preceding boom. In the countries studied economic expansion was usually associated with a boom in exports. *Ceteris paribus*, the higher the rate of expansion, the greater tended to be the share of investment in national income, the share of capital goods in imports, and the share of the imports of capital goods destined for new investment rather than for replacement purposes.[1] It follows that the higher the rate of expansion in the boom the greater tended to be, in the ensuing downswing, the part of the national income directly affected by the decline in investment which accompanied a given decline in exports; and, given the multiplier, the greater tended to be the relative decline in consumption, total income, and prices. Consequently, the higher the rate of expansion in the boom the greater tended to be, in the ensuing downswing, the percentage decline in imports of consumer goods; also, of capital goods, since goods imported for new investment (whose importance tended to be the greater) tended to decline more heavily than replacement goods. The imports of all goods tended to decline the more, both because of this greater decline in imports of consumer and capital goods, and because the share of capital goods in imports tended to be the greater and imports of capital goods tended to decline more heavily than other imports.

The economic expansion of Colombia in the nineteen-twenties originated in good coffee exports and rapid growth of petroleum mining from 1921 onwards: her output of crude petroleum increased from 319,000 barrels in 1922 to 20,381,000 in 1929. These developments were accompanied by large investment of American capital in the oil industry, public utilities, transportation, and other public works, amounting in the years 1924 to 1929 to over $250 million.[2] In 1928-9 capital goods represented about 36 per cent of Colombia's imports.[3] And, while her balance of merchandise trade showed large surpluses in 1921, 1922, and 1924, and again from 1930 to 1936, in the period 1925 to 1929, it showed very small surpluses in 1926 and 1929, a deficit in 1925, and large deficits in 1927 and 1928.

From 1928, and particularly 1929, onwards Colombia's exports declined. The profit outlook in coffee growing, oil mining, and business in general became less clear, and the inflow of capital subsided. As a consequence investment declined heavily. Furthermore, as in Brazil or Cuba, the whole economy was export-oriented. The decline in coffee exports (which in 1928-9 represented about two-thirds of Colombia's exports) tended to affect, more or less directly, every important sector of the economy: the incomes of thousands of farmers, middle-men, distributors, transportation companies, financial institutions, and exporters, as well as the government revenue.[4] As indicated earlier, such a wide spread of the immediate impact of a given decline in exports (implying a low percentage decline per unit of time in many incomes, rather than a high percentage decline in few) tends to be accompanied by a relatively high marginal consumption/income ratio and large over-all effects on the economy.[5]

The foregoing developments, chiefly the relatively large volume of investment in the boom, the heavy decline of investment in the downswing, and the high marginal consumption/income ratio—as well as the increases in Colombia's import duties from May 1931 on, the prohibition of certain imports, and the adoption of exchange control in September 1931—resulted in a heavy decline in Colombia's imports in the downswing.[6] Between 1928-9 and 1931-2 the imports of capital goods (which represented more than one-third of all imports in 1928-9) declined by 81.8 per cent. And the percentage decline in Colombia's exports was well exceeded also by the decline in imports of food (79.8 per cent) and textiles (67.0 per cent)—indeed, by the decline in every class of imports distinguished in Chapter 5 for which data are available.[7]

The relatively high responsiveness of imports of Brazil and Venezuela should be ascribed to factors similar to those outlined with reference to Colombia. In the years before 1930 Brazil experienced an unprecedented and partly artifical prosperity, based largely on expansion of coffee production and bumper crops, combined with price stabilization at a high level and excessive advances to the coffee growers. In the period 1925 to 1930 a large volume of American capital was invested in her public utilities and, to a small extent, her agriculture; and in 1928-9 capital goods represented about 34 per cent of her imports.[8]

In the downswing, coffee prices collapsed, capital imports subsided, investment declined heavily,[9] the immediate impact of the decline in exports was widespread throughout the economy, and the heavy indebtedness of the farmers exerted additional pressure on consumption. Between 1928-9 and 1931-2 Brazil's imports of capital goods declined by 80.0 per cent. Her textile imports, which in 1928-9 represented one-tenth of her imports, also declined very heavily, by 82.2 per cent. The decline was exceptionally large (92.8 per cent) in the case of finished textiles which made up almost two-thirds of the total. Foreign exchange control, initiated in May 1931, and an increase in import duties tended to protect Brazilian industry, particularly the textile industry which was relatively well developed.[10]

In the nineteen-twenties Venezuela, like Colombia, experienced spectacular development in petroleum mining: output increased from 121 thousand barrels in 1917 and 1,471 thousand in 1921, to 19,467 thousand in 1925, and 133,954 thousand in 1929. Over $80 million of American capital were invested in Venezuela's oil industry between 1919 and 1924, and another $140 million followed between 1924 and 1929. The oil boom was accompanied by expansion in manufacturing, building, public works, and industries producing building materials.[11] The share of Venezuela's imports in 1928-9 consisting of capital goods, at about 46 per cent, was the highest of the forty-nine countries. As the value of oil exports levelled off in 1930 and declined thereafter, and as the profit outlook in mining and business in general became less clear, capital imports ceased and investment declined. The imports of capital goods (which had accounted in the boom for almost half the total imports) declined heavily: between 1928-9 and 1931-2 by 75.6 per cent.[12]

In the general pattern of Diagram II, reflecting the relation between import responsiveness and percentage decline in exports of the countries studied, Venezuela's responsiveness is high, but not exceptional: the country lies within the parallel lines cc and c'c' and, in relation to the decline in exports, its responsiveness is lower than that of Brazil and, particularly, of Colombia. Unlike these predominantly coffee-exporting economies, in which the impact of the decline in exports was widespread throughout the economy, in underdeveloped oil-exporting economies like Venezuela short-term changes in exports involved big percentage changes per unit of time in a relatively small number of incomes, to a large extent foreign. In times of rising prices of exports wages were rather "sticky," while the prices of goods bought by the workers increased; also, large increases in production of oil were not paralleled by significant increases in labour employment in the oil industry. On the other hand, profits soared. In the downswing after 1930 oil exports declined mainly on account of the fall in oil prices, and this fall affected chiefly the incomes of foreign capital-owners.[13] Accordingly, consumption was affected less than in countries like Brazil or Colombia. The income of foreign managerial personnel was not greatly affected, and in any event, the income elasticity of demand of these people for many imported goods was limited. In sum, to a considerable extent changes in exports were accompanied by a fall in payment abroad of dividends and related remittances, and in imports of capital goods, rather than in imports of consumer goods.[14]

Australia is another country whose responsiveness of imports in the period studied was considerably greater than the responsiveness of other countries that experienced a similar rate of decline in exports (see Diagram II). In this country too the rates of income growth and investment were high in the nineteen-twenties. Rising exports, a large inflow of foreign capital in the years 1923-8, and liberal expansion of credit were accompanied by vigorous expansion of agricultural and industrial production and of governmental expenditure, notably on public works. In 1927/8-8/9 capital goods represented more than one-third of Australia's imports. Over the period 1919/20 to 1928/9 Australia's real national income increased by about 80 per cent, though the rate of growth was particularly high in the earlier years of the decade and decreased later.[15]

As Australia's exports declined after 1928/9 and as the business prospects became less clear and the inflow of capital subsided, investment declined heavily. Furthermore, the immediate impact of the decline in exports tended to be fairly widespread and, hence, to be accompanied by a relatively high marginal consumption/income ratio. Consumption was further affected by the debt burden of the farming population, which originated in the boom.[16] These factors, plus the policy of deflation (largely through reduction in governmental expenditures and increase in taxes), the heavy burden of service of the external public debt, and the large increase in tariffs in 1930, largely explain the substantial decline in Australia's income and her relatively high import responsiveness. Compared to a decline of 53.0 per cent in her total exports between 1927/8-8/9 and 1931/2-2/3, her imports of capital goods declined by 84.5 per cent, of food by 76.5 per cent, and of textiles by 69.1 per cent.[17]

II

In the foregoing discussion of countries with a relatively high responsiveness of imports, attention was repeatedly drawn to the share of capital goods in imports in the boom. The relation of this feature to the responsiveness of imports of the other countries studied may be discussed briefly.

In comparisons of different countries, differences in the share of capital goods in imports in the boom do not necessarily reflect differences in the rate of investment and economic expansion in these countries: the pattern of demand for, or of domestic supply of, capital goods and other goods may be different in the various countries. However, there was a tendency among the countries studied for the responsiveness of imports of countries with similar percentage declines in exports (i.e., allowing for the variation of the responsiveness of imports with the percentage decline in exports) to vary positively with the share of capital goods in imports. This phenomenon is explained first, by the tendency for the imports of capital goods of the various countries to decline more heavily than other imports; and second, by the fact that, according to available information, in many cases differences in the share of capital goods in imports in fact did tend to parallel differences in the rate of economic expansion in the boom.[18] As indicated earlier,

TABLE XVII

SHARE OF CAPITAL GOODS IN THE IMPORTS OF FORTY-EIGHT
PRIMARY-EXPORTING COUNTRIES IN 1928-9 [*]

Country	Share of capital goods in imports (%)	Country	Share of capital goods in imports (%)
Argentina	34.9	India	22.2
Australia	33.8	Irish F.S.	16.2
Bolivia	31.8	Latvia	19.8
Brazil	34.2	Lithuania	19.0
Bulgaria	34.2	Malaya	12.6
Canada	33.7	Mexico	40.0
Ceylon	11.5	Netherlands	24.5
Chile	32.4	New Zealand	32.7
China	10.7	Nicaragua	20.2
Colombia	35.5	Nigeria	24.8
Costa Rica	25.8	Norway	28.8
Cuba	18.2	Panama	22.5
Denmark	17.2	Paraguay	23.9
Dominican R.	23.5	Persia	14.5
D.E. Indies	21.8	Peru	33.3
Ecuador	31.0	Philippines	24.2
Egypt	19.7	Poland	24.4
Estonia	20.7	Portugal	23.6
Finland	24.6	Roumania	37.2
Greece	16.6	Salvador	26.3
Guatemala	29.0	Siam	18.2
Haiti	16.9	Spain	27.1
Honduras	20.5 [†]	Venezuela	45.6
Hungary	24.2	Yugoslavia	27.4

[*] Data on the composition of Turkey's imports in 1928-9 are not readily available.
[†] 1928-9 only.

the higher this rate the greater tended to be the percentage decline in imports of consumer and capital goods in the ensuing downswing. We may consider the data relating to the countries studied.

The share of capital goods in the imports of each country in 1928-9 is shown in Table XVII. For a ready appreciation of the relation between the responsiveness of imports and the share of capital goods in imports, line dd' has been drawn in Diagram II. Above the line lie twenty-nine countries,[19] and in twenty-four of these the share of capital goods in imports in 1928-9 exceeded 23 per cent; the exceptions, with the respective shares shown in brackets, are Cuba (18.2), Estonia (20.7), Latvia (19.8), Nicaragua (20.2), and Persia (14.5). Below the line dd' lie nineteen countries, and in fourteen of these the share of capital goods in imports in 1928-9 was less than 23 per cent; the exceptions, with the respective shares shown in brackets, are the Netherlands (24.5), Norway (28.8), the Philippines (24.2), Portugal (23.6), and Yugoslavia (27.4). *At given percentages declines in exports*, the responsiveness of imports tended to be the greater the larger the share of capital goods in imports in 1928-9.

We may digress momentarily to account for most of the exceptions noted in the previous paragraph. The reader will notice that of the five countries whose responsiveness of imports was exceptionally low, three (the Netherlands, the Philippines, and Portugal) were almost borderline cases with respect to the share of capital goods in imports. In any event, the relatively low responsiveness of imports of these countries and Norway will be explained later in this chapter. Some comments may be made here about two of the countries whose responsiveness of imports was exceptionally high, namely, Cuba and Persia.

In the boom of the late nineteen-twenties the markets for Cuba's sugar were weak and prices were declining. Her exports were falling, and foreign capital was not attracted to this country on any noteworthy scale. In sum, Cuba's economy was already on a decline, and the share of capital goods in her imports was relatively low.[20]

The relatively high responsiveness of Cuba's imports in the ensuing downswing is explained partly by the fact that the immediate impact of the decline in exports on employment and income tended to be widespread and, hence, to be accompanied by a relatively high marginal consumption/income ratio. The decline in income was widespread because Cuba's economy was affected not only by the decline in the price of sugar, but also by a decline in sugar output, unparalleled in any other important sugar-producing country and exceptional for Class A exports.[21] In addition, the subsistence sector to which partly or fully unemployed labour might have turned in the depression, was much less significant in Cuba than in many other primary-exporting countries. Above all, there were probably few other countries in the world in which so many sectors of the economy depended for employment and revenue so heavily and immediately on the fate of an export crop.[22]

Some other factors also helped to increase Cuba's responsiveness of imports. On account chiefly of the peculiarities of her monetary system, the deterioration in business and the development of substantial deficits in Cuba's balance on current and capital account in the years 1930 to 1932 were accompanied by very severe deflation.[23] Furthermore, Cuba depended heavily on imported foodstuffs (in 1928-9 they represented almost two-fifths of her imports), and a large part of these foodstuffs, such as rice and beans, were Class A goods. Moreover, the protective tariff of 1927 tended in the longer run to reduce Cuba's dependence on imported food. Between 1928-9 and 1931-2 her food imports declined by 70.6 per cent.

The relatively high responsiveness of imports of Persia is explained chiefly by her policy of rigorous control of trade. The country was on a silver standard and, partly because of the heavy decline in the price of silver, in 1930 it experienced balance of payments difficulties. The adoption of foreign exchange control in February 1930, and of related measures in July 1930, proved insufficient for dealing with the problem. Consequently, through the Foreign Trade Monopoly Law passed on February 25, 1931, imports were subjected to a system of quotas and licences: in most cases importers could obtain licences only by presenting transferable certificates of prior export of Persian products of an equal or greater value. The rigour of this measure may be gauged by the fact that mineral oils, whose exports far exceeded all other exports, and fishery products from the

Caspian Sea were not eligible for export certificates; also, exports of products constituting an export monopoly (e.g., opium or red oxide) entitled the exporters to certificates equal to only 20 per cent of their value.[24] Between 1927/8-8/9 and 1931/2-2/3 imports of textiles and food (which in the base period represented about 58 per cent of total imports) declined fairly heavily. They declined relatively more than the imports of capital goods: the obligation of importers to produce export certificates was waived in the case of machinery imported under special licence in order to assist in the development of domestic industry and thereby to reduce the country's dependence on foreign products.

Having considered the exceptional responsiveness of imports of certain countries, we may return to our main argument. In the demonstration based on the use of line dd' in Diagram II the relation of the responsiveness of imports to the share of capital goods in imports reflected the influence of both factors noted earlier: of the effect on total imports of the typically heavier decline in imports of capital goods than of other goods; and of the tendency of imports of consumer and capital goods to decline more heavily in countries in which a large share of capital goods in imports in 1928-9 reflected a high rate of economic expansion in the boom. But it is possible to observe the influence of the latter factor separately. For this purpose, in Diagrams IV, V, and VI, in which the responsiveness of the three important classes of imports (capital goods, food, and textiles) is related to the percentage decline in exports of the various countries, we have drawn lines dd', similar to line dd' in Diagram II. Owing to lack of data Costa Rica, Mexico, Panama, and Turkey are not included in Diagrams IV to VI, so that the number of countries in each diagram is forty-five. Above line dd' in Diagrams IV, V, and VI lie twenty-seven, twenty-eight, and twenty-five countries, respectively; and in twenty-one, twenty, and twenty of these countries, respectively, the share of capital goods in imports in 1928-9 exceeded 23 per cent. Below the line dd' lie eighteen , seventeen, and twenty countries, in the three diagrams respectively; and in twelve, ten, and thirteen countries, respectively, the share of capital goods in imports in 1928-9 was less than 23 per cent.[25]

It is clear that, in the foregoing discussion of the variation in import responsiveness between countries with similar percentage declines in exports, the support presented for the existence of a relation between import responsiveness and share of capital goods in imports was rather crude. The position of several countries above or below line dd' in Diagram II might be the result of a host of other factors that affected their responsiveness of imports, rather than of the relation suggested. While in this chapter we do consider the influence of many of these factors with respect to a number of countries, it is impracticable to try to isolate their effects. One of these factors is the policy of foreign exchange control adopted by a number of countries. Unfortunately, the support of its influence presented below must be as crude as the support of the relation between import responsiveness and share of capital goods in imports.

According to information supplied by the League of Nations and other sources, the following twenty countries adopted exchange control before the middle of 1932: Argentina, Bolivia, Brazil, Bulgaria, Chile, Colombia, Costa Rica, Denmark, Ecuador, Estonia, Greece, Hungary, Latvia, Nicaragua, Paraguay, Persia, Roumania, Spain, Turkey, and Yugoslavia. The remaining twenty-nine countries had not introduced exchange control until the end of 1932.[26] Following our earlier diagrammatic approach, we have drawn line *ee'* in Diagram II. Below this line lie twenty-four countries; twenty of these had not introduced exchange control by the end of 1932. Above the line lie twenty-five countries; sixteen of these had introduced exchange control by the middle of 1932. *At given percentage declines in exports*, the responsiveness of imports tended to be greater in countries which used exchange control.[27]

III

Our intended itinerary along the periphery of the scatter plot in Diagram II was interrupted temporarily by section II. If we resume proceeding clockwise we reach Chile. Her responsiveness of imports is not exceptional: it falls in the general pattern relating import responsiveness to percentage decline in exports. Nevertheless, we may comment briefly on this country. First, we may summarize the main factors which seem to explain the sharp contrast between the import responsiveness of Chile and the much higher responsiveness of Venezuela, another country exporting largely mineral products. Second, we may comment on the fact that Chile's responsiveness of imports increased greatly over the three periods of the downswing distinguished earlier; between 1928-9 to 1930-1 and 1928-9 to 1931-2, or between 1928-9 to 1930-1 and 1928-9 to 1932-3, she experienced a greater increase in responsiveness of imports than any of the other countries.

In 1928-9 more than four-fifths of Chile's exports consisted of copper and nitrate of soda, while more than three-quarters of Venezuela's exports were petroleum products. The percentage decline in Chile's exports in the period 1928-9 to 1931-2 was the greatest of the forty-nine countries, while the decline in Venezuela's exports was the second smallest. In addition to this factor, the difference between the two countries in responsiveness of imports in the earlier stages of the downswing should be ascribed to the difference in their rate of economic expansion in the boom, and particularly to the difference in their rate of contraction in the downswing. These differences may be discussed briefly.

In the years 1925-9 Chile received a substantial volume of foreign capital. In spite of some adverse long-term changes affecting her export industries (particularly, changes in the conditions of production and consumption of nitrate), a certain amount of development did take place in these, and related industries, as well as in the field of public works and utilities.[28] In 1928-9 capital goods represented about 32 per cent of Chile's imports. But this percentage is not remarkably high. First, underdeveloped mineral-exporting countries depended heavily on imported capital goods, and the corresponding percentage in Venezuela, Mexico, and Roumania ranged between 37 and 46 per cent. Second, compared to countries like Venezuela or Colombia, where the petroleum industry and related developments were new, Chile's imports of capital goods included a greater percentage of goods for replacement, rather than new investment. Third, Chile's agricultural hinterland and manufacturing industry were better developed than Venezuela's—she was less dependent on imported food and manufactured goods, such as textiles. By all available evidence the boom was less pronounced

in Chile than in Venezuela. The implications of such differences between countries in the share of capital goods in imports and in the rate of economic expansion in the boom, for the responsiveness of imports in the downswing were
discussed earlier.

The ensuing economic contraction also was less pronounced in Chile, especially
in the earlier stages of the downswing. In 1930 Chile received a certain amount
of foreign capital, chiefly through government borrowing, and as early as the
middle of 1931 central bank credit, to a large extent to the government, eased
monetary conditions.[29] Compared to 1928 or 1929, investment measured in stable
prices was greater in 1930 and 1931; and compared to the average for the years
1927-9, industrial production was moderately lower in 1931, and very slightly
higher in 1932.[30]

As in Venezuela's mining, the relatively heavy decline in the price of Chile's
copper exports in the downswing affected chiefly the incomes of foreign capital-
owners and was accompanied by a fall in payment abroad of dividends and
related remittances, and in imports of mining materials and equipment, rather
than imports of consumer goods. Of course, unlike Venezuela, the quantity of
exports of copper and nitrate declined considerably and this affected domestic
incomes.[31] However, as indicated, Chile's manufacturing and agriculture were
better developed than Venezuela's, and they supplied a large part of the country's
consumption requirements. The dispersion of income changes in these sectors
also was fairly limited—for obvious reasons relating to the conditions in manufacturing in underdeveloped countries, and because of the substantial concentration of the agricultural land in large holdings in the period considered.[32] Consequently, the marginal consumption/income ratio tended to be relatively moderate.
Moreover, the foreign managerial personnel and the big land-owners and manufacturers probably had a limited income elasticity of demand for many imported
goods. In times of falling incomes they scaled down their investment abroad.
Finally, another factor which to some extent eased the pressure on Chilean expenditures and imports was the default on the foreign public debt in the middle
of 1931. In 1930 this debt had represented about one-third of all foreign capital
employed of Chile.

Some of the foregoing factors serve also in explaining the large increase in
Chile's responsiveness of imports over the three periods of the downswing. Thus
the late imports of foreign capital and the late decline in investment are reflected
in the fact that between 1928-9 and 1930-1 imports of capital goods declined only
by 16.3 per cent, while between 1928-9 and 1931-2 they declined by 69.0 per cent,
and between 1928-9 and 1932-3 by as much as 92.5 per cent.[33] Furthermore, in
order to protect the country's gold reserves and the value of the peso, by reducing
chiefly the imports of goods for which Chilean industry, agriculture, and mining
could provide substitutes, Chile increased her customs duties towards the end of
1930, in March 1931, and in April 1932, and introduced foreign exchange control
in July 1931, and quotas and import licences in July 1932.[34] These measures contributed to a large increase, over the three periods distinguished, in the decline
in imports of manufactured goods. The decline in textile imports increased from
36.6 per cent in the period 1928-9 to 1930-1, to 76.0 per cent in the period 1928-9
to 1931-2, and 89.7 per cent in the period 1928-9 to 1932-3.

IV

If we continue our itinerary along the periphery of the scatter plot in Diagram II, we reach China. Her responsiveness of imports was considerably lower than the responsiveness of other countries with a similar percentage decline in exports, and in both the second and the third period distinguished (1928-9 to 1931-2, and 1928-9 to 1932-3), it was the lowest of all forty-nine countries.

Before discussing the factors which seem to explain the low degree of responsiveness of China's imports, we may note that, very probably, this responsiveness was in fact somewhat greater than that indicated by the statistics used. From July 1932 inclusive, the League of Nations and the Chinese official data omit the trade of Manchurian ports, which was more important among China's exports than among her imports.[35] This factor helps to explain why between 1931 and 1932 the decline in Chinese exports is shown to amount to 46.6 per cent, while that in imports only to 27.9 per cent.

By all indications, in the late nineteen-twenties China did not experience any significant economic expansion. Probably, imports of capital in 1928-9 did not exceed U.S. $60-70 million, while in the same period China imported silver amounting to U.S. $70-75 million, as well as a small amount of gold. In 1928-9 capital goods constituted only a little over one-tenth of China's imports (the lowest percentage among the forty-nine countries), which, in turn probably did not exceed one-tenth of her national income.[36] Since, in addition, her domestic output of capital goods was very limited, the supply of capital goods for replacement and new investment was not significant.

Like the boom, the ensuing cyclical decline in China was mild. Available reports characteristically indicate that, while China's exports started declining in 1930, "generally speaking, the world depression did not otherwise greatly affect China till the end of 1931 or the beginning of 1932."[37] Indeed, the year 1931 "was a relatively prosperous year" and the income produced was affected only by the very extensive flood of the Yangtze River. Chiefly because of these conditions the quantity of China's imports of wheat, flour, and rice (which together accounted for one-tenth of the value of her imports in 1928-9) increased between 1928-9 and 1931-2 by 70.5 per cent. On account of the foregoing factors, and of others to be noted presently, the value of imports of food and capital goods declined moderately. These imports, together with the imports of fuel and chemicals, which also declined moderately, represented about one-half of China's imports in 1928-9. Of her important imports only the imports of textile manufactures declined heavily from 1930 onwards, owing largely to increased protection. Even in 1933, the imports of timber reached a level which was "very high and had been exceeded only in two previous years, 1929 and 1931," and the imports of railway sleepers were "exceptionally large."[38]

Some other factors may be noted which probably contributed to the low degree of responsiveness of China's imports. There are reasons for believing that the structure of the Chinese economy and of some of its export industries was conducive to a relatively low marginal consumption/income ratio. Compared to advanced agricultural countries, or even to landowning-peasant economies of Europe included in the countries studied, in China transportation and communication, and hence the movement of goods and information through time and space were much less developed. Exploitation of peasants by landlords and merchants was much more prevalent. As a consequence, the proportion of the export price of agricultural products which accrued to the farmer tended to be much smaller in China than in those other countries.[39] In addition, owing to the greater shortage and subdivision of the land in China, her farmer tended to market a much smaller proportion of his net produce than the farmers of the other countries. For these two reasons the proportion of farm income earned in kind, rather than through the market, was much greater in China. Another significant difference between China and the countries indicated is that, since the Chinese farmer marketed a much smaller proportion of his produce than the others, over the short term the supply of farm produce to the market was probably more elastic in China, and the price received by the farmer tended to fluctuate less in this country.

We may conclude that the farmer's income was much more stable in China than in the more advanced agricultural economies, partly because the prices received by the farmer tended to be more stable, and chiefly because the part of his income which he earned in kind was much greater. In the Chinese setting the heavy decline in the prices of agricultural exports (predominantly Class A and C goods) affected largely the profits and incomes of landlords, middlemen, port merchants, and foreign capital-owners. Large percentage changes per unit of time in a relatively small number of incomes tended to be accompanied by a relatively low consumption/income ratio and, in the case of foreign capital-owner-ship, by reduction in payment abroad of dividends and related remittances.[40]

The pattern of variation in farm credit is another factor which contributed towards a lower marginal consumption/income ratio in China, and in some other Asiatic economies discussed in the next section, than in countries like Brazil, Australia, or Canada. In Brazil and Australia the boom of the late nineteen-twenties was accompanied by large expansion of farm credit for productive pur-poses in the widest sense. In the downswing, the heavy indebtedness of the farmers entailed pressure on consumption—at least to the extent that debts were not adjusted or renewed. By contrast, in China the expansion of farm credit in the boom was much less pronounced, while in the downswing the peasant borrowed in order to supplement his consumption.

Another factor helpful in explaining the low degree of responsiveness of China's imports is found in the importance of certain invisible earnings and the smaller proportional decline in these earnings than in her merchandise exports in the downswing. In 1928-9 China received over 115 million U.S. dollars in emigrants' remittances, over 70 million through foreign governmental expenditure, and about 12 and 10.5 million in "missionary expenditures and philanthropic remit-tances" and tourist revenue, respectively.[41] Her total earnings on account of these four items were equal to a little less than one-third of her merchandise exports.

Between 1928-9 and 1933 China's tourist revenue is shown to have declined by about 84 per cent.[42] But her receipts from missionary expenditures and philan-thropic remittances decreased only by about 15 per cent; and her two most im-portant invisible earnings—emigrants' remittances and foreign governmental ex-penditure—declined by about 65 and 63 per cent, respectively. Consequently, while her merchandise exports declined in this period by 81.6 per cent, her earnings on account of the four invisible items decreased only by about 61 per cent.[43]

Another, more important, change in China's balance of payments (which to some extent made possible, and reflected, the relatively low marginal consumption/income ratio indicated earlier) was the large inflow of silver and gold in the boom and its reversal in the downswing. A net import some 70–75 million U.S. dollars in 1928-9, was followed by a net export of some 26 and 17 million pre-1933 U.S. dollars in 1932 and 1933, respectively.[44] If we add the exports and imports of these "capital goods" in 1928-9 and 1931-2 to the merchandise exports and imports, respectively, China's responsiveness of imports in the period 1928-9 to 1931-2 increases from −15.6, shown in Diagram II, to about −9.1 percentage points.

In concluding the discussion of factors accounting for the low degree of responsiveness of China's imports we may note that China gained tariff autonomy only as late as 1928, and, apart from some protection adopted for her textile industry, generally she imposed new imports duties, or raised the existing ones, only from May 1933 on. Also, she did not apply foreign exchange control until September 1934.

V

Well above and slightly to the left of China, and between lines $c'c'$ and dd', in Diagram II lies a cluster of seven countries: Ceylon, the Dutch East Indies, India, British Malaya, Siam, Egypt, and Haiti. Their responsiveness of imports is shown to be somewhat lower than that of many other countries with similar percentage declines in exports. We can outline the main factors which seem to account for this difference.

A significant cyclical phenomenon common to the five Asiatic countries—probably also to Egypt—was the import of gold and silver in the boom, largely for private hoarding, and the export of such metals in the depression, when incomes and the value of goods in terms of gold declined. The net flows of gold and silver, bullion and specie, in millions of dollars were as follows:[45]

	Net inflow in 1928-9	Net outflow in 1931-2
Ceylon	3.2	0.8
D.E. Indies	6.3	7.7
India	104.8	149.8
Malaya	6.6	14.0
Siam	2.8	5.6

As with China, we may, for each country, add the exports and imports of these "capital goods" in 1928-9 and 1931-2 to the merchandise exports and imports, respectively.[46] The responsiveness of imports of these countries in the period 1928-9 to 1931-2 increases as follows: of Ceylon from −0.9 to +0.5; of the Dutch East Indies from −3.6 to −1.9; of India from −6.1 to +10.8; of British Malaya from −5.4 to −2.1; and of Siam from −2.4 to +5.1 percentage points. The "correction" made in the case of China, although substantial, still left that country with a responsiveness of imports well below that of other countries with a similar percentage decline in exports (the "corrected" decline in China's exports). On the other hand, the original responsiveness of imports of the Asiatic countries discussed at present was much closer to that of other countries with similar percentage declines in exports, and the "correction" made brings their responsiveness very close to that of such other countries. However, their responsiveness of imports is still on the low side, and the responsiveness of the Dutch East Indies remains perceptibly lower than that of other countries with a similar percentage decline in exports.

In the late nineteen-twenties the countries considered in this section did not experience any significant economic expansion. In Ceylon and Malaya the share of capital goods in imports in 1928-9 was as low as 11-13 per cent.[47] In the other countries it was somewhat higher, ranging between 16 and 20 per cent in Siam, Egypt, and Haiti, and being about 22 per cent in the Dutch East Indies and India; however, estimates of the ratio of imports to national income for the period considered or for later years suggest that, in the period considered, this ratio probably did not exceed one-fifth in the first three countries, one-sixth in the Dutch East Indies, and one-tenth in India.[48] Briefly then in 1928-9 the supply of foreign capital goods, both for replacement and new investment, probably did not exceed 2 per cent of India's national income. In the other six countries it probably did not exceed 2-4 per cent of their national incomes, while the domestic supply of such goods was also very limited. The implications of a low rate of economic expansion in the boom and a modest share of capital goods in imports, for the responsiveness of imports in the downswing were discussed earlier.

As in China, in Malaya, the Dutch East Indies, and Ceylon the effects on consumption of the decline in exports tended to be relatively limited. To a large extent these countries exported minerals, chiefly tin and petroleum, or such goods as rubber and tea, of which the larger part was produced in estates. Except for tin, the decline in these exports in the downswing represented mainly a decline in prices, and this decline affected largely the profits and incomes of land-owners, capital-owners, and merchants.[49] Partly or fully unemployed workers of tin mines and estates, and rubber smallholders could turn to the production of food. The large percentage changes per unit of time in the relatively small number of incomes of the former classes tended to be accompanied by a relatively low marginal consumption/income ratio and by reduction in investment abroad, and, in the case of foreign capital-ownership, by reduction in payment abroad of dividends and related remittances.[50] In India and especially Siam, products of estates and mines were much less important among exports. But the position of the peasant in these countries, as well as in the three countries discussed previously, and Egypt, was not unlike that of the Chinese peasant.[51] Another factor which tended to lower the marginal consumption/income ratio in these Asiatic countries and Egypt was that, in the boom, expansion, of farm credit was much less pronounced in these countries than in such countries as Brazil or Australia, while in the downswing the peasant borrowed in order to supplement his consumption. This purpose was served also through the liquidation of private hoards of gold and silver, indicated earlier.

We may conclude this section with a comment on the Dutch East Indies. It was indicated earlier that the "corrected" responsiveness of imports of this country was lower than that of other Asiatic countries which experienced a similar percentage decline in exports. In India, for instance, the decline in imports was enhanced by such factors as the increase in import duties, the service of the external public debt which represented more than two-thirds of foreign investment, and the application of deflationary policies. [52] On the other hand, in the Dutch East Indies the gold value of the gulden was not reduced until 1936, the external public debt represented less than one-third of foreign investment, and international movements of long-term capital were counter-cyclical: a net outflow of long-term capital in the years 1927 to 1929 was followed by a substantial net inflow in the years 1930 to 1933.[53] New foreign long-term investments in the Indies in each of the latter years were equal to, or substantially greater than, those in any of the former years.

VI

To the left of the group of countries just discussed, in Diagram II there is another group of six countries: Denmark, the Irish Free State, the Netherlands, Norway, Panama, and the Philippines. Their responsiveness of imports was much lower than the responsiveness of other countries with similar percentage declines in exports. Though Greece and Portugal had a considerably higher responsiveness of imports than those six countries, they too lie below line $c'c'$. We may outline the main factors which seem to account for the relatively low responsiveness of imports of these countries, especially of the former six. In doing so, we shall reserve the Philippines for consideration at a later stage and deal first with the other seven countries.

By all indications, in these countries the boom of the late nineteen-twenties was mild as was the decline in the ensuing downswing. In 1928-9 over half the exports of Denmark, the Irish Free State, Panama, and Portugal, as well as over half the primary exports of the Netherlands and about three-tenths of the exports of Norway were Class B exports—non-staple and semi-luxury foodstuffs. The profitability of producing such goods did not rise greatly in the boom.[54] In addition, the markets for some important exports of Greece, such as tobacco, were not particularly strong in the late nineteen-twenties. Nor did the countries here discussed experience development of new resources, like Venezuela or Colombia. Furthermore, Portugal had gone through a long period of economic and fiscal troubles, and in the late nineteen-twenties a new political regime was still only laying the groundwork for the restoration of her economy.[55] Largely on account of these factors most of these countries were not among the recipients of significant volumes of foreign capital.[56] In 1928-9 capital goods represented only about 16-17 per cent of the imports of Denmark, Greece, and the Irish Free State— though the low percentage in Denmark was due also to other factors than the mildness of her boom and Greece depended heavily on imported food.[57] In the Netherlands, Panama, and Portugal the percentage was higher, ranging between 22 and 25 per cent, and in Norway it reached about 29 per cent. The Netherlands and Norway also had a substantial domestic supply of capital goods, and the boom in these two countries was probably stronger than in the others.[58] In any event, the decline after 1929 in these two countries, as well as in Denmark, the Irish Free State, Portugal, Greece, and Panama was moderate.[59]

Another significant feature helpful in explaining the mildness of the downswing and the low degree of import responsiveness of the countries considered in this section is found in the importance of certain invisible earnings, and the smaller proportional decline in these earnings than in merchandise exports in the downswing. As indicated by the ratio of imports to exports shown in brackets, in 1928-9 Denmark (1.06) had a modest merchandise deficit, the Irish Free State (1.29), the Netherlands (1.37), and Norway (1.46) had a large deficit, Greece (1.97) and Portugal (2.48) had a very large one, and Panama (4.07) had a huge one. On the other hand, these countries had substantial surpluses in their account on invisible trade and interest and dividends. While the available balance of payments data do not allow precision, we may briefly survey the changes in the downswing of the main invisible earnings, namely those items which, taken individually, were equal to at least 2 per cent of the merchandise exports of the respective countries in 1928-9.[60]

In 1928-9 the main invisible earnings of these countries, listed in order of importance for each country, were the following: Denmark, shipping income; the Irish Free State, income from investments abroad, pensions, and emigrants' remittances; the Netherlands, income from investments abroad, shipping income, and pensions and salaries;[61] Norway, shipping income, tourist revenue, and emigrants' remittances; and Greece, emigrants' remittances, income from investments abroad, tourist revenue and shipping income. In 1928-9 the total value of these earnings were equal, respectively, to about one-sixth of the merchandise exports of Denmark, about one-third of those of the Irish Free State and of the Netherlands, about two-thirds of those of Norway, and over four-fifths of those of Greece.[62] The invisible earnings of Portugal consisted mainly of income from investments abroad, shipping income, emigrants' remittances, and tourist revenue, and of Panama mainly of revenue from activities in the Canal Zone.[63]

Between 1928-9 and 1931-2 the merchandise exports of the first five countries declined by the following percentages:

Denmark	38.3
Greece	45.7
Irish F.S.	42.7
Netherlands	45.6
Norway	42.7

Compared to these changes, the decline in shipping income was smaller in Denmark (34.3 per cent) and much smaller in the Netherlands and Norway (15.5 and 28.0 per cent, respectively); Greece's shipping income increased slightly between 1929 and 1931-2.[64] Emigrants' remittances received by Greece and Norway declined between 1928-9 and 1931-2 by 29.8 and 34.1 per cent, respectively; probably, the decline in the Irish Free State also was relatively moderate.[65] The tourist revenue of Norway declined by 7.2 per cent, and that of Greece increased. Pensions received by the Irish Free State declined between 1928-9 and the average for the years 1931 and 1933 by 22.5 per cent; and pensions and salaries received by the Netherlands declined between 1930 and 1931-2 only by 8.8 per cent.[66] The estimates of income from investments abroad are very rough in the case of the Irish Free State and very unreliable in the case of Greece.[67] These estimates and the composition of the foreign investments of these countries suggest that the income from these investments declined proportionately less than merchandise exports in the Irish Free State (it decreased by about 25-30 per cent) and more than the exports in Greece.

We conclude that, with the only possible exception of Greek (perhaps also of Dutch) income from investments abroad, the main invisible earnings of the five countries declined in the period 1928-9 to 1931-2 substantially less than their merchandise exports.[68] Very probably, so did the main invisible earnings of Panama.[69] Since we are concerned here with the responsiveness of imports, it should be added that, unlike other invisible earnings, the decline in income from investments abroad of countries like Greece or the Netherlands to a large extent tended to be accompanied by curtailment of further investment abroad rather than of merchandise imports. In any event, our discussion indicates that in the countries considered in this section the responsiveness of imports was substantially higher in the total current account than in merchandise trade alone.

The Philippines, which was reserved for separate consideration, may be discussed at this point. With respect to certain important features—such as the existence of large landholdings, the exploitation of farm tenants and workers, and the fact that short-term changes in national income involved large percentage changes in a relatively small number of incomes, of land-owners, capital-owners, and merchants, domestic and foreign—the Philippines came much closer to the Asian economies discussed in the previous section of this chapter than to the countries discussed in this section.[70] Her relatively low responsiveness of imports should be ascribed partly to factors broadly similar to those discussed in that section.[71]

On the other hand, in another respect the Philippines resembled the countries discussed in this section. Her invisible earnings in 1928-9, although relatively less important than the earnings of these countries, were equal to over one-tenth of her merchandise exports; and between 1928-9 and 1931-2 they increased from $16.8 million to $17.8 millon. Such experience was almost unique among the countries studied. Both this remarkable stability of invisible earnings and its probable contribution to the support of imports of consumer and capital goods in the depression and, hence, to the relatively low responsiveness of imports of the Philippines, are explained by the nature of a large part of these earnings. About three-quarters of them in 1928-9 consisted of remittances by the Government of the United States: for covering its own general expenses in the Islands, chiefly on military and naval services; for the account of its Veterans' Administration; and for payment to the Philippines Treasury of excise taxes collected in the United States on certain Philippine products.[72]

In conclusion we may note some other factors which seem to be helpful in explaining the relatively low responsiveness of imports of the countries discussed in this section. Several of these countries (the Netherlands, Denmark, Norway, and the Irish Free State) ranked among the most advanced of the forty-nine countries studied, and the people held a substantial volume of liquid assets which they could liquidate in the downswing in order to supplement expenditure. The gold value of the currencies of Panama and the Philippines was not reduced until 1933, and of the Netherlands not until 1936.[73] Also, of the eight countries discussed in this section only Denmark and Greece introduced exchange control in the depression.[74]

VII

We may conclude our itinerary along the periphery of the scatter plot in Diagram II with the discussion of Lithuania, which had the most exceptional responsiveness of imports of the forty-nine countries. At +4.2 percentage points her responsiveness was much lower than that of Bulgaria and far lower than that of Venezuela, two countries with similar percentage declines in exports.

The exceptionally low responsiveness of imports of Lithuania is explained largely by the mildness of her boom and, particularly, of her downswing. Class B goods (non-staple and semi-luxury foodstuffs) were important among her exports, and the profitability of producing such goods did not rise greatly in the boom. Foreign capital was not attracted to Lithuania on any noteworthy scale: imports of capital in 1928-9 were equal to only about 3 per cent of her merchandise exports. In the same period capital goods represented only 19 per cent of her imports.

Lithuania was a small international trader: next to ten small Central American countries she had the smallest volume of trade (exports plus imports) of the forty-nine countries. Since she could then count on a high price-elasticity of demand for her exports, from 1930 on she generously subsidized certain agricultural exports, notably butter and meat products. This fact must largely account for the exceptionally moderate decline in her exports: at 21.3 per cent in the period 1928-9 to 1931-2, it was the smallest of the forty-nine countries.[75]

In addition to granting export subsidies the Lithuanian government increased its expenditures, notably on public works, defence, and education. Total governmental expenditure in 1930 and 1931 exceeded that in 1928-9 by 16.5 and 21.8 per cent, respectively. In 1932 this expenditure decreased; still, expenditures on agriculture, public works, and education were higher than in 1928-9, and even the total governmental expenditure was very slightly higher.[76]

Since Lithuania's exports and economy fared, in the downswing, better than those of most other countries, she was able to attract foreign capital, chiefly through governmental borrowing, for the construction of public buildings and other works. In the years 1930, 1931, and 1932 she received 3.12, 3.54, and 1.80 million dollars, respectively. While these were small sums in absolute terms, they were large for Lithuania, equal to 9.3, 13.0, and 9.5 per cent of her merchandise exports in the respective years. This was another advantage of her being a small country. Partly on account of the foregoing developments, the gold value of Lithuania's currency remained unaffected throughout the depression; and unlike her sister republics of Latvia and Estonia, which introduced exchange control in the autumn of 1931, Lithuania did not adopt such control until October 1935.[77]

The foregoing developments and policies in Lithuania, in a combination unparalleled among the forty-nine countries, entailed powerful support for the country's expenditures, incomes and prices. They provide the major explanation of her low responsiveness of imports, and account for certain unique features of change in Lithuania's imports. In all the other forty-four countries, imports of capital goods declined between 1928-9 and 1931-2;[78] and in the great majority of these countries the decline in these imports ranked fourth or higher among the percentage declines of the various classes of imports. Lithuania was the only country in which imports of capital goods increased, by 8.4 per cent; and the only country in which these imports fared better than any other class of imports.[79] On account of the heavy decline in prices of imported food the value of food imports declined relatively heavily, by 55.5 per cent. But imports of textiles declined only by 21.9 per cent, and of fuel and chemicals by 5.5 and 27.2 per cent, respectively.

It appears that the world depression affected Lithuania more seriously from the later part of 1932 on. Her exports faced serious restrictions abroad (for instance those on British imports of bacon) and in December 1932 Lithuania introduced a system of import licensing. Public expenditures on public works and agriculture, as well as total governmental expenditure, were reduced. In 1933 imports of foreign capital declined to $0.5 million, equal to only about 3 per cent of Lithuania's merchandise exports in that year.[80] The percentage decline in her merchandise exports increased greatly between 1928-9 to 1931-2, and 1928-9 to 1932-3 (the increase of 19.2 percentage points was the third largest of the forty-nine countries). And her responsiveness of imports, while still relatively low in the period 1928-9 to 1932-3, was not as unique as it had been in the earlier periods (compare Diagram III with Diagrams I and II).

Our purpose in this chapter was to draw attention to important factors helpful in explaining differences in responsiveness of imports between countries which experienced similar percentage declines in exports. It was neither intended, nor was it practicable to treat these factors exhaustively, or to enumerate all the factors which, in one way or another, contributed to variations in import responsiveness. Obviously many of the factors discussed influenced also the responsiveness of imports of the other primary-exporting countries, which were not considered specifically in this chapter. The balance of influence of these and other factors was apparently such as to let these other countries form the spinal core of the scatter plot in Diagram II.

CHAPTER EIGHT

SUMMARY OF CHANGES IN THE TRADE BALANCES OF FORTY-NINE COUNTRIES EXPORTING CHIEFLY PRIMARY PRODUCTS

THE PURPOSE OF THIS, the last chapter, is to draw together and review the relative role of certain factors accounting for the cyclical changes in the merchandise balances of forty-nine primary-exporting countries. We shall do so by discussing five phenomena relating to the changes in these balances: the percentage decline in exports; the import/export decline, defined earlier as the ratio between the percentage decline in imports and the percentage decline in exports; the original relation, defined earlier as the ratio between exports and imports in the base period; the favourable or unfavourable change in the balance; and the relative importance of the original relation and the import/export decline for the change in the balance. Unless otherwise indicated, the changes considered will relate to the period 1928-9 to 1931-2.

The primary exports of the countries studied were divided into four classes. Between 1928-9 and 1931-2 Class A and C exports declined heavily, while Class B and D exports declined considerably less or increased.

On the basis mainly of the composition of exports, the forty-nine countries were divided into two groups (Table (XVIII). For reasons indicated, while Group One comprises only about two-fifths of the forty-nine countries, in 1928-9 it accounted for three-fifths of the total trade (exports plus imports) of these countries; conversely, Group Two comprises about three-fifths of the number of countries, but accounted for two-fifths of their trade in 1928-9.

Among the exports of the countries in Group One, Class A and C goods predominated heavily. As a consequence between 1928-9 and 1931-2 the total exports of each of these countries declined heavily, by more than 54 per cent. By contrast, the total exports of each of the countries included in Group Two declined in the same period by less than 54 per cent. These were countries in which Class B and D goods predominated among exports, countries in which the predominance of Class A and C goods was much smaller than in the countries of Group One, or countries which experienced exceptionally moderate decreases in some Class A or C exports. This difference between the percentage decline in exports of the countries included in the two groups, as well as other differences between the two groups of countries, noted subsequently, are listed in Table XIX.

The direction of change in the merchandise balances of the countries studied can be viewed as depending on the import/export decline and the original relation. The import/export decline, or the responsiveness of imports (defined earlier as the algebraic excess of the percentage decline in imports over the percentage decline in exports), varied inversely with the percentage decline in exports. Consequently, in the period 1928-9 to 1931-2 the import/export decline of eighteen

TABLE XVIII

IMPORT/EXPORT DECLINE, ORIGINAL RELATION, AND CHANGE IN THE MERCHANDISE BALANCES OF FORTY-NINE PRIMARY-EXPORTING COUNTRIES IN THE PERIOD 1928-9 TO 1931-2

Country	Import/ export decline °	Original relation †	Favourable (F) or unfavourable (U) change in the balance	Sole or main determinant of change in the balance: ‡ import/export decline (m/x), or original relation (E/I)
Group One				
Argentina	1.08	1.18	U	E/I
Bolivia	1.07	1.81	U	E/I
Brazil	1.30	1.08	F	m/x
Canada	0.98	1.09	U	E/I
Ceylon	0.98	1.05	U	E/I
Chile	0.91	1.52	U	E/I
China	0.76	0.82	U	m/x
Cuba	1.09	1.28	U	E/I
D.E. Indies	0.94	1.43	U	E/I
Egypt	0.90	1.02	U	m/x
Haiti	0.92	1.05	U	m/x
India	0.90	1.31	U	E/I
Malaya	0.92	1.01	U	m/x
Mexico	1.09	1.60	U	E/I
Nigeria	1.08	1.20	U	E/I
Peru	1.05	1.77	U	E/I
Salvador	1.07	1.19	U	E/I
Siam	0.96	1.40	U	E/I
Spain	1.05	0.74	F	E/I
Group Two				
Australia	1.40	0.99	F	m/x
Bulgaria	1.80	0.82	F	m/x
Colombia	1.80	0.95	F	m/x
Costa Rica	1.59	0.99	F	m/x
Denmark	0.98	0.94	F	E/I
Dominican R.	1.18	1.06	F	m/x
Ecuador	1.35	1.09	F	m/x
Estonia	1.15	0.96	F	m/x
Finland	1.47	0.85	F	m/x
Greece	1.02	0.51	F	E/I
Guatemala	1.29	0.86	F	m/x
Honduras	1.25	1.64	U	E/I
Hungary	1.20	0.82	F	m/x
Irish F.S.	0.84	0.78	F	E/I
Latvia	1.19	0.80	F	E/I
Lithuania	1.20	0.98	F	m/x
Netherlands	0.90	0.73	F	E/I
New Zealand	1.11	1.17	U	E/I
Nicaragua	1.16	0.86	F	m/x
Norway	0.92	0.68	F	E/I
Panama	0.82	0.25	F	E/I
Paraguay	1.43	1.04	F	m/x
Persia	1.64	1.68	U	E/I
Philippines	1.02	1.15	U	E/I
Poland	1.44	0.82	F	m/x
Portugal	1 26	0.40	F	E/I

Country	Import/ export decline *	Original relation †	Favourable (F) or unfavourable (U) change in the balance	Sole or main determinant of change in the balance: ‡ import/export decline (m/x), or original relation (E/I)
Roumania	1.80	0.91	F	m/x
Turkey	1.71	0.69	F	m/x
Venezuela	2.65	1.67	F	m/x
Yugoslavia	1.12	0.93	F	m/x

   * Ratio between the percentage decline in imports and the percentage decline in exports in the period 1928-9 to 1931-2.

   † Ratio between exports and imports in 1928-9.

   ‡ The basis on which the original relation, or the import/export decline is taken to be the sole or main determinant of the direction of change in the merchandise balance was indicated in chap. 2, II.

TABLE XIX

PHENOMENA RELATING TO THE CHANGE IN THE MERCHANDISE BALANCES OF FORTY-NINE PRIMARY-EXPORTING COUNTRIES IN THE PERIOD 1928-9 TO 1931-2

Group One *	Number of countries	Group Two *	Number of countries §
All countries in Group One	19	All countries in Group Two	24 (30)
Whose exports declined by more than 54% †	19	Whose exports declined by less than 54%	24 (30)
Whose import/export decline was 1.09 or less ‡	18	Whose import/export decline exceeded 1.09 ‡	23 (23)
Which had a surplus in 1928-9	17	Which had a deficit in 1928-9	16 (22)
Whose balance changed unfavourably	17	Whose balance changed favourably	20 (26)
In which the original relation was the sole or main determinant of change in the balance ✦	14	In which the import/export decline was the sole or main determinant of change in the balance	18 (18)

   * The countries included in the two groups are listed in Table XVIII.

   † About the decline in Mexico's exports see *supra*, p. 38.

   ‡ The import/export decline is the ratio between the percentage decline in imports and the percentage decline in exports in the period 1928-9 to 1931-2. 1.09 was the median value of the import/export declines of the forty-nine countries.

   § For reasons explained in the text two sets of figures are given for Group Two: those in parenthesis are based on inclusion in, and those without parenthesis on the exclusion from Group Two of Denmark, Greece, the Irish Free State, the Netherlands, Norway, and Panama.

   ✦ The original relation in the ratio between exports and imports in 1928-9.

of the nineteen countries in Group One was 1.09 or less (in ten of these countries it was less than 1.00), while the import/export decline of twenty-three of the thirty countries in Group Two exceeded 1.09 (see Table XIX; 1.09 was the median value of the import/export declines of the forty-nine countries). The exceptions were Brazil in Group One, and Denmark, Greece, the Irish Free State, the Netherlands, Norway, Panama, and the Philippines in Group Two.

The importance of invisible earnings in Denmark, Greece, the Irish Free State, the Netherlands, Norway, and Panama, and the smaller proportional decline of these earnings than of the merchandise exports of these countries, discussed earlier, place these countries, in effect, in a category of their own: these factors account for the exceptional behaviour of these countries in Group Two with respect not only to the import/export decline, but also to some of the other phenomena of the cyclical change in the merchandise balance, discussed subsequently. Accordingly, in Table XIX we have presented two sets of figures for Group Two: those in parenthesis are based on inclusion of these six countries in Group Two, and those without parenthesis on their exclusion.

As indicated, the seventh exception in Group Two (country whose import/export decline was smaller than 1.09) was the Philippines. This country might have been included in Group One. Class A and C goods predominated heavily among its exports—though the decline in its exports was moderate. As Table XVIII shows, in all the other respects reviewed in this chapter the Philippines shares the features which predominated among the countries in Group One: her import/export decline was smaller than 1.09; in 1928-9 she had a surplus; in the period 1928-9 to 1931-2 her balance turned unfavourably; and the original relation was the sole determinant of change in the balance. All the other Asiatic economies examined in this study actually fall in Group One.

The original relation was the second proximate determinant of the direction of change in the merchandise balances studied. As Table XIX indicates, in 1928-9, seventeen of the nineteen countries in Group One had a merchandise surplus, and twenty-two of the thirty countries in Group Two had a deficit.

We may now consider the direction of change in the merchandise balances in the period 1928-9 to 1931-2. As indicated in Table XIX, seventeen of the nineteen countries in Group One experienced an unfavourable change in their balances, while twenty-six of the thirty countries in Group Two had a favourable change.

It will be recalled that seventeen of the nineteen countries in Group One had a surplus in 1928-9, a factor contributing towards an unfavourable change in the balance in the downswing. In sixteen of these surplus countries the balance did in fact change unfavourably: the import/export decline in the period 1928-9 to 1931-2 either was smaller than unity (nine countries), or it exceeded unity, but not enough to prevent a decline in the surplus. Only in Brazil did the surplus increase: the effect of the high import/export decline was stronger than that of the original relation. Of the two deficit countries in Group One, Spain's balance turned favourably because of the original relation and the import/export decline, while China's very low import/export decline (0.76)[1] increased her deficit.

In Group Two, twenty-two of the thirty countries had a deficit in 1928-9, a factor contributing towards a favourable change in the balance in the downswing. The balances of all twenty-two deficit countries did in fact change favourably:

the import/export decline in the period 1928-9 to 1931-2 either exceeded unity (seventeen countries), or was smaller than unity, but not enough to prevent a decline in the deficit. Of the eight surplus countries in Group Two, four (the Dominican Republic, Ecuador, Paraguay, and Venezuela) experienced a favourable change in their balance: a substantial (huge in Venezuela) import/export decline more than offset the influence of the original relation on the change in the balance.[2] In the remaining four countries (Honduras, New Zealand, Persia, and the Philippines) the import/export decline exceeded unity, but not enough to prevent a decline in the surplus.

We may next consider the relative importance of the original relation and the import/export decline as determinants of the change in balances of the two groups of countries. As indicated in Table XIX, in fourteen of the nineteen countries in Group One the sole or main determinant of change in the balances was the original relation. On the other hand, in eighteen of the thirty countries in Group Two—or, if we exclude Denmark, Greece, the Irish Free State, the Netherlands, Norway, and Panama, in eighteen of the twenty-four countries—it was the import/export decline.[3]

We have concluded the examination of five phenomena relating to the changes in the merchandise balances of forty-nine primary-exporting countries. It may be interesting also to indicate the volume of trade represented by countries which displayed each of the characteristics listed in the left-hand or the right-hand column of Table XIX, irrespective of whether these countries belong to Group One or Two.

As indicated earlier, large exports of primary products consisted mainly of Class A and C, rather than B, goods; hence, in 1928-9 the countries listed in Group One accounted for three-fifths of the total trade (exports plus imports) of the forty-nine countries. Consequently, as the following estimates for the period 1928-9 to 1931-2 show, each of the features which predominated in Group One is found in countries accounting for the greater part of the trade of the forty-nine countries:

	Exports plus imports in 1928-9	
Countries in which:	In $ billion	As percentage of the trade of the 49 countries
Exports declined by more than 54%	14.7	60.0
The import/export decline was 1.09 or less [4]	18.1	73.9
In 1928-9 there was a surplus	13.5	55.1
In the downswing the balance turned unfavourably	13.6	55.5
The original relation was the sole or main determinant of change in the balance	16.0	65.3

Countries whose trade in 1928-9 amounted to $9.7 billion, or about two-fifths of the total trade of the forty-nine countries, presented all the five features listed above. The opposite features were all present in countries accounting for only $4.2 billion, or about one-sixth of the total trade.

In concluding our study it might be useful to clear up any possible misunderstanding about its purpose. Our main intention was to contribute to the literature on the great cyclical episode of the years 1927 to 1933, a chapter of account and an explanation of the changes in the trade balances of the countries exporting chiefly primary products.

A comparative study might serve to reveal variations between the behaviour of elements which have certain common characteristics—for instance various kinds of primary exports, or various countries exporting primary products—or, it might help to reveal patterns of behaviour common to several such elements. In our work we emphasized the former goal. While in various parts of our study we did separate exports, imports, or the forty-nine countries into groups, our main purpose in doing so was to study differences between elements belonging to different groups and to foster understanding and appreciation of the character-istics of these elements by bringing them into contrast. Even when similarities were observed, it was not our intention to claim or establish the existence of "types" of countries or of "patterns of behaviour" shared by a number of countries. Efforts in the literature to group primary-exporting, agricultural-exporting, or mineral-exporting countries together and to ascribe to their trade a certain pattern of behaviour have often misled.[5]

Even concerning individual countries, we did not attempt to provide statistical estimates of marginal propensities to consume and import, the foreign trade multiplier, or other composite ratios. Estimates of this type are usually assumed to reflect a "pattern" of behaviour of the trade balance of the country considered, which may serve in predicting changes in the future. Prediction was not a con-cern of our study—our main purpose was to analyse and explain past phenomena. What is more important is that the values of these parameters seem to depend also on factors other than those usually noted in the literature. Thus, as indicated, the marginal propensity to import, and hence also the export multiplier, and the responsiveness of imports or the import/export decline, are likely to vary even with the size of the percentage decline in exports and, hence, the foreign trade multiplicand.[6] Consequently, the task of estimating such parameters of change in the trade balance is more complicated and requires more information than even careful writers have suggested. More significantly, such ratios as the export multiplier or the import/export decline tend to be much less stable from one cycle to another than is usually thought. It is inadmissible to gloss over these variations.

APPENDIX

T. C. CHANG ON CYCLICAL CHANGES IN BALANCES OF MERCHANDISE TRADE

IN AN OFT-QUOTED STUDY of cyclical changes in the balance of payments, Tse Chun Chang reaches a number of conclusions concerning cyclical changes in the merchandise balance which are very different from those presented in this study.[1] It may be useful to note and account for these differences. We shall consider first Dr. Chang's treatment of countries exporting chiefly mineral products, and second, his discussion of countries exporting chiefly agricultural goods.

I

In Chapter XI of his study Dr. Chang discusses countries, which, in the interwar period, exported chiefly mineral products or rubber. He lists as the "main mining and extractive-industry countries," Bolivia, Venezuela, Chile, Mexico, Malaya, Persia, Peru, and Ecuador.[2] The inclusion of Ecuador in this group is puzzling: in 1928-9 ores and petroleum constituted only about one-quarter of her exports, compared to fifty per cent shown by Dr. Chang.

Instead of presenting the merchandise balance of each country separately, Dr. Chang shows the sum of the eight balances in each of the years 1924 to 1938. He observes that there is a surplus in every year of this period, and he concludes that in mineral-exporting countries "the size of the surplus rises in prosperity and falls during depression."[3] Clearly, the procedure of lumping together the balances of the eight countries is unfortunate: large changes in one or two large surpluses could more than offset opposite changes in the majority of balances. In fact, Dr. Chang's procedure concealed a substantial diversity of behaviour. In the period 1928-9 to 1931-2, or 1928-9 to 1932-3, the surpluses of Bolivia, Chile, Mexico, Persia, and Peru decreased. But Malaya had an extremely small relative surplus in 1928-9 (imports were equal to 99 per cent of exports) and in the depression it turned into a deficit; and the surpluses of Ecuador and Venezuela increased.[4]

Even more significant than the actual changes in the balances is the explanation of these changes. At an early stage in his study Dr. Chang notes that the direction of change in the merchandise balance depends on the relation between the import/export decline and the original relation; but he immediately dismisses the original relation as being insignificant in practice.[5] He purports to explain the direction of change in the balances of the mineral-exporting countries by analysis of income elasticities of demand in these countries and abroad, changes in the terms of trade, and other factors, which, taken together, are supposed to account for an import/export decline, or increase, smaller than unity—"a larger percentage change of the value of exports."[6]

Dr. Chang's explanation of the change in the balances does not correspond well with the facts.[7] In four of the eight countries (Bolivia, Mexico, Persia, and Peru) the balance turned unfavourably between 1928-9 and 1931-2, or 1928-9 and 1932-3, because of the original relation and in spite of an import/export decline *exceeding unity*; in Ecuador and Venezuela also the import/export decline *exceeded unity* and turned the balance *favourably* in both periods;[8] and in Chile the original relation accounted for 86 per cent of the total unfavourable change in the balance between 1928-9 and 1931-2, and for the entire change between 1928-9 and 1932-3, as the import/export decline in the latter period slightly *exceeded unity*. Of the eight countries, only in Malaya was the import/export decline the more important determinant of the change in the balance between 1928-9 and 1931-2, or 1928-9 and 1932-3. In fact, this was the only one of the eight countries (in addition to Chile in the period 1928-9 to 1931-2) in which the "larger percentage change of the value of exports," which Dr. Chang purports to analyse and explain, did occur; his analysis cannot relate to the developments in the other countries, since in all those countries the relation between the percentage change in value of exports and imports was the opposite. It may be noted also that, quite unlike Dr. Chang's "typical mining country," Malaya's trade in 1928-9 was almost balanced, and that it was only in such an atypical mining country that the influence of the original relation could have been small. In sum, Dr. Chang's "ratio expressing the cyclical percentage changes in exports and imports" was further from unity than "the ratio of import value to export value" in only three of the eight mining countries, and in two of the three, namely Venezuela and Ecuador, it turned the balance in the opposite direction of that stated by Dr. Chang.[9]

II

The cyclical changes in the merchandise balances of countries exporting chiefly agricultural products are discussed by Dr. Chang in Chapter X of his book. Again, for each of the years 1924 to 1938 he presents only the sum of the balances of *"eleven important world* agricultural countries ... Argentina, Bulgaria, Denmark, Estonia, Finland, Hungary, Latvia, Lithuania, Norway, Poland, Australia and New Zealand."[10]

It is not clear what the criteria of "importance" of these twelve countries are. Nine of these countries are European; Dr. Chang's selection includes no country from Africa and Asia (not even India or China), and from Latin America it includes only Argentina. Moreover, the selection is puzzling with respect to the size of foreign trade of several of the countries included. From our forty-nine countries we may eliminate Dr. Chang's eight "mining and extractive-industry countries" and Canada, which Dr. Chang discusses separately. If we rank the remaining forty countries by the volume of trade (exports plus imports) in 1928-9, we find that the two most important countries, India and the Netherlands, have been neglected by Dr. Chang; so have China and the Dutch East Indies, which rank fourth and sixth, respectively. On the other hand, one-third of Dr. Chang's group of countries consists of Latvia, Bulgaria, Estonia, and Lithuania, which rank from twenty-eighth to thirty-first, and are exceeded in unimportance only by nine small Central American traders.[11]

According to Dr. Chang "the cyclical pattern of the agricultural countries' balance of merchandise trade ... tends to show a deficit in prosperity and a surplus during slump. ..."[12] One cannot criticize too strongly the procedure adopted by Dr. Chang, of lumping together the trade balances of the twelve countries. Ten of these countries did have a deficit in 1928-9, but Argentina—by far the most important trader—and New Zealand had a surplus. Moreover, the deficit in the sum of balances of twelve countries claimed by Dr. Chang hinges precariously on the selection of countries. All Asian, African, and South American countries examined in our study, except China and Colombia, had a surplus in 1928-9. Six of these countries ranked among the twelve largest international traders of the forty countries noted in the previous paragraph. But, as indicated, Dr. Chang's selection includes no country from these continents, except Argentina. If in his group of countries we substitute for Norway and Poland for instance, two far more important traders, namely India and the Dutch East Indies, we obtain for 1928-9 a twelve-country surplus of $361 million, instead of the deficit of $254 million indicated by Dr. Chang.[13]

If instead of his selection of countries Dr. Chang had taken those twelve countries of the forty noted earlier which were the most important in terms of volume of trade, he would have found that as many as five, representing in 1928-9 as much as 44.7 per cent of the total trade of the twelve countries, had a surplus in 1928-9.[14] Again, of the larger group of forty countries no less than sixteen, representing in 1928-9 43.5 per cent of the total trade of the forty countries, had a surplus in 1928-9.[15]

Turning to the slump, we find that only seven of Dr. Chang's twelve countries conform to his view that the balance improves in the slump and a surplus develops. In 1928-9 these seven countries accounted for only 44.5 per cent of the total trade of the twelve. On the other hand, in the period 1928-9 to 1931-2, or 1928-9 to 1932-3, the surpluses of Argentina and New Zealand declined; Denmark and Norway failed to develop a surplus in any of the years 1930 to 1933, and Latvia obtained a small surplus only in 1932. All Asian and African countries examined in our study experienced an unfavourable change in the balance between 1928-9 and 1931-2, or 1928-9 and 1932-3; but none of these countries is included in Dr. Chang's selection. Even if these countries can be neglected, the surplus in the sum of balances of twelve countries in the depression, claimed by Dr. Chang, hinges precariously on the selection of countries. Thus, if for two of the countries included in his selection (Argentina and Australia), we substitute two others (the Irish Free State and Greece), we obtain for 1931-2 a twelve-country deficit of $127 million, instead of the surplus of $218 million shown by Dr. Chang. And if we allow ourselves partly to correct the injustice to Asia committed by Dr. Chang, and we ask Greece to bow out in favour of China (a far more important trader), we obtain a twelve-country deficit of $270 million.

If instead of his selection of countries Dr. Chang had taken the twelve most important countries of the forty noted earlier, he would have found that five countries (of which four ranked among the six most important), representing in 1928-9 as much as 49.1 per cent of the total trade of the twelve countries, experienced an unfavourable change in their balances between 1928-9 and 1931-2;[16] and that six countries, representing 44.5 per cent of the total trade in 1928-9 had a deficit in 1931-2.[17] Again, of the larger group of forty countries, fourteen, representing in 1928-9 45.1 per cent of the total trade of the forty countries, experienced an unfavourable change in their balances in the period 1928-9 to 1931-2; and twelve countries, representing in 1928-9 38.1 per cent of the total trade of the forty countries, had a deficit in 1931-2.

We may summarize some of our comments about the pattern of cyclical change in the merchandise balance advanced by Dr. Chang and the selection of countries he has used to support it. According to Dr. Chang the balance "tends to show a deficit in prosperity and a surplus during slump." Of the forty countries noted earlier only fourteen presented these features in the period 1928-9 to 1931-2, or 1928-9 to 1932-3;[18] these include nine European countries, Australia, three Central American republics, and Colombia. With the exception then of the last country, all South American, Asian, and African countries studied, as well as New Zealand, did not satisfy the pattern of cyclical change in the merchandise balance advanced by Dr. Chang.

Even more significant than the actual changes in the balances is the explanation of these changes. As indicated earlier, Dr. Chang dismisses the original relation as being insignificant in practice. He purports to explain the direction of change in the balances of countries exporting chiefly agricultural products by analysis of income elasticities of demand in these countries and abroad, and other factors, which, taken together, are supposed to account for an import/export decline, or increase, exceeding unity.[19] But in four of Dr. Chang's twelve countries the original relation accounted for the entire change in the balance in the period 1928-9 to 1931-2, while the influence of the import/export decline was in the opposite direction: in Denmark and Norway the balance changed favourably in spite of an import/export decline *smaller than unity*, and in Argentina and New Zealand the balance changed unfavourably even though the import/export decline exceeded unity. In a fifth country, Latvia, the original relation accounted for the greater part of the change in the balance. (These five countries, represented 55.5 per cent of the total volume of trade of Dr. Chang's twelve countries in 1928-9.) In five of the remaining seven countries the original relation accounted for a very substantial part of the change in the balance (ranging from almost one-fifth to almost one-half). If we take all twelve countries we find that the original relation accounted for a slightly larger part of the arithmetic sum of the changes in the balances than the import/export decline.

All Asian countries examined in our study, and Egypt, had an import/export decline in the period 1928-9 to 1931-2 *smaller than unity*; but none of these countries is included in Dr. Chang's selection, even though four of them rank among the twelve largest international traders of the forty countries. If Dr. Chang had actually taken the twelve largest traders, he would have found that in seven of these countries (which in 1928-9 represented 64.6 per cent of the total trade of the twelve countries) the original relation was the sole or main determinant of the change in the balance; also, that it accounted for 57.1 per cent of the arithmetic sum of the changes in the twelve balances. Finally, if we take the larger group of forty countries, we find that the original relation was the sole or main determinant of the change in the balance of twenty countries (which in 1928-9 accounted for 62.8 per cent of the total trade of the forty countries); also, that the original relation accounted for 57.5 per cent of the arithmetic sum of the changes in the forty balances.

As indicated, Dr. Chang claims that in countries exporting chiefly agricultural products the import/export decline exceeded unity, and he purports to explain this phenomenon by analysis of income elasticities of demand and other factors referred to earlier. Because of these factors, he claims, "the effect of the relative quantity changes tends to more than offset the effect of the relative price changes."[20] But this view does not accord with the facts in a number of countries exporting staple foodstuffs or certain agricultural raw materials: in Egypt for instance, the import/export decline in the depression was *smaller than unity* exactly because the relative quantity changes failed to offset the unfavourable impact of the relative price changes.

III

Our final comment on Dr. Chang's study relates to his general approach to the problem of cyclical changes in the merchandise balances of primary-exporting countries.

It is not uncommon for students of the foreign trade of these countries to treat these economies as if they belong to one "type," and hence to outline a "pattern" of cyclical behaviour in their trade balances. Presumably, the attitude of these economists is based on the existence of some common features in these countries, notably features relating to the origin, and hence certain conditions of supply, of their chief exports. Unfortunately, many fundamental differences in important economic conditions of these economies are very often neglected. Our study abounds in examples of such differences: they relate, for instance, to the conditions of demand and even of supply of exports, the distribution among the various income classes of the cyclical changes in total income, and the role of foreign investment, of the service of foreign capital, and of invisible earnings.

Some writers distinguish countries exporting food from countries exporting industrial raw materials, and Dr. Chang has distinguished "mining and extractive-industry" countries from countries exporting agricultural products. But even these smaller groups are much too broad: there are fundamental differences between countries belonging to the one or the other of Dr. Chang's groups. As our analysis has shown, it is totally pointless to attempt to submit to a common "pattern" of cyclical changes in trade in the inter-war period such mineral-exporting countries as Venezuela and Chile, whose experience in the years 1927-33 was strikingly different, or, among the countries exporting chiefly agricultural products such countries as Australia, Lithuania, China, and Norway.

NOTES

ABBREVIATIONS

CDBS	Canada, Dominion Bureau of Statistics
EMB	Empire Marketing Board
GBDOT	Great Britain, Department of Overseas Trade
IBRD	International Bank for Reconstruction and Development
IIA	International Institute of Agriculture
LN	League of Nations
LNEC	League of Nations Economic Committee
NBER	National Bureau of Economic Research
RIIA	Royal Institute of International Affairs
UN	United Nations
UNECAFE	United Nations Economic Committee for Asia and the Far East
UNECLA	United Nations Economic Committee for Latin America
USTC	United States Tariff Commission

INTRODUCTION

1. Tse Chun Chang, *Cyclical Movements in the Balance of Payments* (Cambridge: Cambridge University Press, 1951).

CHAPTER ONE

1. In this list of the forty-nine countries and in various tables in this study the following abbreviations are used: "Dominican R." for the Dominican Republic; "D.E. Indies" for the Dutch East Indies; "Irish F.S." for the Irish Free State; and "Malaya" for British Malaya. Also, articles which normally accompany the names of some countries are omitted.

2. See, e.g., T. C. Chang, *Cyclical Movements in the Balance of Payments*, esp. chaps. X and XI, and the Appendix to this study.

3. Owing to the significance of gold or silver in the production and exports of the following countries, ores or bullion (as indicated for each country) have been included in their merchandise exports. Australia's exports include "domestic" gold and silver. Bolivia's exports include silver ores and bullion produced in the country, and some insignificant amounts of gold. Canada's exports include "gold and silver bullion, etc. obtained direct from mining operations." Colombia's exports include "unmanufactured gold." Ecuador's exports include "gold concentrates and dust." Mexico's exports include gold and silver. Peru's exports include gold and silver, ores and concentrates. The Philippines' exports include gold and silver, ore and bullion. In the case of some other countries small amounts of gold or silver, ores or bullion, are included among their exports of "other metals" or "other articles."
New Zealand's imports include gold and silver bullion from April 1932 on, only because it was impossible to exclude bullion on the basis of the statistics presented in the League of Nations publications or *The New Zealand Official Yearbook*. However, the amounts involved are probably very small; some available estimates suggest that imports of bullion and coin would have represented only about 0.1 of one per cent of all imports (including these items) in 1928 and 1929, about 0.2 of one per cent in 1931 and 1932, and about 1.5 per cent in 1933. (G. H. Brown, *International Economic Position of New Zealand*, Supplement to *Journal of Business*, XIX (April 1946), 74, 84). Since most of our comparisons are between the average values of trade for the years 1928 and 1929, and those for 1931 and 1932, the disadvantage of including bullion in New Zealand's imports from 1932 on is negligible.

4. For six of the countries considered, namely Australia, Canada, Haiti, Honduras, Persia, and Siam, the League of Nations publications present yearly data referring to periods other than the Western calendar year (financial, fiscal, economic, or local civil year). Unless otherwise indicated, the following rule applies throughout this study: reference to the years 1928 and 1929 should be taken to mean, as far as these countries are concerned, the years 1927-8 and 1928-9, respectively; and reference to the years 1930, 1931, 1932 and 1933, means

·2 and 1932-3, respectively, for Haiti, and 1930-1, 1931-2, 1932-3 and
ve countries.
ʳ and VI include, under separate headings, data relating to the eleven
untries.
ıl-exporting countries whose balances improved between 1928-9 and
ium, Germany, Italy, Japan, and the United Kingdom) experienced
cit. Of the five countries whose balances deteriorated, Czechoslovakia
s experienced a decline in their surplus, and France, Sweden, and
e in their deficit.
: Denmark and Norway changed unfavourably in the first period and
Ihe experience of Persia was the reverse. The balance of the Philippines
in the first two periods and favourably in the third.
ange in the balances of the industrial-exporting countries also was the
iods, except for Belgium and the United Kingdom, whose experience
nark's, and Czechoslovakia, whose experience was the same as Persia's.

:ountry's exports and imports in the base period, and x and m are the
ı its exports and imports in the period considered. The balance will
ınfavourably depending on whether $Ex \lessgtr Im$, or $E/I \lessgtr m/x$.
ing exports and imports x and m represent the percentage increases in
vely, the balance will change favourably or unfavourably depending on
$E/I \gtrless m/x$.
the balance is $Im - Ex$, or $Ix(m/x - E/I)$. Hence, given I, the amount
ınce depends on E/I, m/x and x. The change in the balance is also
that, given E, the amount of change in the balance depends on E/I,

the balance is $Im - Ex$, or $(I - E)x + I(m - x)$. Hence, given I the
the balance depends on $I - E$, $m - x$ and x. The change in the balance
$(m - x)$; so that, given E, the amount of change in the balance depends
m.
in the balance consists of $(I - E)x$ and $I(m - x)$ (or $(I - E)m$ and
ler is the original deficit or surplus $(I - E)$, the less important for the
ᵢ is the size of the percentage decline in exports (x) (or imports, m), and
. the relation between the percentage decline in imports and the percent-
s $(m - x)$. Also, the smaller is the percentage decline in exports (or im-
:tant is the size of the original surplus or deficit, and, again, the more
ion between the percentage decline in imports and the percentage decline
her hand, the closer the two percentage declines, the more important is
nal surplus or deficit, as well as the size of the percentage decline in
and the larger the trade imbalance in the base period, the more important
:centage decline in exports (or imports). Thus, of two countries which in
the base period have the same values of imports and exports and a large surplus, the
whose exports decline more heavily may experience a larger decline in the surplus even though
the relation between the percentage decline in its imports and the percentage decline in its
exports is more favourable ($m - x$ is greater than in the other country): the greater amount of
decline in its imports (Im) is more than offset by a greater amount of decline in its exports
(Ex). We shall see however (chap. 6, II), that the difference, or ratio, between the percentage
decline in imports and the percentage decline in exports $(m - x,$ or $m/x)$ varied between the
countries studied inversely, rather than directly, with the percentage decline in their exports.
4. If $E/I > 1$ and $m/x < 1$ $(E/I < 1$ and $m/x > 1)$, both relations contributed to the
unfavourable (favourable) change in the balance. On the other hand, if both E/I and m/x
exceeded unity (both ratios were smaller than unity) the direction of change in the balance
was due to either E/I or m/x, depending on whether $E/I \gtrless m/x$ $(E/I \lessgtr m/x)$.
5. In a number of these forty-three countries the deficit gave place to a surplus, or the
surplus to a deficit. A deficit in 1928-9 changed into a surplus in 1931-2 in those countries in
which the change in the deficit, $Im - Ex$, was greater than the deficit, $I-E$, or, by transforming,
when $E/I > (1 - m)/(1 - x)$. In the opposite case only the size of the deficit changed. Similarly, a surplus either changed into a deficit or merely changed in size depending on whether
$E/I \lessgtr (1 - m)/(1 - x)$. (In other words, a country had a deficit or surplus in 1931-2 depending on whether $E/I \lessgtr (1 - m)/(1 - x)$. In twenty-six of the forty-three countries the deficit
(nine countries) or surplus (seventeen) merely diminished. In the other seventeen countries the
deficit (fourteen countries) or surplus (three) changed into a surplus or deficit, respectively.

CDBS   Canada, Dominion Bureau of Statistics
EMB   Empire Marketing Board
GBDOT   Great Britain, Department of Overseas Trade
IBRD   International Bank for Reconstruction and Development
IIA   International Institute of Agriculture
LN   League of Nations
LNEC   League of Nations Economic Committee
NBER   National Bureau of Economic Research
RIIA   Royal Institute of International Affairs
UN   United Nations
UNECAFE   United Nations Economic Committee for Asia and the Far East
UNECLA   United Nations Economic Committee for Latin America
USTC   United States Tariff Commission

6. The part of the change in the balance which is due to the original relation is $(I - E)x$, and the part due to the import/export decline is $I(m - x)$. Dividing the two parts by Ix we get $1 - E/I$ and $m/x - 1$, respectively. The former part then is greater or smaller than the latter depending on whether E/I or m/x is further away from unity.

It will be noticed that the percentage of the change in the balance which is due to the different percentage decline in imports than in exports depends only on the ratio of these two percentages, *i.e.* the import/export decline, and on the original relation. It is independent of the size of the percentage decline in exports (imports) which is a determinant of the total amount of change in the country's balance.

7. In 1928-9 these twenty-six countries accounted for 65.3 per cent of the total trade (exports plus imports) of all forty-nine countries.

An alternative partitioning of the change in the balance would be to ascribe to the original relation that part of the actual change in the deficit or surplus of each country which would have occurred had the *exports* declined by the same percentage by which the *imports* decreased. Using the same notation, the two parts would be $(I - E)m$ and $E(m - x)$, respectively. It will be noticed that these parts are obtained from the parts based on the partitioning in the text by multiplying $(I - E)x$ by m/x, and $I(m - x)$ by E/I. Since in eighteen of the twenty-seven countries in which both relations were responsible for the change in the balance m/x exceeded E/I, the percentage of the change in the balance ascribed to the original relation would tend to increase in more countries than in those in which it would diminish. The predominant relation would change in only three countries—Hungary, Nicaragua, and Turkey—from the import/export decline to the original relation. By this partitioning then the original relation would be the more important determinant of the change in the balance in twenty-nine of the forty-nine countries.

A third alternative would be to ascribe to the original relation that part of the actual change in the deficit or surplus of each country which would have occurred had the exports and imports declined by the arithmetic mean of the percentages by which exports and imports actually declined. For each country, the part of the change in the balance ascribed to the original relation would be the mean of the parts ascribed to this relation by the two previous methods of partitioning $[(1 - E)(m + x)/2]$, and similarly for the import/export decline $[(1 - E)(m - x)/2]$. By this third method of partitioning the original relation would be the more important determinant of the change in the balance in twenty-seven of the forty-nine countries.

It will be noticed that the two methods of partitioning discussed in this note show the original relation to have been even more important than it was found to be by the method used in the text.

8. For instance, increases in the surpluses of some countries and decreases in those of others, or decreases in the surpluses of some countries and in the deficits of others, are not taken to offset each other, but are added together.

9. Tables V and VI show that the original relation was relatively stronger in those primary-exporting countries in which the balance turned unfavourably. This phenomenon will be discussed after the consideration of the decline in exports and imports.

An alternative partitioning of the change in the balance (chap. 2 n. 7), would be to ascribe to the original relation that part of the actual change in the deficit or surplus of each country which would have occurred had the *exports* declined by the same percentage by which the *imports* decreased. By this criterion the original relation appears even more important than in Table VI; it accounted for 64.1 per cent of the arithmetic sum of the changes in the forty-nine balances (48.0 per cent of the favourable change in twenty-eight balances, and 82.3 per cent of the unfavourable change in twenty-one balances).

10. This involves, in effect, adding to the totals of Table VI twice the negative shares of the original relation and the import/export decline which have been deducted.

11. For obvious reasons in the case of the industrial-exporting countries we have ascribed to the original relation that part of the change in the deficit or surplus of each country which would have occurred had the *exports* declined by the same percentage by which the *imports* decreased; and the remainder to the import/export decline. The two parts are $(I - E)m$ and $E(m - x)$, respectively. By the alternative partitioning, of ascribing to the orignial relation that part of the change in the deficit or surplus which would have occurred had the *imports* declined by the same percentage by which the *exports* decreased, the percentage of the change in the eleven balances due to the original relation is 72.6—higher than that shown in Table VI.

12. For examples of such oversight see the Appendix to this study.

13. In fourteen countries which had a deficit in 1928-9, $E/I > (1 - m)/(1 - x)$, and in three that had a surplus, $E/I < (1 - m)/(1 - x)$. In all seventeen countries $1 - E/I < m/x - 1$.

14.   In nine countries which had a deficit in 1928-9, $E/I < 1 - m/1 - x$, and in seventeen that had a surplus, $E/I > (1 - m)/(1 - x)$.

15.   In the remaining six of the forty-nine primary-exporting countries the surplus or deficit increased because of the import/export decline and in spite of the original relation.

Of the eleven industrial-exporting countries only one changed from a deficit to a surplus; none changed from a surplus to a deficit. In seven countries the deficit or surplus merely declined. In the remaining three countries the deficit increased.

16.   In the eleven industrial-exporting countries, the original relation was the sole or main determinant of change in the balance of four countries in the first period, and seven in the second and third periods.

17.   In the remaining eleven countries the original relation or the import/export decline was, in both periods, the sole determinant of change in the balance.

18.   The eight countries were: Bolivia, Cuba, India, the Irish Free State, New Zealand, Paraguay, the Philippines, and Peru.

19.   In the remaining six of the forty-nine countries the value of the import/export decline changed as follows: in two countries it exceeded unity in the third period by more than in the first; in another two countries it was less than unity in the third period by more than in the first; and in the remaining two countries it exceeded unity in the first period and was less than unity in the third. In none of these countries did the role of the original relation as a determinant of change in the trade balance improve between the first and third period.

20.   See chap. 4, II, and chap. 6, VI.

CHAPTER THREE

1.   In the period examined the manufactured exports of the Balkan countries were of little significance. For instance, in 1928-9 textiles and fibres accounted for only 1.1 per cent of the total exports of Greece, which industrially was the most advanced of the four countries; cement and paper represented 2.1 and 1.1 per cent. respectively, of Yugoslavia's exports.

2.   The dry beans were a staple foodstuff of low-income classes in the importing countries.

3.   In bad times, in an effort to pay taxes and debt service at fixed dates and to mitigate the decline in his real income, the Balkan peasant tended to work harder, and, since agricultural credit was costly, he had to make considerable concessions on the price of his product. See H. Seton-Watson, *Eastern Europe between the Wars, 1918-1941* (Cambridge: Cambridge University Press, 1946), 82-4; J. K. Galbraith and J. D. Black, "The Maintenance of Agricultural Production during Depression: The Explanation Reviewed," *Journal of Political Economy*, 46 (1938), 313-14; D. Gale Johnson, "The Nature of the Supply Function for Agricultural Products," *American Economic Review*, 40 (1950), 543-4, 564; LNEC, *The Agricultural Crisis*, I (Geneva, 1931), 14; LN, *World Production and Prices, 1925-1932*, 103; and UNECLA, *Economic Survey of Latin America, 1949*, 127-8, 135; also J. de V. Graaff, "Income Effects and the Theory of the Firm," *Review of Economic Studies*, 18, 1950-1, esp. 81-3.

4.   For the decline in the prices of Balkan exports of this class see Otto von Franges, "Die wirtschaftlichen Beziehungen Jugoslawiens und die Problematik seiner Eingliederung in die Weltwirtschaft," *Weltwirtschaftliches Archiv*, 37 (1933), 129; C. Evelpidi, "Die landwirtschaftliche Krise in Griechenland," *Weltwirtschaftliches Archiv*, 51 (1940), 348 ff.; RIIA, *South-Eastern Europe: A Political and Economic Survey* (London: Oxford University Press, 1939), 160; and LN Economic Intelligence Service, *Review of World Trade*, 1933, 40.

For some estimates of price elasticities of demand for goods of this Class see H. Schultz, *The Theory and Measurement of Demand* (Chicago: University of Chicago Press, 1938), 399-400, 481-2; W. Malenbaum, *The World Wheat Economy 1885-1939* (Cambridge: Harvard University Press, 1953), 72-7; W. A. Mackintosh, *Economic Problems of the Prairie Provinces* (Toronto: Macmillan of Canada, 1935), 20-1; and LN, Mixed Committee on the Problem of Nutrition, *Final Report on the Relation of Nutrition to Health, Agriculture, and Economic Policy* (Geneva, 1937), 191-3.

For some estimates of income elasticities of demand for foodstuffs, farm products and, particularly, the goods of this class see C. Clark, *The Conditions of Economic Progress* (1st ed.; London: Macmillan, 1940), 436 ff.; T. W. Schultz, *Agriculture in an Unstable Economy* (New York: McGraw-Hill, 1945), 60 ff.; R. Stone, *The Measurement of Consumers' Expenditure and Behaviour in the United Kingdom, 1920-1938*, I (Cambridge: Cambridge University Press, 1954), 313 ff.; S. J. Prais and H. S. Houthakker, *The Analysis of Family Budgets* (Cambridge: Cambridge University Press, 1955), chap. 7, esp. 93-4, 106; and H. S. Houthakker, "The Econometrics of Family Budgets," *Journal of the Royal Statistical Society*, Series A (General), 115 (1952), 6, 15, 18-19. See also J. R. N. Stone, "The Analysis of Market Demand," *Journal of the Royal Statistical Society* (New Series) 108 (1945), 314-21; and C. E. V. Leser, "Family

Budget Data and Price-Elasticities of Demand," *Review of Economic Studies*, 9 (1941/2), 52-6. The short-run income elasticities of demand should be lower than the longer-run elasticities given by some of these authors.

5. The fairly large crops in the year 1928 coincided with large crops in most of the world. Hence, exports from Bulgaria and Roumania were small and their stocks of wheat were increased. See Stanford University, Food Research Institute, *Wheat Studies*, VI (Nov. 1929-Sept. 1930), 41, and XII (Sept. 1935-June 1936), 400. See also J. S. Davis *et al.*, *Wheat in the World Economy* (Stanford: Food Research Institute, Stanford University, 1945), 5-8.

6. See J. S. Davis, *Wheat and the AAA* (Washington: Brookings Institution, 1935), 18-26; F. B. Horner, "Elasticity of Demand for the Exports of a Single Country," *Review of Economics and Statistics*, 34 (1952), 326-9; D. J. Morgan and W. J. Corlett, "The Influence of Price in International Trade: A Study in Method," *Journal of the Royal Statistical Society*, Series A (General), 114 (1951), 329, 344; and S. E. Harris,*Exchange Depreciation* (Cambridge: Harvard University Press, 1936), 32, 36. See also G. H. Orcutt, "Measurement of Price Elasticities in International Trade," *Review of Economics and Statistics*, 32 (1950), 127.

7. For data on production of rye in Bulgaria and Roumania see LN, *Statistical Yearbook 1930/1*, 78, and *1934/5*, 92.

8. In some of these countries (e.g. Portugal) the wine output was exceptionally high in one or both years of the earlier period, while in others (e.g. Greece) it was exceptionally low in one or both years of the later period.

Throughout the present discussion Portuguese wine does not include madeira and port.

In contrast with the countries listed in the text, the wine output of such countries as Germany, Hungary, and Roumania increased during the period considered. See LN, *Statistical Yearbook, 1932/3*, 90, and *1936/7*, 104.

9. LN, *Statistical Yearbook, 1936/7*, 104. In the years 1925-30 Algeria exported about three-quarters of her wine output. See LNEC, *The Agricultural Crisis*, I, 169.

10. Based on comparison of export values and quantities given in LN, *International Trade Statistics*.

11. See LN, Mixed Committee on the Problem of Nutrition, *Final Report on the Relation of Nutrition to Health, Agriculture and Economic Policy*, 186, 256; R. G. D. Allen and A. L. Bowley, *Family Expenditure: A Study of its Variation* (London: Staples Press, 1935), 34-6; E. M. H. Lloyd, *Food Supplies and Consumption at Different Income Levels* (London: Agricultural Economic Society, 1935), quoted in C. M. Wright, *Economic Adaptation to a Changing World Market* (Copenhagen: Ejnar Munksgaard, 1939), 42-3; "An International Survey of Recent Family Living Studies: II," *International Labour Review*, 39, 1939, 836-41; Stone, *The Measurement of Consumers' Expenditure and Behaviour in the United Kingdom 1920-1938*, I, 313 ff.; Prais and Houthakker, *The Analysis of Family Budgets*, chap. 7, esp. 93-4, and 106; Houthakker, "The Econometrics of Family Budgets," *Journal of the Royal Statistical Society*, Series A (General), 115, 1952, 6, 15, 18-19; H. Wold, *Demand Analysis: A Study in Econometrics* (New York: John Wiley & Sons, 1953), 263-5; and N. L. Gold and M. Enlow, "The Demand for Food by Low Income Families," *Quarterly Journal of Economics*, 57, 1942/3, 602. See also Clark, *The Conditions of Economic Progress*, 1st ed., 439-40; Schultz, *Agriculture in an Unstable Economy*, 60; G. S. Shepherd, *Agricultural Price Analysis* (Ames, Iowa: Iowa State College Press, 1941), 210; H. Staehle, "Elasticity of Demand and Social Welfare," *Quarterly Journal of Economics*, 54 (1939/40), 225-9; and C. M. Wright, "Butter as a World Staple," *Index* (Stockholm: Svenska Handelsbanken), 10 (1935), 259.

12. Either the demand for the commodity in general tended to be elastic, or the volume of Balkan exports had little influence on price.

13. See, for example, Mackintosh, *Economic Problems of the Prairie Provinces*, 20-1; F. B. Horner, Elasticity of Demand for the Exports of a Single Country," *Review of Economics and Statistics*, 34 (1952), 334; and United States Department of Agriculture, Agricultural Marketing Service, Marketing Research Division, *Farm-Retail Spreads for Food Products*. Miscellaneous Publication No. 741 (Washington: U.S. Government Printing Office, November 1957), 7, 59-60.

14. Between 1928-9 and 1931-2 ocean freight rates declined in terms of gold only by one-third or less, while the gold prices of agricultural products listed in Classes A and C declined, as a rule, by about one-half to three-quarters, and of meat and dairy products listed in Class B by about two-fifths to one-half. See IIA, *International Yearbook of Agricultural Statistics, 1932/3*, 684; also, United States Department of Agriculture, Agricultural Marketing Service, Marketing Research Division, *Farm-Retail Spreads for Food Products*, 3-4, 8.

About the phenomenon discussed in the text see also J. Tinbergen, "Long-term Foreign Trade Elasticities," *Metroeconomica*, I (1949), 176-7. Generally, in the period considered, prices of Class B goods declined less than prices of Class A goods, but the differences between the declines in prices of Class A and B goods tended to be greater at the f.o.b. export stage, than at the retail stage in the importing countries. See Sections VIII, IX, and pp. 35-6, and compare, for instance, the estimates on the one hand pp. 25-6, 29, and references, and on the other hand in Stone, *The Measurement of Consumers' Expenditure and Behaviour in the United Kingdom 1920-1938*, I, 27-8, 51, 53, 67-8, 95-6, 120-1, 134, 136, 144, 151, 174.

15.   See also C. M. Wright "Butter as a World Staple," *Index*, 10 (1935), 263-4; LNEC, *The Agricultural Crisis*, I, 203, 223.

For producers' behaviour similar to that noted in chap. 3, n. 3, see D. J. Morgan and W. J. Corlett, "The Influence of Price in International Trade: A Study in Method", *Journal of the Royal Statistical Society*, Series A (General), 114 (1951), 337-8; and A. R. Bergstrom, "An Econometric Study of Supply and Demand for New Zealand's Exports," *Econometrica*, 23 (1955), 266-8.

16.   For the output of olive oil see LN, *Statistical Yearbook, 1936/7*, 112. For the great variability of yield in the production of oil see Food and Agricultural Organization, UN, *The Stabilization of the Olive Oil Market*, FAO Commodity Policy Studies, No. 9 (Rome: 1955), 2.

Of the ten years 1926-35 only in 1927 and 1931 was the volume of fig exports from Greece smaller than 14 thousand metric tons; at 9.6 thousand in 1931 it was the lowest. See EMB, *Canned and Dried Fruit Supplies in 1931*. Publication No. 55 (London: HMSO, July 1932), 113-14; *idem, Canned and Dried Fruit Supplies in 1932*. Publication No. 69 (London: HMSO, June 1933), 127-8; and LN, *International Trade Statistics* for the various years.

17.   See Orcutt, "Measurement of Price Elasticities in International Trade," *Review of Economics and Statistics*, 32 (1950), 123; and Wright, *Economic Adaptation to a Changing World Market*, 271.

18.   See chap. 3, n. 14.

19.   E.g., between 1928-9 and 1931-2 the export value of Roumanian oxen declined by 61.8 per cent, while that of pigs decreased only by 36.0 per cent. See also Table VIII, note (*d*).

20.   For changes in prices of Class C exports see Section x; also Otto von Franges, "Die wirtschaftlichen Beziehungen Jugoslawiens und die Problematik seiner Eingliederung in die Weltwirtschaft," *Weltwirtschaftliches Archiv*, 37 (1933), 129.

21.   Not much can be said about the last item in Table VIII, Class C: "other mineral oils." However, it accounted for only about 5 per cent of Roumania's oil exports in 1928-9.

22.   In Table X we include kerosene in Class A. The price of kerosene was affected also by the fact that "the use of kerosene for lighting purposes was in sharp decline" from the mid-twenties to the mid-thirties. See H. Neisser and F. Modigliani, *National Incomes and International Trade* (Urbana: University of Illinois Press, 1953), 227.

23.   While between 1929 and 1932 the world output of pig iron and ferro-alloys decreased from 98.6 to 39.6 million metric tons, of steel from 120.6 to 50.6 million metric tons, and of automobiles from 6.31 to 1.98 millions, the world output of petroleum decreased only from 206 to 180 million metric tons, and of coal and lignite from 1,396 to 1,006 million metric tons. (LN, *Statistical Yearbook 1933/4*).

The short-run income elasticity of demand for motor spirit tended to be moderate because the influence of changes in incomes on the amount of motor spirit consumed "is partly of a direct character, but is in a more important degree transmitted through the change in the number of automobiles in good operating condition" and in the size and quality of the road network. J. S. Bain, *The Economics of the Pacific Coast Petroleum Industry* (Berkeley: University of California Press, 1944), Part I, 202; and R. Cassady, Jr., *Price Making and Price Behavior in the Petroleum Industry*. Petroleum Monograph Series. I (New Haven: Yale University Press, 1954), 79.

24.   For the price elasticity of demand for the first two oil items of Table VIII, which may be considerable, see R. F. Mikesell and H. B. Chenery, *Arabian Oil* (Chapel Hill: University of North Carolina Press, 1949), 158; C. F. Roos, *Dynamic Economics* (Bloomington, Indiana: Principia Press, 1934), 26, 30-5, 38-40; E. V. Rostow, *A National Policy for the Oil Industry* (New Haven: Yale University Press, 1948), 13; and NBER, *Price Research in the Steel and Petroleum Industries* (New York, 1939), 153-4.

For the long-term growth in demand for the oil items considered see American Petroleum Institute, *American Petroleum Industry* (New York: American Petroleum Institute, 1935), 103-5.

The effects on export prices and volumes, of the monopolistic features of the oil industry, and of secret international combinations to control prices, outputs or exports, have not been, and apparently cannot be, fully ascertained. See, e.g., Mikesell and Chenery, *Arabian Oil*, 114-15. In August 1932 Roumania reluctantly became a party to the Paris Agreement on restriction of oil exports, which had been concluded in the previous month. However, in spite of the fact that Roumania's export quota was fixed more liberally than that of other oil-exporting countries, her producers did not, at least until the end of 1932, restrict their exports to conform to the Paris Agreement. See *The Economist*, 115 (1932), 237-8, 425, 1098.

25. See data in IIA, *International Yearbook of Agricultural Statistics*, various years; LN, *World Production and Prices, 1925-1934*, 118-19; and *idem*, *Statistical Yearbook*, various years.

26. See IIA, *International Yearbook of Agricultural Statistics*, various years, and LN, *Review of World Trade, 1934*, 52-54.

The large increase in world exports of maize was due chiefly to large increases in the exports of Argentina, Roumania, Yugoslavia, and Bulgaria. In the late nineteen-twenties Argentina accounted for about two-thirds of the world exports of maize. Owing chiefly to a very small crop in 1928/9 and a huge crop in 1930/1 her maize exports increased between 1928-9 and 1931-2 by 2,701 thousand metric tons, or by 47.3 per cent. (If the three years 1930-2 or 1931-3 are compared with the three years 1927-9, the increase is only about 600-700 thousand metric tons, or about 9-10 per cent.) For reasons indicated earlier the exports of the three Balkan countries increased in the same period by 1,166 thousand metric tons. IIA, *International Yearbook of Agricultural Statistics*, various years; and LNEC, *The Agricultural Crisis*, I, 79, 84.

Between 1928-9 and 1931-2 the quantity of tobacco exports of eleven primary-exporting countries (Algeria, Brazil, Bulgaria, Cuba, the Dominican Republic, the Dutch East Indies, Greece, Hungary, India, Paraguay, and the Philippines) declined by 11.0 per cent. Including the exports of the United States the decline was 15.0 per cent. (LN, *International Trade Statistics*, various years.)

27. LN, *Statistical Yearbook*, various years; IIA, *International Yearbook of Agricultural Statistics, 1932-3*, 582, ff.; and estimates based on comparisons of the values and quantities of exports of primary-exporting countries given in LN, *International Trade Statistics*, various years. See also *idem*, *World Economic Survey, 1933-4*, 142; UNECLA, *Economic Survey of Latin America, 1949*, 230; EMB, *Survey of Vegetable Oilseeds and Oils*. Publication No. 54 (London: HMSO, June 1932), I, 113, 122; *idem*, *Survey of Oilseeds and Vegetable Oils*. Publication No. 61 (London: HMSO, December 1932), II, 168-9; N. A. Cox-George, *Finance and Development in West Africa: The Sierra Leone Experience* (London: Dennis Dobson, 1961), 266; and V. D. Wickizer and M. K. Bennett, *The Rice Economy of Monsoon Asia* (Stanford: Stanford University, Food Research Institute, 1941), 330-1.

28. About Persia's opium exports see LNEC, *The Agricultural Crisis*, I, 246. In 1928-9 opium accounted for 4.1 per cent of the value of Persia's exports.

Many of the differences between coffee, tea, and other Class A goods may be deduced from perusal of V. D. Wickizer, *The World Coffee Economy, with Special Reference to Control Schemes* (Stanford: Food Research Institute, Stanford University, 1943), chap. v-xi; *idem*, *Tea under International Regulation* (Stanford: Food Research Institute, Stanford University, 1944), chap. i-v; P. Lamartine Yates, *Commodity Control: A Study of Primary Products* (London: Jonathan Cape, 1943), chap. ii-iv; E. J. Broster, "Elasticities of Demand for Tea and Price-Fixing Policy," *Review of Economic Studies*, 6 (1939), 167-9, 173-6; UNECLA, *A Study of Trade between Latin America and Europe* (Geneva, 1953), 58; and UNECAFE, *A Study of Trade between Asia and Europe* (Geneva, 1953), 20. See also V. D. Wickizer, *Coffee, Tea and Cocoa: An Economic and Political Analysis* (Stanford: Food Research Institute, Stanford University, 1951).

29. See pp. 21-2.

30. See chap. 3, n. 14; LNEC, *The Agricultural Crisis*, I, 110; Wickizer, *The World Coffee Economy with Special Reference to Control Schemes*, 167, 244; and LN, *World Production and Prices, 1925-1933*, 103.

31. As a tea exporter, China was less important than the Dutch East Indies, and much less important than India or Ceylon. She was not an important competitor of British-grown teas within the British Empire. For more details see Wickizer, *Tea Under International Regulation*, 5, 31-2, 47, 57, 181-2. See also UN, Secretariat, Department of Economic Affairs, *Instability in Export Markets of Under-Developed Countries* (New York: United Nations, 1952), II.A.1., 34-5. In 1928-9 tea represented the following percentages of exports of the countries noted in the text: Ceylon 53.8, the Dutch East Indies 6.1, India 8.1, and China 3.9.

32. Similar differences could be noted between the characteristics of demand for coffee, and hence the changes in consumption, in the United States on the one hand, and certain European countries on the other. On the basis of the principle indicated in the text, of classifying a commodity by the characteristics of demand prevailing in important foreign markets, potatoes belong to Class A, rather than Class B. See Allen and Bowley, *Family Expenditure: A Study of Its Variation*, 36; Stone, *The Measurement of Consumers' Expenditure and Behaviour in the United Kingdom 1920-1938*, I, 313 ff.; Prais and Houthakker, *The Analysis of Family Budgets*, 106; and Houthakker, "The Econometrics of Family Budgets," *Journal of the Royal Statistical Society*, Series A (General), 115 (1952), 18.

33. See also p. 48. For estimates indicative of the low price and income elasticities of demand

for sugar see Allen and Bowley, *Family Expenditure: A Study of its Variation*, 34-6; Schultz, *The Theory and Measurement of Demand*, 229-30; Stone, *The Measurement of Consumers' Expenditure and Behaviour in the United Kingdom 1920-1938*, I, 313-19; Prais and Houthakker, *The Analysis of Family Budgets*, 106; Houthakker, "The Econometrics of Family Budgets," 18; Wold, *Demand Analysis: A Study in Econometrics*, 265; and J. Alienes y Urosa, *Caracteristicas Fundamentales de la Economia Cubana* (Havana: Banco Nacional de Cuba, 1950), 375-6.

For the low elasticity of supply of sugar in the downswing see Foreign Policy Association, Commission on Cuban Affairs, *Problems of the New Cuba* (New York: Foreign Policy Association, 1935), 237-8; also H. C. Wallich, *Monetary Problems of an Export Economy: The Cuban Experience 1914-1947* (Cambridge: Harvard University Press, 1950), 227-8.

34. See EMB, *Cocoa, World Production and Trade*, Publication No. 27 (London, HMSO, May 1930), 96.

35. In the period 1925-9 about three-quarters of Cuba's sugar exports were directed to the United States, where they accounted for about one-half of the sugar consumed. (UNECLA, *A Study of Trade between Latin America and Europe*, 68). For more information about the changes in Cuba's production and export of sugar, the increase in import duties and imposition of quotas on Cuban sugar in the United States, and the attempts towards international regulation (such as the Chadbourne Plan of 1930) see IBRD, Mission, *Report on Cuba* (Washington, 1951), 811 ff.; Foreign Policy Association, Commission on Cuban Affairs, *Problems of the New Cuba*, 235-6, 246 ff.; USTC, *The Foreign Trade of Latin America*. Report No. 146, Second Series (Washington: U.S. Government Printing Office, 1942), Part II, Vol. 2, 235 ff., especially 250-7, and Part III, 189-91; *idem, United States—Philippine Tariff and Trade Relations*. Report No. 18, Second Series (Washington: U.S. Government Printing Office, 1931), 7, 65; *idem, United States—Philippine Trade*. Report No. 118, Second Series (Washington: U.S. Government Printing Office, 1937), 52; V. P. Timoshenko and B. C. Swerling, *The World's Sugar, Progress and Policy* (Stanford: Stanford University Press, 1957), 157-9; B. C. Swerling, *International Control of Sugar, 1918-41*, (Stanford: Stanford University Press, 1949), 42 ff.; J. E. Dalton, *Sugar: A Case Study of Government Control* (New York: Macmillan, 1937), 52-6, 67-8, 188-264; Wallich, *Monetary Problems of an Export Economy: The Cuban Experience 1914-1947*, 226 ff.; and Yates, *Commodity Control: A Study of Primary Products*, 58-9.

36. See LN, *Statistical Yearbook, 1936/7*, 72-3, 80-1; and *idem, World Production and Prices, 1925-1934*, 118.

37. Eggs were one of the few Class B goods whose quantity exported declined substantially. See P. Lamartine Yates, *Forty Years of Foreign Trade* (London: George Allen & Unwin, 1959), 77-8, 83.

38. See IIA, *International Yearbook of Agricultural Statistics*, various years, and LN, *International Trade Statistics*, various years. Dried fish (cod, etc.), split or salted, exported from Norway, is not included in the estimate of fish exports in the text. In 1929 the four exporters of frozen and chilled meat listed in the text accounted for well over nine-tenths of total exports of such meat from Latin America and Oceania. (LN, *Review of World Trade*, 1934, 53.)

In the United Kingdom, one of the foremost importers of meat and dairy products, fairly rigid money wages, unemployment compensation, and reduction of saving helped to maintain consumption in the downswing, and the quantity of food imports increased. Between 1928-9 and 1931-2 net imports of bacon increased in quantity by 42.2 per cent. See A. E. Kahn, *Great Britain in the World Economy* (London: Sir Isaac Pitman and Sons, 1946), 160; EMB, *Dairy Produce Supplies in 1932 (Including Poultry and Pig Products)*, Publication No. 66 (London: HMSO, June 1933), 70; and Stone, *The Measurement of Consumers' Expenditure and Behaviour in the United Kingdom 1920-1938*, Vol. I, Part I. It may be noted that after 1929 the quantity of bacon exported from the Irish Free State decreased. On the other hand, the quantity of Irish pig exports increased between 1928-9 and 1931-2 by 25.2 per cent. For related data and some of the factors accounting for this shift in Irish exports see EMB, *Dairy Produce Supplies in 1932 (Including Poultry and Pig Products)*, 68-70, 86-87; and *idem, Dairy Produce Supplies in 1931*, Publication No. 52 (London: HMSO, June 1932), 75, 82.

39. See D. W. Rodriguez, *Bananas; An Outline of the Economic History of Production and Trade with Special Reference to Jamaica*, Jamaica Department of Agriculture, Commodity Bulletin No. 1 (Kingston: The Government Printer, 1955), 15, 18-19, 29, 51 ff., and Tables II, V. Between 1928-9 and 1931-2 the quantity of bananas imported by European countries such as the United Kingdom, Denmark, France, Germany, and Norway increased considerably —in the case of the United Kingdom by as much as 19.3 per cent. On the other hand, owing partly to the heavy decline in incomes, United States banana imports (accounting in the period examined for the great bulk of the country's fruit imports) declined in quantity by

18.6 per cent. In the late 1920's the United States accounted for more than half the world imports of bananas. See data in EMB, *Fruit Supplies in 1932*, Publication No. 65 (London, HMSO, June 1933), 20, 124-34; and USTC, *The Foreign Trade of Latin America*, Part III, 8-13.

40. See LN, *Statistical Yearbook, 1936/7*, 112, and *idem, International Trade Statistics*, various years.

41. IIA, *International Yearbook of Agricultural Statistics*, various years, and *supra*, chap. 3, n. 39 and references; also EMB, *Canned and Dried Fruit Supplies in 1932*, Publication No. 69 (London: HMSO, June 1933), 13, 42.

42. The estimates of changes in the prices of meat and dairy products are based on data quoted in EMB, *Dairy Produce Supplies in 1932 (Including Poultry and Pig Products)*, 122-4; *idem, Wool Survey: A Summary of Production and Trade in the Empire and Foreign Countries*, Publication No. 57 (London, HMSO, July 1932), 162; LN, *Statistical Yearbook, 1936/7*, 72, 73, 112; *idem, Review of World Trade, 1935*, 13; and IIA, *International Yearbook of Agricultural Statistics, 1932/3*, 633-50. See also Yates, *Forty Years of Foreign Trade*, 68, 77-8, 83. The estimates of changes in the prices of fruits are based on data quoted in EMB, *Fruit Supplies in 1932*, 22, and *idem, Canned and Dried Fruit Supplies in 1932*, 92.

43. See also the *Economist, Commercial History and Review of 1930*, 112 (February 14, 1931), 23; *The Economist, Commercial History and Review of 1931*, 114 (February 13, 1932), 23, 30; and LN, *World Production and Prices, 1925-1933*, 103.

44. Statistics relating to the years 1925 to 1935 show an uninterrupted yearly increase in the world output of butter. The upward trend was shared by almost every important producing country for which data are available, specifically by Australia, Canada, Denmark, Finland, Germany, Latvia, New Zealand, Sweden, Switzerland, the Union of South Africa, and the United States. LN, *Statistical Yearbook 1935/6*, 81, and *1936/37*, 72. See also Wright, "Butter as a World Staple," *Index*, 10 (1935), 261; EMB, *Dairy Produce Supplies in 1932 (Including Poultry and Pig Products)*, 18, 94, 102. See also R. Stone, "The Demand for Food in the United Kingdom Before the War," *Metroeconomica*, 3 (1951), 20-1, 26; and *idem, The Measurement of Consumers' Expenditure and Behaviour in the United Kingdom 1920-1938*, I, 95, 324, 328, 334. In addition to the increase in world output of butter, in the downswing important exporting countries such as Denmark and New Zealand engaged in competitive exchange depreciation. See C. P. Kindleberger, "Competitive Currency Depreciation between Denmark and New Zealand," *Harvard Business Review*, 12 (1933/4), 416-26. On the demand side, some available estimates suggest that in certain advanced countries the income and price elasticities of demand for butter, and cheese, were lower than those for many other Class B goods. The decline in the prices of butter and cheese tended to be greater. See Stone, *Measurement of Consumers' Expenditure and Behaviour in the United Kingdom 1920-1938*, I, 51, 53, 67-8, 95-6, 120-1, 134, 136, 174, 313 ff.; and Prais and Houthakker, *The Analysis of Family Budgets*, 106. See, however, "An International Survey of Recent Family Living Studies: II," *International Labour Review*, 39 (1939), 836-40.

45. It was indicated earlier that while the world output of pork and mutton increased, that of beef declined. (*supra*, 28) Similarly, while the quantity of world exports of bacon and mutton increased, that of beef declined. See Yates, *Forty Years of Foreign Trade*, 78; also, UN, Secretariat, Department of Economic Affairs, *World Economic Survey 1958* (New York, 1959), 45. For an explanation of these differences see W. C. Mitchell, *What Happens during Business Cycles* (New York: National Bureau of Economic Research, 1951), xii, xiv, 33, 39, 62.

46. See, e.g., p. 98.

47. See EMB, *Dairy Produce Supplies in 1931*, 99-100; *idem, Dairy Produce Supplies in 1932 (Including Poultry and Pig Products)*, 105, 111-12; and S. Taussig, "Live Stock Production and Trade in Live Stock Products as Affected by the World Economic Crisis," *International Review of Agriculture*, 25 (1934), 260, 262-3.

48. See F. Benham, *Great Britain under Protection* (New York: The Macmillan Company, 1941), 33-4, 53; E. B. McGuire, *The British Tariff System* (London: Methuen & Co., 1939), 244; and the *Economist, Commercial History and Review of 1932*, 116 (February 18, 1933), 29-30.

49. It is interesting to note that often differences between the declines in quantity exported and in price largely offset each other as to their effects on export values. Thus, between 1928-9 and 1931-2 the gold price of Dutch cheese decreased by 37.6 per cent, while that of New Zealand cheese declined by 47.5 per cent. In the same period the quantity of Dutch cheese exports declined by 13.3 per cent, while that of New Zealand's cheese exports increased by 2.4 per cent. Again, between 1927/8-8/9 and 1930/1-1/2 the gold price of Italian olive oil decreased by 39.4 per cent, while that of Spanish oil declined by 49.0 per cent. Between 1928-9 and 1931-2 the quantity of Italian oil exports declined by 25.2 per cent,

while that of Spanish oil exports decreased only by 4.7 per cent. (Data from EMB, *Dairy Produce Supplies in 1932 (Including Poultry and Pig Products)*, 123; LN, *Statistical Yearbook 1936/7*, 73, 112; *idem, The Agricultural Crisis*, II, 51; and *idem, International Trade Statistics*, various years.)

50.   LN, *International Trade Statistics*, various years. See also USTC, *The Foreign Trade of Latin America*, Part III, 118 ff.

51.   LN, *World Production and Prices, 1925-1934*, 118-19; also IIA, *International Yearbook of Agricultural Statistics*, various years.

In India, which had the virtual monopoly of jute production, "a heavy fall in prices [of jute] during 1930 resulted in very reduced sowings in 1931, and a corresponding increase of area under rice." Between 1930 and 1931 the former area was reduced by 660 thousand hectares, and the latter was increased by 920 thousands. While the low output of jute "in 1931 is mainly due to the reduced acreage, severe flooding of the riparian areas in Bengal also caused considerable damage to the standing crop." (Imperial Economic Committee, *Industrial Fibres* (London: HMSO, 1936), 72-3; LN, *Statistical Yearbook*, various years; US Bureau of Foreign and Domestic Commerce, *Commerce Yearbook 1931*, II, 521-2; and *1932*, II, 524; *The Economist, Commercial History and Review of 1930*, 112 (February 14, 1931), 29; and UNECAFE, *Economic Survey of Asia and the Far East 1957* (Bangkok, 1958), 149.) Part of the trouble of the jute industry in the depression was due to over-expansion of jute production in the nineteen-twenties and the expansion of bulk handling of grain. See D. H. Buchanan, *The Development of Capitalistic Enterprise in India* (New York: The Macmillan Company, 1934), 253; H. Venkatasubbiah, *The Structural Basis of Indian Economy* (London: George Allen & Unwin Ltd., 1940), 132-3, 138-40; *The Economist, Commercial History and Review of 1932*, 116 (February 18, 1933), 28; and L. Dudley Stamp, *Asia: A Regional and Economic Geography* (5th ed.; New York: E. P. Dutton & Co., 1944), 223.

52.   In 1928-9 Ceylon, the Dutch East Indies and Malaya accounted for over nine-tenths of the world rubber output. See IIA, *International Yearbook of Agricultural Statistics*, various years; LN, *Statistical Yearbook, 1936/7* and *idem, Review of World Trade, 1934*, 57.

53.   The quantity of India's exports of coir manufactures (of which four-fifths were yarns) declined by 16.6 per cent. EMB, *Survey of Oilseeds and Vegetable Oils*, II, 13, 114.

For the heavy decline of the world trade in containers and packing material see also chap. 5, III.

54.   LN, *Statistical Yearbook*, various years; IIA, *International Yearbook of Agricultural Statistics, 1932-3*, 624-31; and estimates based on comparisons of the values and quantities of exports of primary-exporting countries given in LN, *International Trade Statistics*, various years. See also EMB, *Wool Survey: A Summary of Production and Trade in the Empire and Foreign Countries*, Publication No. 57 (London: HMSO, July 1932), 156, 162, 218-9; LN, *Review of World Production, 1925-1931*, 94; *idem, World Production and Prices, 1925-1932*, 93; *idem, World Economic Survey, 1933-34*, 142; and USTC, *The Foreign Trade of Latin America*, Part III, 98-9.

55.   For the low elasticity of supply. for instance. of wool see EMB, *Wool Survey: A Summary of Production and Trade in the Empire and Foreign Countries*, 163-4, 74-91. For hides see Mitchell, *What Happens during Business Cycles*, 124, and LN, *Review of World Production, 1925-1931*, 95; also V. N. Murti and V. K. Sastri, "Elasticities of Demand for Certain Indian Imports and Exports." *Sankhyā: The Indian Journal of Statistics*, 11 (1951), 324-6. Rubber prices were depressed also by the increase in productive capacity which originated in the prosperous midnineteen-twenties and became effective in the early nineteen-thirties. See K. E. Knorr. *World Rubber and Its Regulation* (Stanford: Food Research Institute, Stanford University, 1945), 68, 103.

56.   For factors explaining differences in the changes in rubber output in the three countries see P. T. Bauer, *The Rubber Industry: A Study in Competition and Monopoly* (Cambridge: Harvard University Press. 1948), chap. 4.

57.   India's cotton output in 1931/2 was 31.6 per cent lower than in 1927/8-8/9. The acreage under cotton was only 7.4 per cent smaller in 1931/2, but the yield per hectare was low. (LN, *Statistical Yearbook*, various years.) Between 1928-9 and 1931-2 the quantity of raw cotton imported by India increased by 226.7 per cent. In 1928-9 raw cotton had represented 19.6 per cent of India's exports, and 1.3 per cent of her imports.

In spite of the smaller quantity of China's cotton exports and the increase in her cotton output between 1927/8-8/9 and 1930/1-1/2, the quantity of her raw cotton imports increased between 1928-9 and 1931-2 by 88.8 per cent. In 1928-9 raw cotton had represented 3.2 per cent of China's exports and 6.5 per cent of her imports. (LN, *Statistical Yearbook*, and *International Trade Statistics*, various years.)

58.   For the data on mineral output see LN, *World Production and Prices, 1925-1934*, 119, and *idem, Statistical Yearbook, 1936/7*, 138-45, 152.

124   NOTES, P. 33

The following remarks supplement the information about the changes in the quantity of exports of various minerals, given in Table XI:

Copper. The exports of copper ("bars, ingots, plate, wire, etc.") from the United States, which in 1928-9 represented 3.3 per cent of the value of her exports, declined in quantity by 59.6 per cent.

Lead. The quantity of lead exports of Australia, Canada, India, and Spain either increased, or declined considerably less than that of Mexico. For Australia and Canada the explanation lies largely in the development of new ore bodies, significant technological gains in production, the preferential position in the British market, and the depreciation of their currencies, particularly of Australia. Factors similar to the last two mentioned largely explain the relatively modest decline in the quantity of India's lead exports. Spain's lead exports benefited from government assistance to the industry, as well as from the favourable treatment 'of these exports by France and Germany, due chiefly to the fact that the capital invested in the industry was largely French and German. For more details on these factors, and those explaining the generally smaller decline in the quantity of lead, than of several other mineral, exports see A. Skelton, "Lead," in W. Y. Elliott *et al., International Control in the Non-Ferrous Metals* (New York: Macmillan, 1937), 624-33, 649-51.

Silver. The smaller decline in the quantity of silver exports of such countries as Australia and Canada than of countries like Mexico or Peru is explained largely by factors of the kind noted in the previous paragraph.

Zinc. Canada and, especially, Australia benefited from the depreciation of their currencies vis-a-vis the currencies of the European gold bloc countries and Mexico. Also, between 1927 and 1931 Australia and, particularly, Canada experienced a very substantial expansion of low-cost zinc-smelting capacity. Consequently, even though in 1931/2-2/3 their plants (especially of Canada) operated well below capacity (partly on account of the membership of these countries in the International Zinc Cartel established in July 1931), they produced more zinc than in 1927/8-8/9. As indicated by the percentage changes in the quantities of exports from Australia, of zinc concentrates on the one hand and zinc (bars, blocks, slabs, ingots and cakes) on the other, there was a very considerable shift in relative importance from the former to the latter type of exports. A similar shift in relative importance, from exports of zinc ore to exports of zinc spelter, occurred in Canada. See CDBS, *Trade of Canada,* various years. See also Skelton, "Zinc," in Elliott *et al., International Control in the Non-Ferrous Metals,* 710-18, 743, 746, 761, and UN, Department of Economic and Social Affairs, *Non-Ferrous Metals in Under-Developed Countries* (New York, 1956), 51-3.

59.   See LN, *World Production and Prices, 1925-1932,* 94, 103; *idem, Statistical Yearbook,* various years; Elliott *et al., International Control in the Non-Ferrous Metals,* 321, 507-8, 652,3, 751-2; Peru, Ministerio de Fomento, *Boletin del Cuerpo de Ingenieros de Minas del Perú,* No. 122 (*La Industria Minera en el Perú 1937,* por Jorge Hohagen) (Lima, 1938); UNECLA, *Economic Survey of Latin America, 1949* (New York, 1951), 386; and O. W. Main, *The Canadian Nickel Industry: A Study in Market Control and Public Policy* (Toronto: University of Toronto Press, 1955). The price of synthetic nitrate of soda decreased only by 8.4 per cent.

60.   The relatively small number of producers of some minerals facilitated control of their supply, for instance, through national or international agreements. Elliott *et al., International Control in the Non-Ferrous Metals,* chap. vii, viii, xii; Yates, *Commodity Control: A Study of Primary Products,* 146 ff; UN, Department of Economic and Social Affairs, *Non-Ferrous Metals in Under-Developed Countries,* chap. 3 and references; K. E. Knorr, *Tin under Control,* (Stanford: Food Research Institute, Stanford University, 1945), chap. v-viii; and LN, *World Economic Survey, 1932-33,* 61.

61.   With respect to nitrate of soda, the large decline in the quantity exported from Chile to a large extent reflects the growth of production of synthetic nitrates from World War I on. See P. T. Ellsworth, *Chile: An Economy in Transition* (New York: The Macmillan Company, 1945), 139, and C. Lewis, *America's Stake in International Investments* (Washington: The Brookings Institution, 1938), 260-1. See, however, also J. J. Polak, *An International Economic System* (London: George Allen & Unwin, 1954), 149.

62.   In 1928-9 wood accounted for the following percentages of the value of exports of the countries indicated: Canada 7.4, Finland 50.0, Latvia 29.8, Lithuania 28.8, Nicaragua 11.6, Norway 19.5, Paraguay 9.7, Poland, 18.4, Roumania 16.1, and Yugoslavia 18.0. Timber exports represented 14.7 per cent of the value of Sweden's 1928-9 exports, and declined in quantity between 1928-9 and 1931-2 by 42.8 per cent.

In 1928-9 cork represented 15.9 and 7.4 of the value of exports of Portugal and Spain respectively. These two countries produced the great bulk of the world's output of cork. (LN, *The Agricultural Crisis,* II, 52, and *idem, International Trade Statistics.*)

63.   Estimates based on comparisons of the values and quantities of exports of primary-exporting countries given in LN, *International Trade Statistics,* various years. The price of

raw cork exported from Portugal declined by 59 per cent, of cork sheets by 9 per cent, and of cork stoppers by 19 per cent.

64. For estimates of factor proportions relating to the United States see W. Leontief, "Factor Proportions and the Structure of American Trade: Further Theoretical and Empirical Analysis," *Review of Economics and Statistics*, 38 (1956), 403-4.

Concerning the relatively small decline in the price of wood in the period 1928-9 to 1931-2, it may be noted also that owing, among other factors, to the expansion of European timber production and to the reappearance of Russian wood exports in 1927, timber prices started declining as early as 1928. They showed serious weakness in the middle of 1929, when Central European building activity slackened and supplies from Russia increased suddenly. (LN, *World Production and Prices, 1925-1932*, 71, and *1925-1933*, 36.)

65. The nine countries exporting unrefined mineral oil were the Dutch East Indies, Persia, Peru, Roumania, the U.S.S.R., the United States, Colombia, Mexico, and Venezuela. The seven countries exporting petrol were the first six in the previous list and British Malaya. (LN, *World Production and Prices, 1925-1934*, 119; *idem*, Review of World Trade, 58; and *idem*, *International Trade Statistics*, various years.)

66. During the downswing after 1929 the prices of crude oil and petroleum products fluctuated greatly over short periods. Further, the changes in export prices varied with the distance of the producing countries from the consuming areas. The estimates in the text are based on comparisons of values and quantities of exports given in LN, *International Trade Statistics*, various years. See also data in *idem, Statistical Yearbook, 1936/7*, 126; *idem, Review of World Trade, 1931*, 9, *1932*, 9, *1933*, 45, *1935*, 13; *idem*, World Economic Survey, *1933-34*, 142; Bain, *The Economics of the Pacific Coast Petroleum Industry*, Part II, 168-71; Cassady, *Price Making and Price Behavior in the Petroleum Industry*, 137; *The Economist, Commercial History and Review of 1933*, 118 (February 17, 1934), 73; UNECLA, *Economic Survey of Latin America, 1949*, 457.

67. Of the forty-nine countries considered, petroleum exports represented more than 5 per cent of the value of exports in 1928-9 in the nine countries listed in the text.

68. It may be noted also that Poland's coal output was exceptionally large in the years 1928 and, especially, 1929. Except for these two years, in no year of the period 1922 to 1936 did output exceed 40 million metric tons. (LN, *Statistical Yearbook*, various years.)

In all the estimates in the text the coal exports of Poland and the Netherlands include, besides coal, a very small volume of coke and briquettes. For the changes in prices see LN, *Statistical Yearbook 1936/7*, 127. See also *idem*, Review of World Trade, *1933*, 40, 42, 44-46, and *idem*, World Economic Survey, *1932-33*, 51, and *1933-34*, 142.

69. In 1928-9 wood pulp represented 3.6, 4.7, 17.4, and 13.7 per cent of the value of exports of Canada, Estonia, Finland, and Norway, respectively.

Between 1928-9 and 1931-2 the quantity of pulp exported from Czechoslovakia, Estonia, Finland, and Germany increased, and the quantity exported from Norway and Sweden declined only by 8.9 and 9.4 per cent, respectively. But Canada's pulp exports were affected adversely from 1927/8 on by non-cyclical factors, and between 1927/8-8/9 and 1931/2-2/3 the quantity exported declined by as much as 41.1 per cent.

In 1928-9 paper represented 10.5, 5.8, 6.5, and 12.8 per cent of the value of exports of Canada, Estonia, Finland, and Norway, respectively.

For the changes in production of wood pulp and paper see LN, *Statistical Yearbook, 1936/7*, 121-2, and *idem, World Production and Prices, 1925-1934*, 77, 143.

70. LN, *Statistical Yearbook, 1936/7*, 121, and *idem*, Review of World Trade, *1934*, 14. See, however, E. Marcus, *Canada and the International Business Cycle 1927-1939* (New York: Bookman Associates, 1954), 12, 35, 41-2.

71. The short-run income elasticity of demand for pulp and paper was lower also than the elasticity for agricultural raw materials. The difference between the income elasticities of demand for the respective imports was in some cases enhanced by the greater possibility of substitution of domestic production for imports, e.g., of hides as compared to pulp and paper. However, the quantity of exports of several agricultural raw materials was maintained fairly well in the depression owing to the limited elasticity of supply of such goods.

72. See also the discussion of the decline in paper imports of the countries studied in chap. 5, III.

73. Compare also the changes in gold price and quantum of exports of a number of the countries considered, shown in LN, *Review of World Trade, 1935*, pp. 72 ff. See also F. C. Mills, *Price-Quantity Interactions in Business Cycles* (New York: National Bureau of Economic Research, 1946), 106-8; also 78-9.

74. Of course, as suggested by the data and Table XI (pp. 31-3), the relation between the declines in price and quantity exported of each mineral varied substantially among the various exporting countries.

75. The reader may be interested in some estimates of instability of prices and values of certain primary exports in the period 1950-8, in J. D. Coppock, *International Economic Instability: The Experience After World War II* (New York: McGraw-Hill, 1962), 42-7.

76. See, for example, pp. 27, 29-30, and chap. 3, n. 71.

CHAPTER FOUR

1. Spain also experienced a relatively heavy decline in exports of olive oil and olives, Class B goods, which in 1928-9 accounted for 11.0 per cent of her total exports. The output of olive products is very variable. (chap. 3, n. 16) In 1927/8 and 1929/30 Spain produced huge olive crops and between 1927/8-8/9 and 1930/1-1/2 the prices of her olive products declined very considerably. (See LN, *Statistical Yearbook, 1936/7*, 112, and chap. 3, n. 49.) Between 1928-9 and 1931-2 Spain's exports of olive oil and olives declined by 53.9 and 65.0 per cent, respectively, compared to the decrease of 59.8 per cent in her total exports.

In 1928-9 petroleum products, listed in Class D, represented about one-third of Peru's exports. As indicated in chap. 3, II, unlike the oil exports of almost every other oil-exporting country among the forty-nine considered, the quantity of oil exported from Peru declined substantially between 1928-9 and 1931-2. As a consequence, the relative decline in value of her oil exports was about as great as that of her total exports.

2. See chap. 1, n. 3. In 1928-9 Mexico's exports of gold were negligible. In 1931-2 they amounted to over $22 million and represented about one-sixth of all her exports.

In Uruguay (a country not included in our study) Class A and C goods accounted, in 1928-9, for roughly three-fifths of all exports. Between 1928-9 and 1931-2 her total exports declined by 63.8 per cent. See LN, *The Agricultural Crisis*, I, 298-9, and *idem, International Trade Statistics*.

3. With respect to Ecuador it may be noted also that 8.0 per cent of her 1928-9 exports consisted of "gold concentrates and dust," and another 14.8 per cent of petroleum products. Between 1928-9 and 1931-2 the former exports declined only by 16.1 per cent, and the latter increased by 6.5 per cent.

4. The "flood . . . covered an area of about eighty-seven million mow" (or over fifteen million acres) "in the Yangtze and Hwai river valleys between Hankow and the sea. . . ." (China, Ministry of Industries, Committee for the Study of Silver Values and Commodity Prices, *Silver and Prices in China* (Shanghai: Commercial Press, 1935), 15, 27.) The quantity of China's wheat, flour, and rice imports increased between 1928-9 and 1931-2 by 70.5 per cent, while in 1934-5 it was only 7.9 per cent higher than in 1928-9. In 1931-2 China imported 1,150 thousand metric tons of wheat, against only 210 thousand in 1928-9; in 1934, 1935 and 1936 the volume of wheat imports declined to only 460, 520, and 120 thousand tons, respectively. See also GBDOT, Report by A. H. George *et al., Trade and Economic Conditions in China, 1933-1935* (London: HMSO, 1935), 7.

5. Australia's large wheat crops in the years 1930/1 to 1932/3 were due to expansion of wheat acreage (fostered by governmental assistance and encouragement to producers) and high yields due to good seasons. See W. R. Maclaurin, *Economic Planning in Australia, 1929-1936* (London: P. S. King & Son, 1937), 192-6, 202-9, 271, and Stanford University, Food Research Institute, *Wheat Studies*, IX, Oct. 1932-Sept. 1933, 266, and XII, Sept. 1935-June 1936, 171, 173, 395.

6. Gold exports represented 2.0 per cent of Australia's total exports in 1927/8-8/9, and increased from $13.9 million in that period to $47.0 million in 1931/2-2/3.

7. See p. 27 and Wickizer, *The World Coffee Economy, with Special Reference to Control Schemes*, chap. v-xi.

8. The quantity of Nicaragua's coffee exports in 1931 was slightly higher than in 1928-9. But in 1932 it was only about half as large. Consequently, between 1928-9 and 1931-2 the quantity of her coffee exports declined by as much as 21.4 per cent. In the same period the coffee exports of all other countries in which coffee represented more than 3 per cent of exports in 1928-9 (except Haiti and Mexico), specifically of Brazil, Costa Rica, Colombia, the Dominican Republic, the Dutch East Indies, Ecuador, Guatemala, El Salvador, and Venezuela, either declined in quantity by less than 8 per cent, or increased.

9. In 1928-9, 20.3 and 2.5 per cent of Colombia's exports consisted of petroleum (a Class D good) and unmanufactured gold, respectively. Between 1928-9 and 1931-2 her petroleum exports declined by 39.9 per cent, and her gold exports increased by 40.6 per cent.

10. See the main factors in Timoshenko and Swerling, *The World's Sugar, Progress and Policy*, 18 ff., 200-5, 240-2, and Schultz, *The Theory and Measurement of Demand*, 229 ff. The exports of sugar of the Dominican Republic declined from $16.1, $15.3, $17.3, and $18.5 million in 1925, 1926, 1927, and 1928, respectively, to $13.2 million in 1929, and $7.7 and $7.4 million in 1931 and 1932.

The Dominican Republic did not participate in the ("Chadbourne") International Sugar Agreement of May 9, 1931, which restricted production and exports. See Timoshenko and Swerling, *The World's Sugar, Progress and Policy*, 23, 243, and Swerling, *International Control of Sugar, 1918-41*, chap. VI.

11. It may be noted also that the quantity of Paraguay's tobacco exports was exceptionally low in 1930, and exceptionally high in 1931. One reason for the decline in quantity of her exports of quebracho extract was the armed conflict between Paraguay and Bolivia over the quebracho-producing region of Northern Chaco. See *Encyclopaedia Britannica*, 5 (1943), 184-5. For data on Paraguay's production and exports of these products see LN, *Statistical Yearbook*, various years, *idem, International Trade Statistics*, various years; and IIA, *International Yearbook of Agricultural Statistics*, various years. For the change in the price of quebracho extract exported from Argentina and Paraguay see also USTC, *The Foreign Trade of Latin America*, Part. II, vol. 1, 21, 199-200.

12. The share of sugar in the Philippines' exports increased to 48.1, 62.7, and 60.8 per cent in 1931, 1932 and 1933, respectively. See USTC, *United States-Philippine Tariff and Trade Relations*, Report No. 18, Second Series, 7, 65; *idem, United States-Philippines Trade*, Report No. 118, Second Series, 52; and P. E. Abelarde, *American Tariff Policy Towards the Philippines 1898-1946* (New York: King's Crown Press, 1947), 148. In 1928-9 and 1931-2 the United States took 95.1 and practically 100 per cent of the quantity of Philippines sugar exports, respectively. The quantity exported to the United States increased from 632.8 thousand metric tons in 1928-9 to 884.8 thousand in 1931-2 (1,016.3 thousand in 1932). The share of the United States in the total exports of the Philippines increased from 74.6 per cent in 1928 and 75.7 in 1929, to 86.7 per cent in 1932. See also GBDOT, report by T. J. Harrington, *Economic Conditions in the Philippine Islands, 1933-34* (London: HMSO, 1935), 6 ff.; P. E. Abelarde, *American Tariff Policy Towards the Philippines 1898-1946*, 123, 127-8, 133-4, 202; and S. Jenkins, *American Economic Policy Toward the Philippines* (Stanford: Stanford University Press, 1954), 32 ff.

The rapid expansion of gold mining and exports from 1930 on was another factor that helped to moderate the decline in the exports of the Philippines. Her exports of gold and silver increased from $2.6 million, or 1.6 per cent of her total exports in 1928-9, to $4.4 million, or 4.2 per cent of total exports in 1931-2. See USTC, *United States-Philippine Trade*, Report No. 118, Second Series, 9, 43, 122-5.

13. The changes in the average decline in exports of the forty-nine countries between the three periods may be summarized as follows:

	Number of countries
Increase between the 1st and 2nd, and the 2nd and 3rd, period	10
Larger increase between the 1st and 2nd period, than decrease between the 2nd and 3rd period	17
Smaller increase between the 1st and 2nd period, than decrease between the 2nd and 3rd period	8
Decrease between the 1st and 2nd, and the 2nd and 3rd, period	14
Total	49

The second group, of seventeen countries, includes Columbia and Venezuela; each of these countries had the same average decline in exports in the second and third period.

See also Ilse Mintz, *American Exports During Business Cycles, 1879-1958*, NBER, Occasional Paper 76 (New York, 1961), 53-7, 83-5.

14. In the first period, 1928-9 to 1930-1, the countries listed in Group One, except Spain, experienced a decline in exports exceeding 32 per cent; the exports of the countries in Group Two, except Australia, the Dominican Republic, New Zealand, and Nicaragua, declined by less than 32 per cent. In the second period, 1928-9 to 1931-2, as indicated, the countries in Group One, with the slight exception of Mexico, experienced a decline in exports exceeding 54 per cent; the exports of all countries in Group Two declined by less than 54 per cent. In the third period, 1928-9 to 1932-3, the countries in Group One, except Haiti, experienced a decline in exports exceeding 62 per cent; the exports of the countries in Group Two, except the Dominican Republic, Estonia, Guatemala, the Irish Free State, Latvia, and Nicaragua, declined by less than 62 per cent.

15. We may consider the ten (fifteen) countries with the smallest, and the ten (fifteen) countries with the largest percentage decline in exports in the first period, 1928-9 to 1930-1. The percentage decline in exports of the former countries in the third period exceeded the decline in the first period by an average of 39.2 (36.7) percentage points. In the latter countries the excess was only 22.6 (23.5) percentage points. The difference between these two

changes is 16.6 (13.2) percentage points; it was 7.6 (6.1) percentage points between the first and second period, and 9.0 (7.1) between the second and third period.

16.   The data in the previous note and the changes in differences between decile values shown in the text indicate that the decrease of the differences between the percentage declines in exports of the various countries was somewhat greater between the second and third period than between the first and second. On the other hand, as indicated by the following differences between various decile values of the average yearly percentage decline in exports of the forty-nine countries, the decrease of the differences between the yearly declines in exports of the various countries was greater between the first and second period:

	1st to 9th decile	2nd to 8th decile	3rd to 7th decile	4th to 6th decile
1928-9 to 1930-1	17.1	12.2	8.0	5.1
1928-9 to 1931-2	10.3	7.2	5.1	2.7
1928-9 to 1932-3	6.9	4.3	3.0	1.2

17.   See also H. K. Zassenhaus, "Direct Effects of a United States Recession on Imports: Expectations and Events," *Review of Economics and Statistics*, 37 (1955), 241, 246.

18.   For the changes in quantities of exports and prices see, for instance, LN, *World Production and Prices, 1925-1933*, 36-7, and *1925-1934*, p. 76. The terms of trade of several countries exporting the raw materials indicated in the text improved in 1933; for instance the terms of trade of the Dutch East Indies recovered to the 1930 level. LN, *World Economic Survey, 1933-34*, 150-1, 195.

In a few cases the changes over the three periods compared in the relative declines of quantities or prices of various exports were so significant as substantially to change the ranking of a country with respect to the percentage decline in exports. For instance, in 1928-9 raw cotton represented 80.2 per cent of Egypt's exports. While in the period 1928-9 to 1930-1 only six of the other forty-eight countries had a heavier decline in total exports, in the period 1928-9 to 1932-3 the percentage decline in Egypt's exports was exceeded by that of twenty countries.

In a few cases the ranking of a country by percentage decline in exports changed considerably owing to special conditions relating to the exports of that country, rather than to the type of goods exported. Thus, in the period 1928-9 to 1930-1 only five of the countries considered had a smaller percentage decline in exports than that of the Irish Free State. But, owing largely to the "economic war" with Great Britain, in the period 1928-9 to 1932-3, as many as thirty-one other countries had a smaller decline in exports.

19.   See p. 40.

20.   RIIA, *The Problem of International Investment* (London: Oxford University Press, 1937), 260; italics supplied.

21.   RIIA, *The Problem of International Investment*, 253-4, 277-80.

22.   See also M. Michaely, *Concentration in International Trade* (Amsterdam: North-Holland Publishing Company, 1962), 70 ff.

CHAPTER FIVE

1.   The commodities included in our eight classes accounted as a rule for about 80-90 per cent of the 1928-9 imports of each country, and in no case for less than 75 per cent.

2.   Data for estimating the changes in the various classes of imports of Costa Rica and Turkey are not readily available. Appropriate data are lacking also for the following countries in the years indicated: Honduras in 1927/8 and 1933/4, Mexico and Panama in 1932 and 1933, and Nicaragua in 1933. Throughout this chapter we use as a base period for Honduras the year 1928/9 alone; and in some parts of our discussion of the changes between 1928-9 and 1931-2 it seems permissible to include Mexico and Panama by comparing, for these two countries, 1928-9 with 1931 alone.

As is indicated later, for some other countries data are not available for some classes of imports.

Probably, some articles which might have been included in one or another of the eight classes of imports are hidden, in the primary statistics, in such residual classes as "other articles" or "miscellaneous." Accordingly, our estimates of the percentage declines in the various classes of imports are less accurate than our practice of presenting the relevant percentages to the first decimal might suggest.

3.   As indicated, Table XII shows the fourth smallest percentage decline of imports of capital goods. The sixth smallest decline in the period 1928-9 to 1930-1 was that of the Irish Free State, which, at 9.3 per cent, exceeded the dividing point of 7 per cent.

4. Countries for which declines in more than three classes of imports cannot be estimated were excluded from the present discussion. Consequently, forty-five, forty-seven, and forty-three countries were considered in the three periods respectively. No data are available for estimating the percentage decline in the imports of hides in eleven, ten, and eleven of these countries in the three periods respectively, of containers in twenty-three, twenty-four, and twenty-one countries, of fuel in two, one, and two countries, and of paper in six, six, and five countries.

5. While the quantity of sugar imported by the United States declined between 1928-9 and 1931-2 by 29.8 per cent, the quantity imported by India decreased by 40.6 per cent.

6. See L. Juréen, "Long-Term Trends in Food Consumption: A Multi-Country Study," *Econometrica*, 24 (1956), 4-5, 8-9.

7. See LN, *World Production and Prices, 1925-1933*, 102, and *idem, Review of World Trade, 1935*, 13.

8. Norway's imports of all capital goods increased by 9.8 per cent between 1928-9 and 1930-1, and decreased by 36.3 per cent between 1928-9 and 1931-2, and by 64.9 per cent between 1928-9 and 1932-3. On the other hand, when ships are excluded, her imports of capital goods declined by 18.9, 42.5, and 54.0 per cent, in the three periods respectively.

9. For the large change of the terms of trade against the farmer, and the consequent heavy decline in imports of farm machinery in Argentina, for instance, see UNECLA, *Economic Survey of Latin America, 1949*, 122-3.

10. Capital goods ordered in the boom are imported in the early stages of the downswing at boom prices. Some goods may be ordered after the downturn in order to complete projects started in the boom. See also Mills, *Price-Quantity Interactions in Business Cycles*, 21-24.

In some of the countries considered, the production of substitutes for certain imported capital goods, for instance cement, increased in the longer period. See, e.g., UNECLA, *Economic Survey of Latin America, 1949*, 117, 218, 250, 358. and R. C. Simonsen, *Brazil's Industrial Evolution* (São Paulo: Escola Livre de Sociologia e Politica, 1939), 53.

11. In Argentina, imports of "spares for agricultural machinery" declined in the depression very much less than imports of agricultural machinery. See UNECLA, *Economic Survey of Latin America, 1949*, 122.

12. The available data, relating to a large number of the countries considered, indicate that the quantity of cotton imports (raw, semi-manufactured and manufactured) declined in the period 1928-9 to 1931-2 more than the quantity of tobacco imports.

13. Such composite items as "wool and manufactures of" or "other textiles" have been included in the latter subclass.

14. The thirty-four countries are: Argentina, Bolivia, Brazil, Bulgaria, Canada, Ceylon, Chile, China, Colombia, Cuba, the Dominican Republic, the Dutch East Indies. Egypt, Estonia, Finland, Greece, Guatemala, Hungary, India, Latvia. Lithuania, Mexico, the Netherlands, Nicaragua, Norway, Paraguay, Persia, Poland, Portugal, Roumania, El Salvador, Siam, Spain, and Venezuela. The seven countries in which the decline in imports of raw and semi-manufactured textiles exceeded the decline in imports of finished textiles are: Canada, Ceylon, Egypt, Estonia, the Netherlands, Norway, and Poland.

15. The eleven countries are: Bulgaria, China, Colombia, Greece, Hungary, India, Latvia. Poland, Finland, Guatemala, and Roumania. The quantity of imports of cotton yarns and threads declined relatively less (increased relatively more) than the quantity of imports of raw cotton in the last three countries. See also p. 31.

16. See A. C. Harberger, "A Structural Approach to the Problem of Import Demand," *American Economic Review*, 43 (May, 1953), 154-7, and P. J. Thomas, "India in the World Depression." *Economic Journal*, 45 (1935), 477, 479. See also H. Venkatasubbiah, *The Foreign Trade of India 1900-1940: A Statistical Analysis* (London: Oxford University Press, 1946), 50, 58, 70-1.

17. See also the statistics of Canada's imports of textiles in CDBS, *Trade of Canada, 1931*, 230 ff., and *1933*, 425 ff.

18. It may be noted also that Egypt's imports of "raw and semi-manufactured textiles" include only yarn and thread, and that the percentage decline in the value of these semi-manufactured imports (61.4 per cent) was only slightly greater than that of finished textiles (59.2 per cent).

19. The exceptions were Poland, Roumania, and Spain.

20. See, however, p. 50.

21. See LN, *World Production and Prices, 1925-1933*, 102, and *idem, Review of World Trade, 1935*, 13.

22. See also Mills, *Price-Quantity Interactions in Business Cycles*, 21-4.

23. The percentage of countries in which the decline in hide imports ranked first increased slightly between the first and second period and declined substantially between the

second and third period. However, the percentage in which it ranked first, second, or third declined throughout, especially between the first and second period.

24. In 1933, for instance, prices of hides declined very little compared to prices of important foodstuffs, such as wheat or rice. See LN, *World Production and Prices, 1925-1933*, 102.

25. It ranked first in as many countries as the decline in food imports. But there is a substantial difference between the percentages of countries in which the decline in the two classes of imports ranked first, second, or third.

26. E.g., Bolivia, Brazil, Canada, Chile, Cuba, Denmark, Hungary, British Malaya, the Netherlands, New Zealand, Norway, the Philippines, and Spain.

27. In some of these countries widespread underemployment and lack of library facilities made the daily newspaper indispensable.

28. See pp. 34-5. The available data, relating to many of the countries considered, indicate that, generally, the decline in quantity of paper imports was relatively moderate—comparable to that of tobacco or coal imports.

29. Bolivia, Bulgaria, Ceylon, Chile, Denmark, the Dominican Republic, the Dutch East Indies, Ecuador, Egypt, Estonia, Finland, Greece, Haiti, Honduras, India, the Irish Free State, Latvia, Lithuania, Mexico, the Netherlands, New Zealand, Nicaragua, Nigeria, Panama, Paraguay, Persia, Peru, the Philippines, Roumania, El Salvador, Siam, Spain, and Venezuela.

30. For some estimates of the decline between 1928-9 and 1931-2 in the consumption of fertilizers in some of the countries studied see IIA, *Annuaire International de Statistique Agricole 1931-32*, 720 ff., and *International Yearbook of Agricultural Statistics, 1934-35*, 830 ff.

31. Probably, some articles which might have been included in one or another of the eight classes of imports are hidden, in the primary statistics, in such classes as "other articles" or "miscellaneous." Accordingly, our estimates of the relative importance of each class of imports are less accurate than our practice of presenting the relevant percentages to the first decimal might suggest. In any event, it seems certain that a more complete classification would not materially affect our argument in the text. See also chap. 5, n. 1.

32. See also Michaely, *Concentration in International Trade*, 6-15.

33. See also USTC, *The Foreign Trade of Latin America*, Part II, vol. 1, 29, and P. R. Olson and C. A. Hickman, *Pan American Economics* (New York: John Wiley and Sons, 1943), 4.

34. In 1928-9 almost half of all (liquid, solid, and vegetable) fuel consumed in Argentina was imported. See UNECLA, *Economic Survey of Latin America, 1949*, 156.

CHAPTER SIX

1. Estimates have not been possible for Bulgaria, China, Estonia, Hungary, Latvia, Lithuania, Poland, and Roumania. The estimates for India exclude Pakistan.

The estimates of national incomes are found mainly in M. H. Watkins, *Estimate of World Income*, 1953 (Cambridge, Mass.: Massachussets Institute of Technology, mimeo, 1956); see also UN, Secretariat, Statistical Office, *Per Capita National Product of Fifty-five Countries: 1952-1954*, Statistical Papers, Series E, No. 4 (New York, 1957), 7-8. For the great majority of the countries considered the available estimates of national income, for 1953 or, in some cases, for the period studied, relate to net national income. Hence, both here and elsewhere in this study reference is made to this concept of national income. See, however, S. Kuznets, "Toward a Theory of Economic Growth," in R. Leckachman (ed.), *National Policy for Economic Welfare at Home and Abroad* (Garden City, N.Y.: Doubleday, 1955), 46-7.

The foreign trade data for 1953 are found in UN, Department of Economic and Social Affairs, Statistical Office, *Yearbook of International Trade Statistics, 1955*, 12-19. The area and population data are found in UN, Statistical Office, *Demographic Yearbook, 1955*, 99 ff., 116 ff., and *1954*, 99.

2. The thirty-two countries are: Argentina, Colombia, Egypt, Greece, Haiti, Nigeria, Panama, Paraguay, (in the following countries the ratio exceeded 20 per cent) Australia, Bolivia, Canada, Ceylon, Chile, Costa Rica, Cuba, Denmark, the Dominican Republic, Ecuador, Finland, Guatemala, Honduras, the Irish Free State, Malaya, the Netherlands, New Zealand, Nicaragua, Norway, Peru, the Philippines, El Salvador, Thailand (Siam), and Venezuela.

3. The nine countries are: Brazil, India, Indonesia (Dutch East Indies), Iran (Persia), Mexico, Portugal, Spain, Turkey, and Yugoslavia. In 1953 Iran's trade/income ratio was less than 9 per cent. It has been higher in more normal years.

4. In our estimates the huge area of Greenland has been excluded from Denmark's area. For Egypt only the inhabited and cultivated territory of about thirty-five thousand square kilometres has been considered.

The nine countries whose area exceeded 500 square kilometres were Argentina, Australia,

Colombia, Nigeria, Bolivia, Canada, Chile, Peru, and Venezuela. In the first four countries the trade/income ratio was lower than 20 per cent, barely exceeding 15 per cent in the first two. Large areas of Australia, Bolivia, Canada, Colombia, Peru and Venezuela are "unsettled or sparsely inhabited" and presumably rather unexplored; in effect, they are not a part of their economies. See *Canadian Oxford Atlas of the World* (2nd ed.; Toronto: Oxford University Press, 1957), Part II, vi-vii. Furthermore, the natural resources of some of these countries are not markedly diversified.

5. About the relation between a country's trade/income ratio and the size of its population and area, see also C. P. Kindleberger, *Foreign Trade and the National Economy* (New Haven: Yale University Press, 1962), 32-6; S. Kuznets, *Six Lectures on Economic Growth* (Glencoe, Illinois: Free Press, 1959), 91 ff.; *idem*, "Economic Growth of Small Nations," in E. A. G. Robinson (ed.), *Economic Consequences of the Size of Nations* (London: Macmillan, 1960), 18-21; K. W. Deutsch and A. Eckstein, "National Industrialization and the Declining Share of the International Economic Sector, 1890-1959," *World Politics*, 13 (1960/1), 289, 291; and K. W. Deutsch, C. I. Bliss, and A. Eckstein, "Population, Sovereignty and the Share of Foreign Trade," *Economic Development and Cultural Change*, 10 (1961/2), 353 ff. For an examination of the relation between the trade/income ratio and the size of countries measured by the gross national product, see J. Tinbergen, *Shaping the World Economy* (New York: Twentieth Century Fund, 1962), 59-66 and Appendix VI. See also S. Kuznets, "Quantitative Aspects of the Economic Growth of Nations. IX. Level and Structure of Foreign Trade: Comparisons for Recent Years," *Economic Development and Cultural Change*, 13 (1964/5), no. 1, Part II, 7 ff.

6. Economic and social conditions and the organization of labour in many of the countries considered were much less conducive to the defence of money-wage standards in the period studied than they have been since the Second World War.

7. In the great bulk of the countries studied, which were less developed economies, the trade/income ratio becomes substantially higher if we exclude the income of subsistence agriculture. In this sector of the economy changes in income relate chiefly to weather conditions —not to cyclical changes in foreign trade or in domestic factors affecting employment and income, with which we are concerned.

8. With reference to Siam for instance, see J. C. Ingram, *Economic Change in Thailand Since 1850* (Stanford: Stanford University Press, 1955), 206, 237, 242.

9. Given the points of impact, the effects of a disturbance are likely to be the more widespread the greater the magnitude of the disturbance. Usually compartmentalization is not complete. A large increase in prices, for instance, is more likely to break through the barriers of isolation—natural, institutional or economic—than a small increase.

10. The traditional concept of elasticity relates the proportional change in the dependent variable to a "one per cent" or "small" proportional change in the independent variable. See A. Marshall, *Principles of Economics* (8th ed.; New York: Macmillan, 1948), III. iv. 1, and n. 1. A concept of responsiveness is required which is the ratio of the proportional change in the dependent variable to a given proportional change *of any chosen magnitude* in the independent variable. This responsiveness will tend to vary with the proportional change in the independent variable per unit of time. See R. G. D. Allen, *Mathematical Economics* (2nd Ed.; London: Macmillan, 1960), 2, 6-7, 11.

11. The phenomenon described in the text is different from that with which lag theory has been concerned. This theory considers the variation in the adjustment of a person's consumption *with the length of the period* after a *given change* of income. The discussion in the text is concerned with the change in consumption in a *given period* after the change in income and the variation in the marginal saving/income and consumption/income ratios *with the rate of change in income* by which the new level of income was reached.

It will also be noticed that the discussion in the text is not concerned with whether the marginal saving/income ratio tends to be different at different *levels* of income.

12. The relationship described in the text tends to be attenuated by a reverse influence. due to the factor noted in chap. 6, n. 9: the more concentrated is the immediate impact of a disturbance of a given overall magnitude, the greater will be the size of the immediate impact at each point affected; hence, the tendency for the effects to spill over into other sectors will be the greater, and, therefore, the tendency described in the text (for the overall effects of a concentrated disturbance to be small because of the reason described in the previous paragraph of the text) will weaken somewhat.

13. The statement in the text is particularly true if the sector of subsistence agriculture is neglected and only the exchange sectors of the economy are taken into consideration.

14. In a few underdeveloped economics which exported mainly minerals or plantation crops the impact of a change in exports was less widespread: a considerable part of the impact was borne, or enjoyed, by the domestic or foreign capital-owner.

15. For the tax structure of a large number of the countries studied see LN, Economic Intelligence Service, *Public Finance 1928-1935*, and *1928-1937* (Geneva, 1936-1938); see also R. Magill and C. Shoup, *The Cuban Fiscal System 1939* (1939), 3-5, 8, and G. B. Sherwell, *Mexico's Capacity to Pay* (Washington, 1929), 101.

A considerable part of the tax revenue in the less developed countries was raised through taxes on necessities consumed by the broad masses, for example, salt, alcohol, matches, or flour, Since these taxes were usually specific rather than *ad valorem*, and since also the income elasticity of demand for these goods was low, these taxes tended to cushion the decline of government revenue in the downswing. Formally, a land tax assessed at infrequent intervals should have similar effects. But in practice low prices were often accompanied by default on tax payments.

16. See, for instance, UNECLA, *A Study of Trade between Latin America and Europe*, 33.

Other current items of the balance of payments were of some significance in only a very few of the countries studied. The effects of changes in the downswing in these items and in the international flow of capital on the expenditures, incomes and commodity imports of particular groups of countries are considered in the next chapter. It should be remembered, however, that some of these changes, notably in the international flow of capital, were related to changes in foreign merchandise trade.

17. The difference between the second and eighth decile values of percentage decline in imports of the forty-nine countries was 18.3 percentage points, while in exports the corresponding difference was 21.7 points. The contrast is more striking when in-between deciles are considered: the differences between the third and seventh decile values were 8.8 and 15.2 points, for the declines in imports and exports respectively, and between the fourth and sixth deciles 4.0 and 8.0 points.

18. The median and mean values of the import/export declines of the forty-nine countries in the period 1928-9 to 1931-2 were 1.09 and 1.20 respectively. While the import/export decline was less than 1.00 in only sixteen countries and less than 0.90 in only three (about China, however, see pp. 90-1), it was as high as 1.20 or more in eighteen countries, and 1.40 or more in eleven.

19. The term "responsiveness of imports" also has no relation to Marshall's responsiveness which is tantamount to elasticity (*Principles of Economics* (8th ed.), III, iv, 1), or to the concept of responsiveness suggested earlier (chap. 6, n. 10).

20. In the diagrams we might have related the percentage decline in imports, rather than the responsiveness of imports, to the percentage decline in exports. (The vertical distance of each country from a 45 degree line drawn through the origin of such alternative diagrams would have been equal to the distance of the same country from the horizontal line of zero responsiveness in our diagrams.) However, later we examine also the relation of the responsiveness of total, or of given classes of, imports to some other economic variables. Therefore, for the sake of uniformity we treat throughout the responsiveness of imports as the dependent variable and the factors to which it might be related as the independent variable. Another advantage of our diagrams over the alternative indicated is that it is visually easier to compare the vertical distance of the various countries from a horizontal line of zero responsiveness than from a diagonal at which the percentage declines in imports and exports are equal.

21. In Diagram II thirty-six of the forty-nine countries lie between the parallel lines cc and $c'c'$. Two other countries (Brazil and Portugal) lie close to these lines. The vertical distance from these lines of four other countries (Colombia, Australia, China and Greece) is considerably greater. Finally, a constellation of six countries (Denmark, the Irish Free State, the Netherlands, Norway, Panama and the Philippines) and, especially, Lithuania lie much below line $c'c'$. The main factors accounting for the exceptionally high or low responsiveness of imports of the countries lying outside the lines cc and $c'c'$ are discussed in the next chapter.

For reasons which will become obvious in that chapter the problem of import responsiveness of some of the countries lying outside the lines cc and $c'c'$ differs in essence from that of the great bulk of the countries considered. Thus, the constellation of six countries indicated in the previous paragraph and Lithuania had significant invisible earnings or experienced conditions which in many ways were unique. If then we neglect these countries, we obtain for the remaining forty-two countries a coefficient of simple linear correlation of import responsiveness and percentage decline in exports of –0.822, and a regression coefficient of the former on the latter of –0.821. For thirty-eight countries (neglecting, in addition to the previous seven, also Australia, China, Colombia, and Greece) the coefficient of correlation is –0.868. And for the thirty-six countries lying between lines cc and $c'c'$ the coefficient of correlation is –0.897, and the regression coefficient of responsiveness on decline in exports is –0.812, which is the slope given to lines cc and $c'c'$.

22. See p. 11.

23. Owing to lack of data Costa Rica, Mexico, Panama, and Turkey are not included in Diagrams IV-VI.

24. An inverse variation of responsiveness of imports and percentage decline in exports (much stronger than that observed in the examination of total, or of individual classes of imports) could be obtained in the unlikely case in which the percentage decline in imports would vary among the countries more than the percentage decline in exports, but inversely with it.

25. The equalizing effect appeared strong for instance in the case of staple foodstuffs or textile fibres.

In a diagramatic presentation such as that of Diagrams I-VI the effect of a uniform decline in import price is to change the slope of the scatter plot towards –1.

26. It was indicated earlier that the imports of the various countries were much more diversified than their exports. (57) This observation is different from, though related to, the observation in the text.

27. The number of countries for which estimates were possible ranges for the various goods from twenty-two to twenty-eight.

28. The ratio $g/(g + a)$ might be called the marginal import/export ratio. However, we shall keep referring to it by the former term $g/(g + a)$.

29. The import/export decline is not affected by the argument in the text. I and E are a country's imports and exports in the base period, and m and x are the percentage declines in its imports and exports in the period considered. It is assumed in the text that I/E is the same for all countries, and that $I/E > g/(g + a) = Im/Ex = (I/E)(m/x)$. It follows that m/x is the same for all countries and smaller than unity; and, hence, that the responsiveness of imports $(m - x)$ will be smaller the greater the x.

30. If I/E is the same for all countries, and if $I/E < g/(g + a) = Im/Ex = (I/E (m/x)$, m/x is the same for all countries and exceeds unity; hence, the responsiveness of imports $(m - x)$ will be greater the greater the x.

31. If $g/(g + a)$, or $Im/Ex = (I/E) (m/x)$, and x are the same for all countries, the greater is the original relation (i.e. the smaller is the I/E) the greater will be the m/x or the $m - x$.

32. If $g/(g + a) = Im/Ex$ is the same in two countries, the country with the much lower I/E (i.e., the much higher original relation) may have a greater $m - x$ even though its x exceeds that of the other country. The tendency for this to occur is greater the greater the difference in I/E and the greater the Im/Ex or $g/(g + a)$ of the two countries, and if for both countries $I/E > g/(g + a) = Im/Ex$, so that $m/x < 1$, the smaller the difference in x between the two countries.

33. Of eighteen countries whose exports declined between 1928-9 and 1931-2 by more than 55 per cent, sixteen had a surplus in 1928-9; and of twenty-five countries whose exports declined by less than 52 per cent, nineteen had a deficit. See Tables I and III.

34. For instance, some countries which had small deficits in the boom received a large volume of long-term foreign investment. Thus, in addition to paying for their deficits, they accumulated foreign exchange reserves which could be drawn upon to maintain imports in the downswing. Again, some countries balanced their deficits by substantial invisible earnings; and in the downswing, the considerably lighter decline in these earnings than in merchandise exports contributed towards a relatively low responsiveness of merchandise imports.

35. The marginal propensity to purchase consumer and capital goods of the kind which was largely imported (e.g., a number of consumer durables, or agricultural and mining equipment) may also have tended to vary with the percentage decline in income in a given period. But it is difficult to speculate on the direction and extent of this variation.

Another factor contributing towards an inverse variation of responsiveness of import quantity and percentage decline in exports might be found in the variation among the countries in the change of governmental expenditure. In many of the countries studied the tax revenue depended heavily on foreign trade, directly or indirectly. However, it might be reasonable to expect that, *ceteris paribus*, the decline in governmental expenditure tended to vary among the countries less than proportionately with the variation in the decline in foreign trade and tax revenue: the economic, political, social, institutional, and technical difficulties of restricting largely inflexible current expenditures, and of terminating in a given period investment schemes which had been initiated, or of cancelling plans for starting new ones, were relatively greater the larger the part of such expenditures whose restriction was called for by the decline in governmental revenue.

36. The argument in the text neglects differences between countries in the ratio of exports to national income, about which our information is very incomplete. If this ratio is greater in one country than in another, domestic prices may decline more in the former country even though the percentage decline in exports is the smaller in that country.

Naturally, several other factors also influenced the rate of decline in domestic prices in various countries. Some of these factors are discussed in the next chapter.

37. As previously (chap. 6, n. 36), differences between countries in the ratio of exports to national income are neglected.

38. It may be added that, while the probable direction of, and intercountry variation in, the effects of substitution are generally those indicated in the text, the "final" effects of such substitution on imports were probably moderated by the reverse income effects by which substitution is followed: as domestic goods are substituted for imports, the increase in production and incomes leads to an increase in imports.

39. Of the twenty-seven countries whose responsiveness increased between the first and third period, ten had a positive responsiveness in both periods, four had a negative responsivenes in both periods, and thirteen had a negative responsiveness in the first period and a positive one in the third. Of the twenty-two countries whose responsiveness declined between the first and third period, sixteen had a positive responsiveness in both periods, four had a negative responsiveness in both periods, and two had a positive responsiveness in the first period and a negative one in the third.

40. The changes in responsiveness of the forty-nine countries between the three periods may be summarized as follows:

	Number of countries
Increase between the 1st and 2nd, and the 2nd and 3rd period	17
Larger increase between the 1st and 2nd period, than decrease between the 2nd and 3rd period	8
Smaller increase between the 1st and 2nd period, than decrease between the 2nd and 3rd period	7
Decrease between the 1st and 2nd, and the 2nd and 3rd period	12
Larger decrease between the 1st and 2nd period, than increase between the 2nd and 3rd period	3
Smaller decrease between the 1st and 2nd period, than increase between the 2nd and 3rd period	2
Total	49

41. We may divide the countries into two groups: twenty-one countries whose responsiveness in the second period, 1928-9 to 1931-2, exceeded +8.0, and twenty-eight countries whose responsiveness was smaller than +6.0. In the earlier period, 1928-9 to 1930-1, only one country of the first group had a responsiveness lower than +4.5, and one of the second group had a responsiveness exceeding that value. In the later period, 1928-9 to 1932-3, only four countries of the first group had a responsiveness lower than +7.0, and four of the second group had a responsiveness exceeding that value.

42. Compared to 1929, the terms of trade of the United Kingdom improved greatly in 1930 and 1931; but between 1931 and 1932 they slightly deteriorated (LN, *World Production and Prices, 1925-1932*, 111.)

43. See p. 40.

44. The exceptions in the first group were Chile, Cuba, and Lithuania, and in the second group Brazil, Colombia, the Dominican Republic, Haiti, Honduras, Nigeria, and Portugal. The ranking of the forty-ninth country, the Dutch East Indies, did not change between the first and third period either by percentage decline in exports or by responsiveness.

CHAPTER SEVEN

1. See chap. 5, IV, and chap. 6, I. Probably also, the higher the rate of economic expansion and, hence, the share of investment in national income, the more did investment depend on imported capital goods—that is, the share of capital goods in imports increased more than proportionately with the increase in the investment/income ratio.

2. See USTC, *Mining and Manufacturing Industries in Colombia* (Washington, 1949), 33; US Department of Commerce, Office of International Trade, *Investment in Colombia* (Washington, 1953), 11-26; C. Lewis, *America's Stake in International Investments* (Washington: Brookings Institution, 1938), 378-9, 588, 603, 624; UN, Department of Economic and Social Affairs, *Foreign Capital in Latin America* (New York, 1955), 68-9, 155.

3. The percentage shown in the text and similar percentages shown later for other countries are probably underestimates. See Chap. 5, n. 31.

4. There were some large coffee estates; but most of the coffee was produced on small

properties averaging under ten acres. For the heavy decline in governmental revenue and expenditure see LN, *Public Finance, 1928-37.* XXXIX. *Colombia* (Geneva, 1939), 2, 5, 8.

5. See pp. 65-6.

6. See US Department of Commerce, *Investment in Colombia*, 34, 54; USTC, *Mining and Manufacturing Industries in Colombia*, 22; and LN, *World Economic Survey, 1931-32*, 288.

7. Imports of containers and fuel are not shown separately in the League of Nations statistics for Colombia.

8. See, for instance, J. W. F. Rowe, *Markets and Men: A Study of Artificial Control Schemes in Some Primary Industries* (Cambridge: Cambridge University Press, 1936), 35 ff.; Lewis, *America's Stake in International Investments*, 590, 603, 624, 655; and UN, Department of Economic and Social Affairs, *Foreign Capital in Latin America*, 49, 51, 155. Under the stimulus of favourable coffee prices Brazil's coffee output increased from 888 thousand tons in 1925 to 1,101 thousand in 1927, and to 1,671, 1,577, and 1,634 thousand in 1928, 1929, and 1930, respectively. The magnitude of these volumes can be gauged by comparison with the years 1945 to 1949, when Brazil's coffee output ranged between 830 and 1,040 thousand tons only. (Data in UNECLA, *Economic Survey of Latin America, 1949*, 230.)

9. The ratio of the total supply of capital goods (imported and domestic) to the total agricultural and industrial output (minus exports plus imports) declined from 13–16 per cent in 1928 and 1929, to about 5–5.5 per cent in 1931 and 1932. (Based on data in UNECLA, *Economic Survey of Latin America, 1949*, 203, 218.)

10. See USTC, *Mining and Manufacturing Industries in Brazil* (Washington, 1949), 15, 66. For the very heavy decline in the quantity of textile imports see UNECLA, *Economic Survey of Latin America, 1949*, 239.

11. See USTC, *Mining and Manufacturing Industries in Venezuela* (Washington, 1949), 7, 24; UNECLA, *Economic Survey of Latin America, 1949*, 457; Lewis, *America's Stake in International Investments*, 588; US Department of Commerce, Office of International Trade, *Investment in Venezuela* (Washington, 1953), 4, 7, 50, 57; and GBDOT, *Economic Conditions in Venezuela, March 1935*, report by J. P. MacGregor (London: HMSO, 1935). 5.

12. See LN, *Public Finance, 1928-1937.* LIV. *Venezuela* (Geneva, 1938), 8. The imports of iron, tin, and lead pipes, which in 1928-9 represented about 10 per cent of all imports, declined between 1928-9 and 1931-2 by 89 per cent; those of wood and manufactures thereof, which represented about 4 per cent of all imports, declined by 83 per cent; the imports of non-agricultural machinery, which accounted for about 9 per cent of all imports, declined by 53 per cent; and those of railway materials declined by 78 per cent.

13. The quantity and value of Venezuela's exports of crude petroleum reached their peak in 1930. The quantity exported increased very slightly between 1928-9 and 1931-2, and declined very slightly between 1928-9 and 1932-3.

In the late nineteen-twenties practically the entire production of petroleum in Venezuela was in the hands of foreign-controlled companies, chiefly the Standard Oil Company of New Jersey, the Dutch Shell group, and the Gulf Oil Corporation. See USTC, *Mining and Manufacturing Industries in Venezuela*, 2, 23, and LN, *Balances of Payments, 1936*, 234-5.

14. With respect to the distribution of changes in export income and its effect on merchandise imports in countries exporting products of mines or estates see also J. V. Levin, *The Export Economies: Their Pattern of Development in Historical Perspective* (Cambridge: Harvard University Press, 1960), 6-10, 170-7, 182-3, 187-8.

Unlike many underdeveloped countries, Venezuela had no external public indebtedness whose rigid service might have enhanced her responsiveness of imports in the downswing. (RIIA, *The Problem of International Investment*, 225.)

15. See W. R. Maclaurin, *Economic Planning in Australia, 1929-1936* (London: P. S. King & Son, 1937), 13, 20-1, 26-7, 31-3; E. R. Walker, *Australia in the World Depression* (London: P. S. King & Son, 1933), 25-7, 32-40, 66-71; G. Wood, *Borrowing and Business in Australia* (London: Oxford University Press, 1930), 186-7, 209-11; R. Wilson, *Capital Imports and the Terms of Trade* (Melbourne: Melbourne University Press, 1931), 31, 36; D. B. Copland, "The Australian Problem," *Economic Journal*, 40 (1930), 639 ff.; J. W. M. Eddy, "Public Expenditure," in "An Economic Survey of Australia," *Annals of the American Academy of Political and Social Science*, 158 (Nov. 1931), 202 ff; C. Clark, *The Conditions of Economic Progress* (2nd ed.; London: Macmillan, 1951), 141; C. Clark and J. G. Crawford, *The National Income of Australia* (Sydney: Angus & Robertson Ltd., 1938), 65, 71; and D. Copland, *Australia in the World Crisis, 1929-1933.* Alfred Marshall Lectures delivered in the University of Cambridge, October and November 1933. (Cambridge: Cambridge University Press, 1934), chap. I.

16. For the decline in investment see Clark and Crawford, *The National Income of Australia*, 89. Some relief was provided to the farmers through farm relief and assistance Acts, and reduction in interest charges on loans to primary producers. See Maclaurin, *Economic Planning in Australia, 1929-1936*, 215 ff., 228; F. B. Horner, "The Multiplier in Australia: A

Further Comment," *Economic Record,* 15 (1939), 221; W. Malenbaum, *The World Wheat Economy 1885-1939* (Cambridge: Harvard University Press, 1953), 10-11, 13-14; and Paul de Hevesy, *World Wheat Planning and Economic Planning in General* (London: Oxford University Press, 1940), 347-50.

17. For the strong deflationary measures adopted in 1931 and 1932 see LN. *Public Finance 1928-1937.* LXI. *Australia* (Geneva, 1938), 11; W. H. Maclaurin, *Economic Planning in Australia, 1929-1936,* 27, 49-56, 78-106, 180; and Walker, *Australia in the World Depression,* chap. v. In 1931/2-2/3 the interest on the external debt of government and local bodies was equal to about one-third of Australia's merchandise exports. About the increase in Australian tariffs see L. F. Giblin, "The Tariff—Its Costs and Effects," in "An Economic Survey of Australia," *Annals of the American Academy of Political and Social Science,* 158 (Nov. 1931), 119-20.

About the decline in Australia's income and imports see also Copland, *Australia in the World Crisis 1929-1933,* 32, 185 ff.; RIIA, *The Problem of International Investment,* 223, 225, 291-2; and D. B. Copland, "The Australian Problem," *Economic Journal,* 40 (1930), 641 ff. Real national income declined by about 17-18 per cent between 1928/9 and 1930/1, after which it started rising slowly—though gross investment continued falling until 1931/2. (See Clark and Crawford, *The National Income of Australia,* 65, 89; Clark, *The Conditions of Economic Progress,* 2nd ed., 141; and Copland, *Australia in the World Crisis 1929-1933,* chap. II.)

Australia's responsiveness of imports decreased slightly between the periods 1927/8-8/9 to 1930/1-1/2 and 1927/8-8/9 to 1931/2-2/3, and more substantially between the latter period and 1927/8-8/9 to 1932/3-3/4. This is partly explained by the early revival of the Australian economy, indicated earlier, and the downward adjustment of tariffs from 1932 on. See Maclaurin, *Economic Planning in Australia, 1929-1936,* 40, 164-8; also, the references chap. 7, n. 16.

18. See chap. 5, IV. Compare, for instance, the developments in Colombia or Venezuela, described in section I of this chapter, with the developments in countries exporting non-staple and semi-luxury foodstuffs, or in certain Asiatic economies, described later, in sections IV and VI.

19. Data on the composition of Turkey's imports in 1928-9 are not readily available. Therefore, this country has been excluded from the present argument.

20. See Wallich, *Monetary Problems of an Export Economy: The Cuban Experience 1914-1947,* 39; IBRD, Mission, *Report on Cuba,* 40-2, 51, 729; USTC, *The Foreign Trade of Latin America,* Part II, vol. 2, 235-6; IIA, *International Yearbook of Agricultural Statistics, 1929-30,* 542; and Lewis, *America's Stake in International Investments,* 590, 602-3, 625.

21. While between 1927/8-8/9 and 1930/1-1/2 the sugar output of the Philippines, Hawaii, Puerto Rico, Formosa, the Dominican Republic, Peru, India, Brazil, and Australia increased, and the output of the British West Indies, Java, and Argentina declined by percentages ranging between 4 and 8 per cent, the output of Cuba declined by as much as 37.2 per cent. See also p. 28.

22. See IBRD, Mission, *Report on Cuba,* 7, 25, 44-6, 173, 194, 668, 723-6, 730-1; Magill and Shoup, *The Cuban Fiscal System 1939,* 3-5, 8; and UNECLA, *A Study of Trade Between Latin America and Europe,* 70.

23. See Wallich, *Monetary Problems of an Export Economy: The Cuban Experience 1914-1947,* 31 ff., 68, 76-7, 95-8, 186-7, 190; Foreign Policy Association, Commission on Cuban Affairs, *Problems of the New Cuba,* 350, 370-1; and LN, *Public Finance, 1928-1937.* XLI. *Cuba* (Geneva, 1938), 2, 4, 6; also, IBRD, Mission, *Report on Cuba,* 173, 530 ff., 566 ff., 729.

24. See also GBDOT, report by S. Simmonds, *Economic Conditions in Iran (Persia), July 1935* (London: HMSO, 1935), 1 ff, 10, 13 ff.

25. As one might have expected, the exceptions above and below line *dd'* in Diagrams IV, V, and VI are somewhat more numerous than those observed in Diagram II.

26. About Paraguay see USTC, *The Foreign Trade of Latin America,* Part I, vol. 1, 196. Portugal adopted exchange control in 1922. In the late nineteen-twenties she started recovering from a long period of economic and fiscal troubles, and from 1932 on she gradually relaxed her exchange control. See LN, *Statistical Yearbook 1937/8,* 226, 230; GBDOT, report by A. H. W. King, *Economic Conditions in Portugal, September 1934* (London: HMSO, 1934), 5, 14; and *infra,* chap. 7, VI, esp. n. 74. In the text Portugal is classed with the countries that "had not introduced exchange control until the end of 1932."

27. It was noted earlier that our examination of the role of exchange control in relation to the responsiveness of imports was bound to be rather crude. For several of the countries listed in the text the information about the purposes for which exchange control was adopted, its scope or coverage, the success of its application, and other equally significant features, is not

readily available. Also, what some countries sought to achieve through exchange control, alone, or in combination with other measures, others attempted to secure through tariff changes, trade controls, currency devaluation, or other policies. In Norway, for instance, the banks exercised some unofficial exchange control. See LN, *World Economic Survey, 1931-32*, 287-8.

28. See Lewis, *America's Stake in International Investments*, 584, 624; UN, Department of Economic and Social Affairs, *Foreign Capital in Latin America*, 61, 63, 155; LN, *Balances of Payments, 1934*, 180; and USTC, *Mining and Manufacturing Industries in Chile* (Washington, 1949), 10.

29. Between 1928-9 and 1931-2 ordinary budget receipts declined by 43 per cent. On the other hand, ordinary budget expenditures (excluding the service on the foreign debt, which was suspended in July 1931) decreased only by about 14 per cent; and expenditures under the ordinary and extraordinary budgets and "special laws" (excluding again the foreign debt service) decreased by about 24 per cent. The ordinary budget changed from surpluses in the years 1928 and 1929 (a yearly average of 41 million pesos) to deficits in 1931 and 1932 (a yearly average of 163 million pesos), and this change occurred in spite of the fact that no service was paid on the foreign debt after July 1931. For more details see Lewis *America's Stake in International Investments*, 624; LN, *Balances of Payments, 1934*, 180; Ellsworth, *Chile: An Economy in Transition*, 35 ff., 167, 171; LN, *Public Finance 1928-1937. XXXVIII. Chile* (Geneva, 1939), 3, 5-7, 12-14; and GBDOT, report by A. J. Pack, *Economic Conditions in Chile, November 1934* (London: HMSO, 1935), 17-18.

30. For estimates of changes in investment and industrial production see LN, *World Production and Prices, 1925-1934*, 28; UNECLA, *Economic Survey of Latin America, 1949*, 287, 293-5, 357-9; also Ellsworth, *Chile: An Economy in Transition*, 13. In the boom industry accounted for roughly one-fifth of Chile's national income. (L. M. Dominguez, "National Income Estimates of Latin American Countries," in NBER, *Studies in Income and Wealth. X.* (New York, 1947), 189.) From March 1931 on various Chilean industries were assisted by restrictions on imports, noted later in the text.

31. In 1928 the price of electrolytic copper was 14.57 US cents per pound. Of this sum, 2.20 cents were paid to Chileans as domestic production costs, 1.01 cents went for taxes, 6.92 cents were spent on imported materials and machinery, and 4.44 cents were paid abroad as profits, interest, and reserve against mine depletion. By 1932 the price of copper had fallen to 5.56 cents per pound. Expenditures on imported materials and equipment had fallen to 3.70 cents. The domestic production costs had remained practically unchanged, at 2.19 cents, and tax payments had fallen to 0.29 cents. Domestic real incomes were affected chiefly by the decline in the quantity of copper produced. On the other hand, the payment abroad for profits, etc., had disappeared; instead, the foreign investor was paying 0.62 cent per pound of copper, the difference between the foregoing costs and the price of copper. It may be added that even as late as 1948 foreign-owned companies produced as much as 95.6 per cent of Chile's copper output. (These estimates are based on data given in UNECLA, *Economic Survey of Latin America, 1949*, 275, 280, 381.)

32. As late as 1949 more than 52 per cent of the crop and planted land area of Chile was in holdings exceeding 1,250 acres, and another 25 percent was in holdings of 250-1,250 acres. Only 1.9 per cent of the area was occupied by holdings smaller than 12 acres. (UNECLA, *Economic Survey of Latin America, 1949*, 326.)

33. Between 1931 and 1932 total public and private investment, measured in stable prices, declined by about 56 per cent, and purchases of iron and steel products declined greatly. (UNECLA, *Economic Survey of Latin America, 1949*, 294-5, 359.)

34. Domestic coal to a large extent substituted imported fuel oil, and the output of such goods as cloth, paper, and glass increased very considerably, particularly from 1933 on. See Ellsworth, *Chile: An Economy in Transition*, 9-12, 49-51, and UNECLA, *Economic Survey of Latin America, 1949*, 344, 356, 367.

35. See China, Ministry of Industries, Committee for the Study of Silver Values and Commodity Prices, *Silver and Prices in China*, 139, 141-8. For estimates of the exports and imports in 1927-8 of Manchuria, and of China excluding Manchuria, see J. B. Condliffe, *China To-day: Economic* (Boston: World Peace Foundation, 1932), 200-1.

36. See LN, *International Trade Statistics, 1930*, 69. Large-scale import and hoarding of precious metals and jewelry during periods of relative prosperity was a significant phenomenon in several Far Eastern and some Middle Eastern economies. For its important economic and social causes and consequences see, C. F. Remer, *The Foreign Trade of China* (Shanghai: Commercial Press, 1926), 209 ff., and P. J. Thomas, "Indian Currency in the Depression," *Economic Journal*, 48 (1938), 241 ff.

Pao-San Ou has estimated China's total income produced in 1931 at about 23,000 million Chinese dollars. ("A New Estimate of China's National Income," *Journal of Political Economy*, 54 (1946), 553.) China's imports in 1931 amounted to 2,233 million Chinese dollars. See also Chi-ming Hou, "External Trade, Foreign Investment, and Domestic Development: The Chinese Experience, 1840-1937," *Economic Development and Cultural Change*, 10 (1961/2), 23.

37. GBDOT, report by A. H. George *et al.*, *Trade and Economic Conditions in China, 1933-1935* (London: HMSO, 1935), 5.

38. See p. 38; and GBDOT, *Trade and Economic Conditions in China, 1933-1935*, 11. The decline in China's imports of capital goods between 1928-9 and 1931-2 was among the smallest of the forty-nine countries. And the responsiveness of imports of capital goods to the decline in exports was smaller in China than in any of the other countries, except Lithuania, where imports of capital goods increased. The corresponding responsiveness of China's food imports was the smallest among the forty-nine countries. (Diagrams IV and V)

39. In China, partly on account of high transportation costs and inefficient marketing, and partly because of practices which have been likened to "medieval forestalling and regrating, the peasant farmer often receives a pathetically small proportion of the final value of his product. ... The multiplication of middlemen, nearly always organized strongly in monopolistic gilds, deprives the peasant of a large part of his share of the price. ... A picul of tea purchased in Anhwei for $1.50 can be marketed in Shanghai (perhaps 500 miles away) for $14, ..." (One picul equals about 133 lbs.) (Condliffe, *China To-day: Economic*, 64-5.) In 1930 the Roumanian peasant received more than one-half of the c.i.f. export price of wheat. Probably, Spain's producers of farm products received similar percentages of the export prices, and Poland's producers received substantially higher shares. (LNEC, *The Agricultural Crisis*, II, 103) "The New Zealand dairy farmer, operating through a cooperative producing and marketing system and selling his product 13,000 miles away, is able to secure for himself 81% of the wholesale price of his butter in London." (Coldliffe, *China Today: Economic*, 65.) For the farmer's share of retail cost of foods in the United States see US Department of Agriculture, Agricultural Marketing Service, Marketing Research Division, *Farm-Retail Spreads for Food Products*, 2, 53, 59-60, and W. E. Hamilton, *A Current Look at the Farmer's Percentage of the Consumer's Food Dollar*, Special Report No. 55 (Washington: National Planning Association, 1959), 1-2, 10.

The Chinese Communist Party has estimated that in 1947 70-80 per cent of the arable land was owned by landlords; according to other estimates, 50 per cent of the arable land was owned by 4 per cent of the land-owners. The National Agricultural Research Bureau of the Republic of China has estimated that in 1947 some 60 per cent of China's farmers were tenants or part tenants, and the remainder were owners. (Estimates quoted in UN, Secretary General, *Land Reform: Defects in Agrarian Structure as Obstacles to Economic Development* (New York, 1951), II.B.3, 55, and A. R. Burns, *Comparative Economic Organization* (New York: Prentice-Hall, 1955), 617.)

40. See pp. 65-6, and our earlier discussion in this chapter relating to Venezuela and Chile. Unlike many other underdeveloped countries (for instance, India or the Balkan countries), the external public debt accounted for a very small part of the total foreign investment in China—less han 15 percent in 1930. (See RIIA, *The Problem of International Investment*, 225; also C. F. Remer, "Investments in Kind," *Explorations in Economics: Notes and Essays Contributed in Honor of F. W. Taussig* (New York: McGraw-Hill, 1936), 93-94.) In 1928-9 about three-quarters of China's net interest and dividend payments abroad were dividends. (Estimates by C. F. Remer, quoted in LN, *Balances of Payments, 1931 and 1932*, 64.) Owing largely to this factor and to the greater variability of dividend than interest payments, China's net interest and dividend payments declined from about U.S. $116 million in 1928-9 to only about 22 million pre-1933 U.S. dollars in 1933. (The decline in the gold value of creditor currencies, such as the pound in 1931 and the U.S. dollar in 1933, reduced the debt service measured in pre-1933 U.S. dollars.)

41. LN, *Balances of Payments*, various years, and sources quoted therein. "Foreign government expenditure" includes "diplomatic expenditure" and "foreign military and naval establishments."

42. However, in the earlier period "tourist receipts" include also "the expenditure of crews of foreign merchant vessels and for repairs of such ships." LN, *Balances of Payments, 1932 and 1932*, 64, n. 5.)

43. Data on invisible earnings in the years 1931 and 1932 are not readily available. It may be noted that, for 1933, Manchuria is excluded from both the merchandise trade data and the data on invisible earnings, and that the effect of this exclusion may have been different for these two accounts.

44. LN, *International Trade Statistics, 1930*, 69, *1933*, 66, and *1936*, 67. In 1931 China had a small net import of silver and gold: as indicated earlier, the world depression did not greatly affect China until the end of 1931 or the beginning of 1932.

45. Except for 1927/8, Siam's data include leaf and ornaments in addition to bullion and

coin. LN, *International Trade Statistics*, 1930, 154, 182, 1931 and 1932, 179, 1933, 151, 1935, 179, 1936, 62, 148-9; *idem, Balances of Payments*, 1933, 146, and 1936, 182; and GBDOT, report by L. B. S. Larkins, *Economic Conditions in the Netherlands East Indies, 1933-1935* (London: HMSO, 1936), 80; LN, *The Network of World Trade*, 74, 104.

Data for Egypt are not readily available. However, there is some evidence of net imports of gold and silver in 1928-9 and of exports in the downswing. LN, Economic Intelligence Service, *The Network of World Trade* (Geneva, 1942), 103.

46. In chap. 1 we adopted the principle of including gold and silver only in the exports of countries producing these metals. (chap. 1, n. 3) It might be suggested that the flows of gold and silver into and out of Asiatic hoards should have been included from the outset in the merchandise trade of the respective countries. But, first, it would be difficult to isolate these flows from the amounts of gold and silver flowing into and out of currency reserves. The latter flows are of a different nature and have been excluded from the merchandise trade of the countries studied. See P. J. Thomas, "Indian Currency in the Depression," *Economic Journal*, 48 (1938), 242-3. Second, it seemed desirable to include among exports only the flows of products of the countries studied and, as far as possible, to exclude reductions in the stock of capital, which in the Asiatic countries involved reduction of metallic hoards, and in more advanced countries, such as Canada, involved liquidation of holdings of foreign securities. It would appear inadvisable to include gold and silver only among imports. Finally, the approach followed serves better in drawing attention to this significant cyclical phenomenon of countries like India or China.

47. The low share of capital goods in the imports of Ceylon and Malaya was to some extent related to the heavy dependence of these countries on imported food. In 1928-9 the share of food in their imports exceeded two-fifths and it was higher than in any of the other countries studied (Table XV). However, even if the value of food imports had been half as large, the share of capital goods in the reduced total imports would still have been quite low.

48. See V.K.R.V. Rao, *The National Income of British India* (London: Macmillan, 1940), 186; Clark, *The Conditions of Economic Progress*, 2nd ed., 123-4, and the sources noted in chap. 6, n. 1.

49. Between 1928-9 and 1931-2 the quantity of tin exported from Malaya or the Dutch East Indies declined by a little over one-third. On the other hand, the quantity of petroleum exports of these countries increased substantially; the quantity of tea exported from Ceylon and the Dutch East Indies increased; and the quantity of rubber exported from Malaya, the Dutch East Indies and Ceylon declined only by 3.7 per cent.

For the relative importance of estates in Ceylon, the Dutch East Indies and Malaya see, for instance, Bauer, *The Rubber Industry*, 3, 8; IBRD, Mission, *The Economic Development of Ceylon* (Baltimore: Johns Hopkins Press, 1953), 228-9, 238; *idem, The Economic Development of Malaya* (Baltimore: Johns Hopkins Press, 1955), 14-15; UN, Secretary General, *Land Reform: Defects in Agrarian Structure as Obstacles to Economic Development*, 18 ff.; and A. R. Burns, *Comparative Economic Organization*, 88 ff.

50. For instance, for the Dutch East Indies see D. Finch, "Investment Service of Underdeveloped Countries," *Staff Papers* (International Monetary Fund), 2 (1951/2), 67. See also UN, Economic and Social Council, *Repercussions of Changes in Terms of Trade on the Economies of Countries in Process of Development*. Report by the Secretary-General, Mimeo, E/2456 (11 June 1953), 38-40.

51. In the period considered over two-thirds of Siam's exports consisted of rice, a product of small-scale farming by peasants. Rubber represented only about 4.3 per cent of her exports in 1927/8-8/9, and it was all produced by smallholders. (Bauer, *The Rubber Industry*, 3.) The quantity of her tin exports (which in 1928-9 accounted for 8.2 per cent of the value of all her exports) increased between 1928-9 and 1931-2.

In 1928-9 tea and rubber (commodities in whose production estate farming was important) represented 53.8 and 21.2 per cent, respectively, of Ceylon's exports, but only 8.1 and less than 1 per cent of India's.

In Egypt about 95 per cent of all land-owners owned less than 5 acres each—in many cases much less; and these farms represented only about one-third of the total farm area. On the other hand, another third of the farm area was owned by only 0.4 per cent of all land-owners. (UN, Secretary General, *Land Reform: Defects in Agrarian Structure as Obstacles to Economic Development*, 9, and Burns, *Comparative Economic Organization*, 85, 617.)

About the economic position of the Malayan peasant see, for instance, T. H. Silcock, *The Commonwealth Economy in Southeast Asia* (Durham, N. C.; Duke University Press, 1959), 17, and T. B. Lim (ed.) *Problems of the Malayan Economy* (Singapore: Donald Moore, 1956), 13-14, 29. For the relatively satisfactory position of Malayan rubber smallholders in the depression see Bauer, *The Rubber Industry*, chap. 5.

52. See, for instance, P. J. Thomas, "India in the World Depression," *Economic Journal*,

45 (1935), 473-6, 479, and LN, *Public Finance, 1928-1935.* LVI. *India* (Geneva, 1937), 4, 6, 9-11.

53.   See LN, *Balances of Payments, 1930,* 77-8, and *1933,* 130-1. Owing to lack of information, investments in the Dutch East Indies of the undistributed profits of foreign enterprises are not included among capital imports.

54.   In 1928-9 Class B goods represented over half the exports of only two other of the forty-nine countries: Honduras and New Zealand. In 1928-9 capital goods represented only about one-fifth of Honduras' imports. As indicated in Diagram II, compared with other countries that had a similar percentage decline in exports, the responsiveness of imports of Honduras was on the low side.

In the late nineteen-twenties New Zealand's economy was in a "semi-chronic structural disequilibrium." The boom was not intense; it was considerably milder than in Australia. (See J. H. Auten, "Income, Expenditure, and the Terms of Trade for New Zealand, 1929-38," *Journal of Political Economy,* 66 (1956), 392-3; and G. H. Brown, *The International Economic Position of New Zealand,* supplement to the *Journal of Business,* XIX (April 1946), 183-4, where also the modest growth of New Zealand's exports in the nineteen-twenties is shown.) While capital goods represented a little less than one-third of New Zealand's imports in 1928-9, one-third of these goods were automobiles, which, unlike materials and equipment, need not be paralleled in the short-run by complementary domestic investment. See also Clark, *The Conditions of Economic Progress,* 2nd ed., 141, 148; GBDOT, report by W. D. Lambie, *Economic Conditions in the Dominion of New Zealand, to October 1929* (London: HMSO, 1930), 9-10, 38-9.

In the period 1928-9 to 1931-2 New Zealand's responsiveness of imports was much lower than Australia's or Brazil's. But compared with the responsiveness of several other countries which experienced a similar percentage decline in exports, it was not exceptionally low. As indicated, capital goods had represented a fairly large proportion of her boom imports, and between 1928-9 and 1931-2 they declined by as much as 69.1 per cent. (The value of imports of machinery fell by 57.0 per cent, and of "other manufacturing metals" by 65.5 per cent; but imports of "motorcars and parts" declined by 78.7 per cent.) The decline in export income was spread fairly widely, and hence the marginal consumption/income ratio tended to be substantial. (Compare with the conditions in China, described pp. 91-2.) The burden of service of the external public debt was considerable: in the years 1931 to 1933 it was equal to between one-fifth and one-quarter of merchandise exports. Farmer indebtedness, to a large extent originating in the speculative land boom, exerted pressure on consumption—though some relief was provided through the Mortgage Relief Acts. Deflationary policies were pursued, and import duties were increased. About some of these factors that helped the responsiveness of New Zealand's imports see Brown, *The International Economic Position of New Zealand,* 38-44, 58-60, 74, 87, 122-5, 154-6, 159, 162-4, 167, 170, 185-7; LN, *Public Finance, 1928-1937.* LXII. *New Zealand* (Geneva, 1938), 12-14; GBDOT, *Economic Conditions in the Dominion of New Zealand, to October 1929,* 13; idem, report by R. Boulter and T. G. A. Muntz, *Report on Economic and Commercial Conditions in New Zealand, April 1936* (London: HMSO, 1936), 4-5, 46; *New Zealand Official Yearbook, 1931,* 318-19, and *1934,* 237-9; D. B. Copland, "New Zealand's Economic Difficulties and Expert Opinion," *Economic Journal,* 42 (1932), 371 ff.; and RIIA, *The Problem of International Investment,* 223, 225.

Gold has not been included in our data of New Zealand's exports. Her gold exports increased from 1932 on, however, in 1928-9 they would have represented less than one per cent of her exports including gold, and in 1931-2 less than two per cent. Hence, inclusion of gold in New Zealand's exports would have reduced the percentage decline in exports, and increased the responsiveness of imports, only very slightly.

55.   See GBDOT, report by A. H. W. King, *Economic Conditions in Portugal, September 1934,* 2; and idem, report by A. H. W. King, *Report on Economic and Commercial Conditions in Portugal, July 1936* (London: HMSO, 1936), 1. Though the value of Portugal's exports had increased considerably in 1928 and 1929, the value of her imports in these years was only about 5-10 per cent greater than in 1923, 1925, or 1926, and lower than in 1924.

56.   Greece and Norway received a considerable amount of foreign capital in the years 1924-8 and 1927-30, respectively. Greece secured foreign capital chiefly through public borrowing, and to a smaller extent through foreign direct investment in private enterprise. The bulk of the foreign loans was used for the settlement of 1.2 million refugees from Asia Minor, for stabilization of the currency and establishment of the Bank of Greece, and for repayment of floating debt. A smaller part was used for the construction of public utilities and public works. For details see LN, *Balances of Payments, 1930,* 131-4; Lewis, *America's Stake in International Investments,* 622; LN, *Public Finance, 1928-1935.* XIII. *Greece,* 13-16; UN, Department of Economic Affairs, *Public Debt, 1914-1946* (New York, 1948), 73; RIIA, *The Balkan States.* I. *Economic,* 142-3; and M. Lamer, "Die Wandlungen der ausländischen Kapital-

anlagen auf dem Balkan," *Weltwirtschaftliches Archiv*, 48 (1938), 482-3; also RIIA, *The Problem of International Investment*, 247.

57.   See p. 59. In 1928-9 food represented about two-fifths of Greece's imports—next to Ceylon and Malaya the largest percentage of the forty-nine countries.

58.   It will be recalled that Class B goods were less important among the exports of Norway than of Denmark, the Irish Free State, Panama, or Portugal; also, that Norway received a considerable amount of foreign capital in the boom.

59.   At constant prices, the national income of the Netherlands declined between 1930 and 1933 only by about 8 per cent—while Canada's gross national product, for instance, declined in the same period by about 23 per cent. (Based on estimates in J. J. Polak, *An International Economic System* (London: George Allen and Unwin, 1954), 100-1, and CDBS, *National Accounts, Income and Expenditure 1926-1950*, 28-9.) Between 1928-9 and 1931-2 the ordinary receipts of the Netherlands' state budget declined by 17 per cent. On the other hand, the ordinary expenditure increased very slightly, and the capital expenditure increased greatly. Total expenditure increased by 16 per cent, or, if the redemption of the public debt is excluded, it rose by 19 per cent. The budget (excluding the redemption of debt) changed from surpluses in 1928 and 1929 (a yearly average of 58.5 million gulden) to deficits in 1931 and 1932 (a yearly average of 114.2 million gulden). For more details see LN, *Public Finance, 1928-1935. XX. Netherlands* (Geneva, 1936), 3, 6-7, 10-14.

The very moderate decline in Norway's real national income is reflected in estimates found in Clark, *The Conditions of Economic Progress*, 2nd ed., 103. Between 1928-9 and 1931-2 (1932-3) the volume of Norway's industrial output declined only by 9.9 (1.7) per cent, compared to declines of 38.4 (45.3) per cent in Poland and 19.4 (11.6) per cent in Finland, other countries with a similar percentage decline in exports in the period 1928-9 to 1931-2. The decline in the period 1928-9 to 1931-2 in the industrial output of countries like Belgium, Czechoslovakia, or Italy was about 25 per cent or more, and in the United States, Germany, and Austria it exceeded 35 per cent. (LN, *Statistical Yearbook 1936/7*, 164.)

National income estimates indicative of the mildness of the boom and subsequent downswing in the Irish Free State and Denmark are found in Clark, *The Conditions of Economic Progress*, 2nd ed., 60-1, 106. Between 1928-9 and 1931-2 Denmark's industrial output declined only by 1.0 per cent, and between 1928-9 and 1932-3 it increased by 1.6 per cent. (LN, *Statistical Yearbook 1936/7*, 164.) Denmark's dairy industry depended considerably on imported fodder, which in 1928-9 represented about 11 per cent of the country's imports; and in the downswing, particularly in the earlier years, her farmers benefited substantially from the greater decline in the price of fodder than in the price of their products. With 1928 as the base year, in 1931 the ratios of the price of butter to the price of oil-cake, and of the price of bacon to the price of maize, had risen to 119 and 130, respectively. (LN, *World Economic Survey, 1931-32*, 163.) A similar benefit accrued to aggriculture in the Irish Free State. (See *The Economist, Commercial History and Review of 1931*, CXIV (Feb. 13, 1932), 30.) Developments in Denmark are summarized in the statement that she "has managed to escape the troughs of the depression, as she never presumed or aspired to ride on the crest of the boom. ... Even in outward appearance Denmark is [in 1933] a prosperous country, whether judged by the new construction going on ...; the intensive cultivation and prosperous look of her countryside; or the crowded attendance at her places of entertainment and restaurants. It is clear that money circulates freely in the country and that its inhabitants have no fear of spending." (GBDOT, report by E. G. Cable, *Economic Conditions in Denmark, February 1934* (London: HMSO, 1934), 11; also *The Economist, Commercial History and Review of 1931*, CXIV. (Feb. 13, 1932), 23.)

From the late nineteen-twenties on, under the leadership of a new political regime, Portugal experienced a long-term recovery from a protracted period of economic stagnation and fiscal and financial disorder. Throughout the depression Portugal "has been less vulnerable than most nations to the increasing pressure of world-wide depression, ... It is true that the general economic crisis has hampered the policy of national effort, ... but, ... the rate of progress has amply demonstrated what possibilities the future holds. ... Visitors to the country ..., as well as the Portuguese themselves, are impressed by the marked improvement which has taken place in every direction within the last few years. Apart from the public works programme, ... there is evidence in every village and hamlet of a renewed prosperity and confidence in the future, in the shape of new buildings and houses, the repair of dilapidated dwellings, the installation of electric power plants and improved water supplies, etc. These are only a few examples of the general background which reflect the growth of a larger economic life. ... The practical achievements of the Government, and their unremitting efforts to secure further progress, if impeded somewhat have in no way been seriously prejudiced by the continuance of the crisis." (GBDOT, *Economic Conditions in Portugal, September 1934*, 1-2, 5.) Partly because of the foregoing developments, and partly because of the very substantial increase in

Portugal's food output in the depression, of the heavy decline in prices of imported staple foodstuffs, and of the protection and expansion of textile production, capital goods represented a somewhat greater percentage of Portugal's imports in each of the years 1930 to 1933 than in 1928-9.

In Greece there was "not much of a boom" in the late nineteen-twenties, and the ensuing downswing was very mild. In the years 1930 and 1931 Greece received foreign loans for the construction of public works, which amounted to $4.9 and $20.9 million, respectively. (See the references in chap. 7, n. 56.) The latter sum was equal to about 40 per cent of her merchandise exports in 1931. From 1929/30 on governmental expenditure on agriculture and public works increased greatly. (See LN, *Public Finance, 1928-1935*. XIII. *Greece*, 11.) As in Denmark and Norway, industrial production was more important in Greece than in the bulk of the forty-nine countries: in 1928 industry employed about 28 per cent of the country's active population. In every one of the years 1930 to 1934 Greece's industrial output was higher than in 1928 or 1929; and the percentage increase in this output in the period 1930-4 was almost as great as in the period 1926-30. (Political and Economic Planning, *Economic Development in S. E. Europe* (London: Oxford University Press, 1945), 129; Supreme Economic Council of Greece, *The Greek Economy in 1939* (in Greek) (Athens: 1940), 41; RIIA, *South-Eastern Europe: A Brief Survey* (London: Oxford University Press, 1940), 100; and *idem, The Balkan States*. I. *Economic,* 122-3.

About Panama see chap. 7, n. 69.

60. The data used are found chiefly in LN, *Balances of Payments,* various years.

61. "Shipping income" in Denmark, the Netherlands, and the other countries noted in the text includes some or all of the following items: freight, passenger money, ships stores and bunkers, port fees and receipts on account of transit, transshipment, commissions, wages, insurance, and repairs.

The pensions received in the Irish Free State from abroad were mainly "war pensions" and "Royal Irish Constabulary pensions." The pensions and salaries received in the Netherlands were paid by the governments of the Dutch East Indies, Surinam, and Curacao, and by private concerns.

62. In the first four countries the surplus on account of invisible trade and interest and dividends in 1928-9 ranged from an amount equal to about two-thirds of the merchandise deficit to an amount exceeding it. In Greece it was equal to a little less than half the merchandise deficit.

63. In 1929 emigrants' remittances to Portugal, chiefly from Brazil, amounted to about $10 million, being equal to about one-fifth of Portugal's merchandise exports. (GBDOT, report by A. H. W. King, *Economic Conditions in Portugal, March 1930* (London: HMSO, 1930), 12.)

Panama's revenue from activities in the Canal Zone included: government receipts from rentals in the Panama Canal Zone; receipts from passenger and commodity trade through the Canal, including income from sales of commodities and services to tourists, travellers, and crews of merchant vessels; income from sales of commodities and services to Panama Canal employees, and officers and men of the United States services; and import duties levied on commodities consumed in the Canal Zone. See GBDOT, report by C. F. W. Andrews, *Report on Economic and Commercial Conditions in the Republic of Panama and the Panama Canal Zone, 1933-35* (London: HMSO, 1936), 2, 10, and L. M. Dominguez, "National Income Estimates of Latin American Countries," in NBER, *Studies in Income and Wealth.* X. 210.

64. Satisfactory estimates of Greek shipping income in 1928 are not readily available.

65. The estimates of emigrants' remittances to Greece are found in X. Zolotas, *Monetary Stabilization* (in Greek) (Athens: Greca, 1929), 214; *idem, The Debt Burden of Greece* (in Greek) (Athens: Greca, 1931), 74; and LN, *Balances of Payments, 1931 and 1932,* 103.

The available estimates of emigrants' remittances to the Irish Free State show a large increase between 1928-9 and 1931-2. But this is due to underestimation for the years prior to 1931. See LN. *Balances of Payments, 1931 and 1932,* 117-9, and *1933,* 109.

The shipping income of the countries discussed declined proportionately less than their merchandise exports (or increased) in all three periods, 1928-9 to 1930-1, 1928-9 to 1931-2, and 1928-9 to 1932-3 (except for Denmark in the first period, in which shipping income declined by 17.4 per cent, and exports fell by 14.1 per cent). On the other hand, emigrants' remittances to countries like Greece or Norway were maintained fairly well up to 1931 inclusive, but declined very substantially after. Consequently, by 1932-3 the relative decline in these remittances was somewhat greater than the decrease in merchandise exports in Norway, and roughly equal in Greece. But while in Norway and the Irish Free State emigrants' remittances represented only about 5-10 per cent of the main invisible earnings in 1928-9, in Greece they accounted for more than half of such earnings, and were equal to over two-fifths of the merchandise exports. The heavy decline in remittances to Greece after 1931 may partly explain the improvement between 1928-9 to 1931-2, and 1928-9 to 1932-3 in the ranking of Greece among the forty-nine countries by responsiveness of imports. (Compare Diagrams II and III).

66. The estimate of Greek revenue from tourism in 1929 quoted in LN, *Balances of Payments, 1931 and 1932,* 103, seems to be too high. In any event, in 1928 the tourist revenue was equal to only about one-third of that in 1929. (See Zolotas, *Monetary Stabilization,* 214, and *idem, The Debt Burden of Greece,* 74.) Compared to 1928-9, the tourist revenue increased moderately in 1931-2, and very considerably in 1933.

Estimates of pensions or salaries received are not readily available for the Irish Free State in 1932, and for the Netherlands in 1928 and 1929. The decline in the Irish pensions in terms of pre-1933 U.S. dollars reflects largely the devaluation of the pound. In terms of pounds they decreased only by 4.8 per cent.

67. Greek income from investments abroad was estimated together with "other invisible resources, etc., . . . as a balancing item. . . ." (LN, *Balances of Payments, 1931 and 1932,* 103, 105-6, and *1934,* 106.) Estimates for the Netherlands for the years prior to 1931 are not readily available.

68. From 1931 on the invisible earnings of the Irish Free State included the net foreign proceeds of the Irish Hospitals Sweepstakes. In the years 1932 and 1933 these proceeds were of about the same size as the pensions received from abroad.

Another development which helps in explaining the low responsiveness of imports of Greece was the very large reduction from 1932 on in the service of her foreign public debt. In 1931/2 the full annual service of this debt would have amounted to about $24.5 million. (LN, Commission of Enquiry for European Union, *Report by the Stresa Conference for the Economic Restoration of Central and Eastern Europe, Submitted to the Commission of Enquiry for European Union* (Geneva, 1932), 7, 33-4.) This sum was equal to about 46 per cent of Greece's merchandise exports in 1931, and 65 per cent in 1932. Outright default or arrangements with the creditors involved suspension of amortization payments and large reductions in interest payments. See RIIA, *The Balkan States. I. Economic,* 102-3; LN, *Balances of Payments, 1931 and 1932,* 103-5, and *1933,* 93-5; and RIIA, *The Problem of International Investment,* 247.

69. Probably Panama's receipts from rentals in the Canal Zone and from passenger and commodity trade through the Canal declined quite moderately. The consequences of the reductions effected by the United States Government in the salaries of the employees, officers, and men of the Canal Zone may have been somewhat more severe. In any event, "the depression resulting from the world crisis . . . was on the whole less acute in Panama than in a number of other States." (GBDOT, *Report on Economic and Commercial Conditions in the Republic of Panama and the Panama Canal Zone, 1933-35,* 1.)

Portugal's invisible earnings depended more than Panama's on emigrants' remittances and income from investments abroad; and while her net tourist revenue increased greatly in the downswing, emigrants' remittances, originating chiefly in Brazil, declined rather heavily, and Portuguese creditors suffered from defaults abroad, such as the moratorium on Brazilian Government bonds. (See GBDOT, *Economic Conditions in Portugal, September 1934,* 22, 54-5, and *idem, Report on Economic and Commercial Conditions in Portugal, July 1936,* 40, 62.) Probably, Portugal's invisible earnings declined more heavily than the earnings of most of the other countries discussed in this section. If so, this factor might help to explain the relatively greater responsiveness of imports of Portugal than of these countries.

70. In 1930 direct investment accounted for about four-fifths of the foreign capital invested in the Philippines. (H. G. Callis, *Foreign Capital in Southeast Asia* (New York: Institute of Pacific Relations, Mimeo, 1942), 23, USTC, *United States-Philippine Tariff and Trade Relations,* Report No. 18, Second Series, 61-3, and *idem, United States-Philippine Trade,* Report No. 118, Second Series, 189 ff.)

About the features noted in the text, and other related features, and about their implications for the responsiveness of imports see *supra,* 94 ff.; J. E. Spencer, *Land and People in the Philippines* (Berkeley: University of California Press, 1952), 10, 122-3, 126, 128, 200-6; K. K. Kurihara, *Labor in the Philippine Economy* (Stanford: Stanford University Press, 1945), 8, 44-8; Jenkins, *American Economic Policy Toward the Philippines,* 26, 41; US Economic Survey Mission to the Philippines, *Report to the President of the United States* (Washington: US Government Printing Office, Department of State Publication 4010, 1950), 55-6; Callis, *Foreign Capital in Southeast Asia,* 16-19; W. S. Thompson, *Population and Peace in the Pacific,* (Chicago: University of Chicago Press, 1946), 277; and J. C. Hobbes, "Manila Hemp Production—A Problem for the Filipinos," *Foreign Agriculture,* 13 (1949), 250-2.

71. In Diagram II the Philippines comes closer to the countries discussed in the present section because of her extraordinarily low decline in exports, which in turn was due to the

important advantages secured in the downswing in the United States market at the expense of other exporters.

72. For data on the Philippines' invisible earnings see USTC, *United States-Philippine Trade*, Report No. 118, Second Series, 35, 37-8.

73. In 1928-9 the Philippines depended on the United States for over three-quarters of her exports, but less than two-thirds of her imports. Other important suppliers of the Philippines were Japan, China, and Britain. In the same period about one-third of Panama's imports also originated in countries other than the United States, mainly Europe and China.

74. Greece adopted exchange control in September 1931, and Denmark in November 1931. See, however, chap. 7, n. 27, and GBDOT, report by C. L. Paus, *Economic Conditions in Norway, May 1934* (London: HMSO, 1934), 14, 25. About Portugal see chap. 7, n. 26. In Portugal "it has not been necessary to resort to quotas or contingents or any other devices to support the national currency. ... The Government has so far done nothing to restrict or regulate imports, by tariffs, quotas, or control of currency." (GBDOT, *Economic Conditions in Portugal, September 1934*, 5.) However, some tariff protection to the textile industry was extended from 1928, and particularly 1930, on. See GBDOT, *Economic Conditions in Portugal, March 1930*, 26 ff.

Another factor which may help in explaining the relatively low responsiveness of imports of Portugal and, especially, the Irish Free State is the large change in emigration between the boom and the downswing.

In the late nineteen-twenties Portugal's population was about six millions, and the rate of natural growth of population was about 1.3 per cent per year, or about 75-80 thousands. While in the years 1927 to 1929 the country experienced an average annual net emigration of about 18 thousands, in 1931 and 1932 it had a net yearly return of emigrants of over 9 thousands. (The annual gross outflow declined from 31 to only 5 thousands in the two periods respectively, mainly because of restrictions imposed on immigration by Brazil.) The long-term improvement in Portugal's agricultural and industrial production, indicated earlier, "assisted the absorption of the surplus." (LN, *Statistical Yearbook, 1936/7*, 18, 40-1; Deutsches Reich, Statistisches Reichsamt, *Statistisches Jahrbuch für das Deutsche Reich*, 56 (1937), Internationale Übersichten, 35°-6°; and GBDOT, *Report on Economic and Commercial Conditions in Portugal, July 1936*, 68-9.)

In the late nineteen-twenties the population of the Irish Free State was about 3 millions, and the rate of natural growth of population was about 0.6 per cent, or about 15-20 thousands. While in the years 1927 to 1929 the country experienced an average annual net emigration of over 22 thousands, in the years 1931 to 1933 it had a net yearly return of emigrants of almost 2.5 thousands. (The statistical sources are those in the previous paragraph.)

75. While the value of such Class A and C exports of Lithuania as linseed, flax, and unmanufactured wood declined by percentages ranging between 70 and 80 per cent, her exports of butter and fresh meat increased by 72.1 and 76.9 per cent, respectively, and her exports of all foodstuffs (except grain and flour) doubled. About her policy of subsidizing certain agricultural exports see GBDOT, report by T. H. Preston, *Economic Conditions in Lithuania, November 1935* (London: HMSO, 1936), 5, 35.

76. While in 1928 and 1929 the government had surpluses of 80 and 2,920 thousand dollars, respectively, in 1930, 1931, and 1932 it ran deficits of 740, 2,020, and 1,220 thousand dollars, respectively. For more details see LN, *Public Finance, 1928-1935*. XVIII. *Lithuania* (Geneva: 1936), 2, 7-9.

77. As indicated by the ratio of merchandise exports to imports shown in brackets, while Lithuania had a very small deficit in 1928-9 (0.98), she had about as small a deficit in 1931 (0.98), when imports of foreign capital were highest, and a surplus in 1930 (1.07), 1932 (1.13), and 1933 (1.13). (Data on the flow of foreign capital to Lithuania are found in LN, *Balances of Payments, 1930*, 118, 121, and *1931 and 1932*, 124, 127.)

78. Data for Costa Rica, Mexico, Panama, and Turkey are not available.

79. Notice Lithuania's extraordinary position in Diagram IV. Imports of capital goods increased from 5.6 million dollars in each of the years 1928 and 1929 to as much as 7.4 million in 1930 and 8.1 million in 1931. In 1932 and 1933 they declined to 4.1 and 3.4 million, respectively. (LN, *International Trade Statistics*, various years). The share of capital goods in imports was greater in every year from 1930 to 1933 than in 1928-9: in 1930, 1932, and 1933 it amounted to about one-quarter of all imports, and in 1931, when imports of foreign capital were highest, it reached as much as three-tenths.

80. About these developments see GBDOT, *Economic Conditions in Lithuania, November 1935*, 2; LN, *Public Finance, 1928-1935*. XVIII. *Lithuania*, 2, 8-9; and *idem, Balances of Payments, 1933*, 122.

CHAPTER EIGHT

1. See, however, pp. 90-1.
2. As indicated by the ratio of exports to imports shown in brackets, the surpluses of the Dominican Republic (1.06), Ecuador (1.09), and Paraguay (1.04) were relatively small. In Venezuela (1.67) the surplus was very large. (Of the forty-nine countries only Bolivia and Peru had a larger relative surplus, and Persia had an approximately equal one.) But Venezuela's import/export decline, at 2.65, was the highest of all forty-nine countries.
3. The six countries listed in the text are in a category of their own: the very low original relation (except in Denmark) and the low import/export decline (smaller than unity, except in Greece) are related to the importance of invisible earnings and the relatively moderate change of these earnings in the downswing. In five of these countries the original relation was the sole determinant of the favourable change in the balance, and in Greece it was the main.
4. As indicated earlier, 1.09 was the median value of the import/export declines of the forty-nine countries.
The import/export decline was less than 1.00 in countries whose trade in 1928-9 amounted to $13.7 billion, or 55.9 per cent of the total trade of the forty-nine countries.
5. See the Appendix to this study.
6. *Supra*, 65, 78.

APPENDIX

1. Tse Chun Chang, *Cyclical Movements in the Balance of Payments* (Cambridge: Cambridge University Press, 1951).
2. *Ibid.*, 188.
3. *Ibid.*, 188.
4. The surpluses of Ecuador and Venezuela in any of the years 1930 to 1933 exceeded their respective surpluses in 1928-9.
5. "The average ratio of import value to export value [the inverse of our original relation] is not much above unity. As a matter of fact, the most common values seem to lie within the range from 1.1 to 1.3. On the other hand, the values for the ratio expressing the cyclical percentage changes in exports and imports [the inverse of our import/export decline] are, in general, much above unity." (Chang, *Cyclical Movements,* 17-18.)
6. *Ibid.*, 17-18, 187.
7. While Dr. Chang dismissed the original relation as being insignificant in practice, we found that, in the period 1928-9 to 1931-2, it was the sole, the main, or a secondary determinant of the change in balance of as many as forty-three of the forty-nine primary-exporting countries studied (and eight of the eleven industrial-exporting countries listed *supra*, 5; see *supra*, Table IV). Thus one could predict the direction of change (favourable or unfavourable) in the balance of any one of these forty-three primary-exporting (and eight industrial-exporting) countries in the period 1928-9 to 1931-2 upon being told whether the country had a surplus or deficit in the base period.
8. Venezuela's import/export decline, at 2.65, was by far the highest of all forty-nine countries of our study.
9. The values of the original relation and the import/export decline in the period 1928-9 to 1931-2, for the eight countries are found *supra*, Table III or XVIII.
10. Chang, *Cyclical Movements,* 169 (italics supplied).
11. There are some significant differences between the cyclical trade experience of small and large traders. See, e.g., *supra*, 21, 27, 38-9, and chap. 7, vII.
12. Chang, *Cyclical Movements,* 169.
13. It may be noted that for the twelve countries selected by Dr. Chang we have estimated a deficit in 1928-9 only about one-third as large as the one he indicates. By our estimate then the surplus for the twelve countries which exclude Norway and Poland, and include India and the Dutch East Indies, is correspondingly greater than the surplus shown in the text. While Dr. Chang lists twelve countries, he notes having selected "eleven." (*Cyclical Movements,* 169.) Perhaps, in estimating the sum of all balances for 1928 and 1929 he neglected the very large surplus of Argentina—this surplus is very close in size to the discrepancy between Dr. Chang's and our estimates of the total deficit. On the other hand, our estimates indicate that Argentina's surplus in 1931-2 is included in the twelve-country surplus for that period claimed by Dr. Chang.
14. The surplus countries, ranked by the size of their trade, were India, Argentina, the Dutch East Indies, Brazil, and Egypt; the deficit countries were the Netherlands, China, Australia, Spain, Denmark, Poland, and the Irish Free State.

15.   In nine of the sixteen countries the surplus equalled or exceeded 15 per cent of their exports.

16.   The five countries, ranked by the size of their trade, were India, Argentina, China, the Dutch East Indies, and Egypt.

17.   The six countries, ranked by the size of their trade, were the Netherlands, China, Spain, Denmark, Egypt, and the Irish Free State.

18.   A fifteenth country, Latvia, had a minute surplus in 1932-3, but a deficit in 1931-2.

19.   See *supra,* 109, and Chang, *Cyclical Movements,* 17-18, 170. Only if the import/export decline, or increase, were the sole or main determinant of change in the balance, could Dr. Chang's pattern of change be obtained: a change between a deficit in prosperity and a surplus in the slump. If, on the other hand, the sole or main determinant was the original relation, there would be a change only in the size of the surplus or deficit.

20.   Chang, *Cyclical Movements,* 170.

INDEX

AGAVE FIBRES: prices, changes in, 31
Apples
  exports: changes in, 29
  prices: changes in, 29
Apricots: exports, changes in, 29
Argentina
  exports: changes in, 7-9, 19, 37-8; composition of, 37-8; of specific commodities, 27, 28, 30, 31, 39, 120 n 26
  imports: changes in, 7-9, chap. 5-6; composition of, 43-4, 56-60, 86; of specific commodities, 50-2, 129 n 9, 129 n 11
  trade balance: changes in, 7-9, 12-13
Australia
  exports: changes in, 7-9, 19, 37-8, 41-2; composition of, 37-8, 41-2, 114 n 3; of specific commodities, 27, 28, 122 n 44, 30, 31-3, 38, 123 n 58, 126 n 6
  imports: changes in, 7-9, chap. 5-6, 82, 85; composition of, 43-4, 56-60, 86; responsiveness of, chap. 6, 82, 85
  trade balance: changes in, 7-9, 12-13

BACON, see Meat
Bags, see Containers
Balkans exports: composition of 18-19; changes in, 18-25; of foodstuffs, non-staple, 18-19, 22-4; of foodstuffs, staple, 18-22; of petroleum products, 18-19; 24-5; of raw materials, 18-19, 23-4
Bananas
  exports: changes in, 28-9, 30, 39, 41, 121 n 39
  output: changes in, 28
  prices: changes in, 29
Barley
  exports: changes in, 19-21
  prices: changes in, 25-6
Beans (dry) exports: changes in, 18-21
Bolivia
  exports: changes in, 7-9, 19, 37-8; composition of, 37-8, 114 n 3; of various minerals, 31-3
  imports: changes in, 7-9, chap. 5-6; composition of, 43-4, 56-60, 86; of textiles, 50-2
  trade balance: changes in, 7-9, 12-13
Brazil
  exports: changes in, 7-9, 19, 37-9; composition of, 37-9; of specific commodities, 27, 28, 31, 38-9, 126 n 8
  imports: changes in, 7-9, chap. 5-6, 82, 83-4; composition of, 43-4, 56-60, 86; responsiveness of, chap. 6, 82, 83-4; of textiles, 50-2

trade balance: changes in, 7-9, 12-13
British Malaya, see Malaya
Bulgaria
  exports: changes in, 7-9, 18-24, 37-8; composition of, 18-19, 20, 37-8; of specific commodities, 18-24, 30-1, 38, 120 n 26
  imports: changes in, 7-9, chap. 5-6; composition of, 43-4, 56-60, 86; of textiles, 50-2
  trade balance: changes in, 7-9, 12-13
Butter, see also Dairy products
  exports: changes in, 28, 30
  output: changes in, 28, 29, 122 n 44
  prices: changes in, 29, 41, 122 n 44

CANADA
  exports: changes in, 7-9, 19, 37-8, 42; composition of, 37-8, 42, 114 n 3; of specific commodities. 27, 31-3, 33-4, 34-5, 123 n 58, 124 n 62
  imports: changes in. 7-9, chap. 5-6; composition of, 43-4, 56-60, 86; of textiles, 50-2
  trade balance: changes in, 7-9, 12-13
Capital, foreign: movements of, and change in merchandise imports, 83-5 passim, 89-91 passim, 94-5, 98-9, 141 n 59; service on, and change in merchandise imports, 84-5 passim, 90, 92, 94-5 passim, 138 n 40, 140 n 54, 143 n 68
Capital goods imports, 43-4; changes in, 44-8, 49; share in total imports, 56-9, 85-8, 89
Cement imports, 43-4; changes in, 49, 129 n 10
Cereals, see Grain
Ceylon
  exports: changes in. 7-9, 19. 37-8; composition of, 37-8, 94; of specific commodities, 27. 30-1, 94, 139 n 49
  gold and silver: trade in, 93, 94
  imports: changes in, 7-9, chap. 5-6, 93-4; composition of, 43-4, 56-60, 86; responsiveness of, chap. 6, 93-4; of textiles, 50-2
  trade balance: changes in, 7-9, 12-13
Chang, T. C., 4, 109-13, 114 n 2
Cheese, see also Dairy products
  exports: changes in, 20, 22-3, 28, 30. 41, 122 n 49
  output: changes in, 28
  prices: changes in, 29, 122 n 44. 122 n 49
Chemicals imports, 43-4; changes in, 44-8, 55-6; share in total imports, 56-8
Chile
  exports: changes in, 7-9, 19, 37-8, 89, 90; composition of, 37-8; of various minerals, 31-3, 90, 124 n 61
  imports: changes in, 7-9, chap. 5-6, 89-90;

output: changes in, 25

Tourist revenue: changes in, 92, 95-7

Trade
foreign: as percentage of national income, 62-4
international: share of various countries, 5, 100, 104

Transportation: cost of, 23, 24, 27, 118 n 14

Turkey
exports: changes in, 7-9, 19, 37-8; composition of, 37-8
imports: changes in, 7-9, chap. 5-6, 128 n 2
trade balance: changes in, 7-9, 12-13

URUGUAY EXPORTS: changes in, 126 n 2; composition of, 126 n 2; of meat, 28, 30

VEGETABLES
exports: changes in, 20, 22-3, 28-9
output: changes in, 28, 29
prices: changes in, 29

Venezuela
exports: changes in, 7-9, 19, 37-8, 42; composition of, 37-8, 42; of specific commodities, 34, 125 n 65, 126 n 8
imports: changes in, 7-9, chap. 5-6, 82, 84, 89-90; composition of, 43-4, 56-60, 86; responsiveness of, chap. 6, 82, 84, 89-90; of textiles, 50-2
trade balance: changes in, 7-9, 12-13

WHEAT
exports: changes in, 19-22, 25, 38

imports: changes in, 48-9
output: changes in, 21-2, 25
prices: changes in, 25-6, 41, 49

Wine
exports: changes in, 19-22, 25
output: changes in, 21-2, 25
prices: changes in, 21-2

Wood
exports: changes in, 20, 23-4, 30, 33-4, 35-6, 41
imports: 44-5; *see also* Capital goods, imports
prices: changes in, 33-4, 35-6, 41, 125 n 64

Wool
exports: changes in, 30-1, 35, 41
imports: 43-4; changes in, 50-3
output: changes in, 30
prices: changes in, 31, 41, 52, 53

YANGTZE RIVER: flood of, 38, 91, 126 n 4

Yugoslavia
exports: changes in, 7-9, 18-24, 37-8; composition of, 18-19, 20, 37-8; of specific commodities, 18-24, 28, 33-4, 120 n 26, 124 n 62
imports: changes in, 7-9, chap. 5-6; composition of, 43-4, 56-60, 86
trade balance: changes in, 7-9, 12-13

ZINC
exports: changes in, 31-2, 123 n 58
output: changes in, 31
prices: changes in, 31-3